DIESE

From 'The Barr

DIESEL TAFF
From 'The Barracks' to Tripoli

AUSTIN HUGHES

AN IMPRINT OF
ANNE LOADER
PUBLICATIONS

Special thanks to Kathryn Allingham for
word-processing the manuscript and
to Gladys Roberts for advising on
the contents of the book
Austin Hughes

ISBN
1 901253 14 7

Published April 2000

Published by:
Léonie Press
an imprint of Anne Loader Publications
13 Vale Road, Hartford
Northwich
Cheshire CW8 1PL
Gt Britain
Tel: 01606 75660 Fax: 01606 77609
e-mail: anne@aloaderpubs.u-net.com
website: http://www.aloaderpubs.u-net.com

Edited, designed and printed by:
Anne Loader Publications

About the author
AUSTIN HUGHES

AUSTIN HUGHES, February 2000

After the Second World War was over, Austin Hughes was set free from the Royal Engineers to return to what might be called 'normal life', driving all sorts of heavy vehicles and bulldozers. Eventually he met a new girlfriend, Mary, and within a few months, on March 12, 1949, they were married at Hope Church. They set up home in Chester and were together for 46 years. They had one son, Trevor, who now lives in Canada.

After years of telling the stories of his youth in North Wales and his time travelling the world in the Army, Austin was persuaded by his family to write them down. "I have tried to be as truthful as possible and cause no offence to anyone," he says.

The events in this book are written from memory. As far as possible, the names of most of the places Austin visited have been checked and standardised, but a handful cannot be found on modern maps and others have Army nicknames which are meaningless nowadays. The author would be glad if anyone could give him the current names and the definitive spellings.

Contents

List of Illustrations

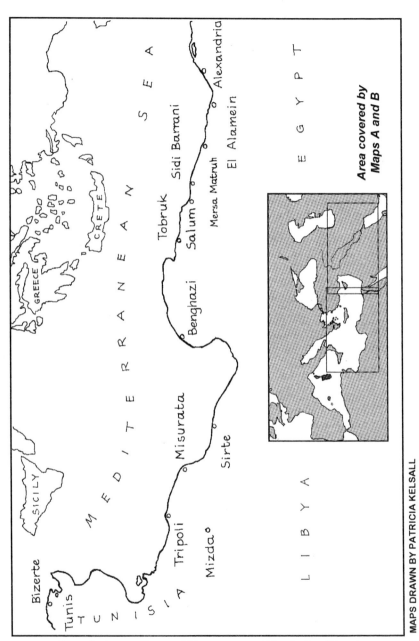

Area covered by
Maps A and B

Map A: From Tunis (West) to the Nile Delta (East)

iii

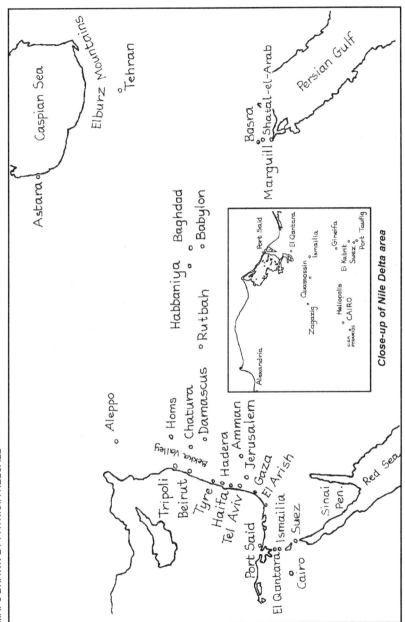

Close-up of Nile Delta area

Map B: From the Nile Delta to Astara (North East) & Basra (East)

'The Barracks' from a watercolour by Merion Pugh Roberts

PREFACE

My family had given me strict instructions: I was to start writing my memoirs on 26th January 1989 aboard Jumbo Jet flight No. BA0283 from Heathrow to Los Angeles.

We were going on holiday to visit my son Trevor, his wife Margaret, and our grandchildren Beverley (10), Karen (8½) and Michael (2½). They then lived at Loma Avenue, Long Beach, Los Angeles.

The point of the exercise was to keep my mind OFF flying, as I was allergic to heights and scared stiff of getting my feet off the ground. At Manchester Airport I was dithering, but managed to get on the domestic flight to Heathrow for an afternoon flight. We boarded the Jumbo for a 12.30pm take off. My wife, Mary, did everything to try to comfort me and, as usual, her magic must have worked. To our surprise, we were ushered to the top deck, which we supposed was first class, and we had a very comfortable seat. It particularly suited me to be in the centre, so that I couldn't see out of the windows. Unfortunately there was not enough elbow-room to write, so I packed in the idea as a bad job.

I was also annoyed when the Captain announced over the tannoy that because of a fault in the automatic pilot we would be delayed on take-off for half an hour.

When we eventually took off, my wife kept nudging me to look out. I was staring either straight ahead or at my feet.

"No way, man, am I going to look out!" I thought.

I'd never expected that anyone would get me in a plane, let alone persuade me to fly the Atlantic for twelve hours. Yet here I was, thousands of feet up in the air – what grandchildren make you do!

The flight went well, with good food, drink and excellent service.

We arrived over Los Angeles ahead of schedule. We were right over the wings and when I finally dared to glance out I noticed with trepidation that the flaps didn't seem to be working properly. They were not folding smoothly but were clunking as the

1

hydraulics worked them – it wasn't a gradual movement. I have spent my life with big machinery and, I can tell you, I was worried! However, we landed safely, so everything must have gone well.

We met our family for the start of a wonderful holiday at Long Beach, where I began to write this life story.

I have travelled the world, east and west, and had some memorable experiences in the Second World War. I was in bomb disposal during the London blitz, helped to build the only sinking bridge in the world across the Tigris and Euphrates rivers and lived in the back of a wagon for four years, working with earth-moving equipment all over the Middle East. We built roads and airfields as well as clearing avalanches and landslides, and ferrying refugees. Then just when I thought I was coming home for good I found myself off on a Royal Engineers' battlefield tour of liberated France.

This book covers my early life in a North Wales village and the war years. I hope that my tale is of interest to those who read it.

Austin ('Diesel Taff') Hughes

Chapter 1

'THE BARRACKS'

I was born in North Wales, not far from the Cheshire border, in an old farmhouse cottage forming part of a square which had probably been converted from old stables or even shippons some time early during the last century. It was called 'The Barracks'. The nearest village was Cymau.

My mum was just an ordinary country girl who had lived on Mount Horeb, better known as Hope Mountain, overlooking the village of Hope in Clwyd. She was born in 1886. My dad, who was a master baker, was born in the village of Bersham in or about 1866, making him 20 years my mum's senior. As far back as I can remember, he worked for a William Lewis as a baker, for thirty shillings and free bread a week. The rent for the cottages was 1/9d per week (in 'old' money), which included the rates of approximately 11d per week.

I came into the world at No. 3 Plas Maen Cottages on 19th February 1922. I can clearly remember back to the age of four. The houses were in an 'L' shape, five on the back row and three on the side row. I was born in the last of the row of three. Outside the blocks of houses was a large square yard made from old ashes which had hardened over the years. Uneven as it was, it was our play area. What games we used to play with the rest of the families who lived there!

As you entered the group of cottages, through a large opening where a gate had once swung, the three houses were on the right:

At No. 1 were the Rowlands: Ethel, Bobby, Dorothy, Kenneth, Edith, Bessy and their parents. Mrs Rowlands was small and neat.

At No. 2 were the Roberts: Tom Roberts, his wife, Johnny, Rosy, Fendolene and Victor.

Living at No. 3 were us, the Hughes: William Henry (Dad), Mary Gladys (Mum), Hope, George William, Estella (Stella),

3

myself and Betty my younger sister. I can remember her being born. I was called 'Austin' after Judge Austin Jones – I think from Plas Teg Hall.

On the back row in the 'L' shaped corner was No. 4, with another Roberts family, who were no relation to those at No 2: Mr and Mrs Roberts and their one daughter Maggy, a very reserved but beautiful girl, a loner who always went to school on her own.

At No. 5 were the Peters family: the 'Old Gnat', as my dad called Mrs Peters, and her son Les.

At No. 6 lived the Gittins: Mr and Mrs Gittins, one son Charlie (and he was a Charlie, too!).

At No. 7 were the Pryderch family: Mr and Mrs Pryderch, Elsie, Ronald, Connie and two more girls, but I can't remember their names. Pryderches lived in No. 8 also, which belonged to the 'Lucky' family in the Ffrwd. I used to call Mrs Pryderch 'Auntie Elsie'. Her eldest son was Leslie and I would go to see if he was coming out to play so that I could have a treacle butty off his mum. I can visualise his mother, cutting into an oven-bottom loaf in her lap, digging deep into it with her pointed knife, spreading it with margarine and slapping treacle over it – and me waiting there in anticipation for my treacle butty. I would sit on the rug and eat it and when I got home my mum would say: "You've been to Auntie Elsie's, eating your treacle butties again, haven't you?" All the kids went to No. 7 for a treacle butty. As far as I can remember the family went to live in Llay. I think I saw Leslie there, once or twice, some time after we moved from The Barracks.

My dad was a son of a miller and I have a very faint recollection of seeing him once at the Old Mill in the village of Bersham (which is no longer there). This is where he must have learned his trade as a master baker, and at The Cross Bakery at Cymau. As you go up into Cymau, from Abermorddu, when you reach the crossroads, the bakehouse used to be through the gates directly opposite the road you are in, parallel to the Talbot Public House. Go past the Bryn Yorkin Road and it's the double gates there. He walked about a mile and a half from The Barracks to the Cross in Cymau via the small hamlet of Pant Hyfryd.

Dad worked hard for his 30 shillings a week and free bread. He had to hump two-hundredweight bags of flour up a flight of

4

stairs to feed the mixing bin. Everything was mixed by hand, then it had to be kneaded, left to rise, then kneaded again. The temperature had to be high for the fermentation of the yeast, and then the dough was cut up in portions to suit the trays. A big blob on top of a small blob made what was called 'an oven bottom loaf.' This was beautiful bread, not like the bread you have to eat today. Dad was always wringing wet with sweat and wore a nice clean white sweatcloth around his neck. He sported a beautiful moustache with long whiskers about four inches wide, and with his white hair at the side of his sideburns, he was a good-looking man.

At about this time my brother George and sister Stella must have started school, because I used to go with my dad to the bakehouse. I was only allowed to go as high as the first three steps and I could sit on them eating the handful of currants he always gave me to keep me quiet. They wouldn't last long and I soon got into trouble and had my backside smacked. I didn't stay there all day. Mum came up for shopping and took me home. The groceries were booked till the weekend and paid for out of Dad's wages. As we walked home, we were always on the look-out for trees that had shed a branch or two so we could either pick them up on the way home or return for them when the family were all together. We were very shrewd and had to be or there was simply no chance of survival in those days.

"The good old days!" Where they found that phrase I'll never know. Good old days for the capitalists, yes, maybe!

We were a happy family. Comfort in those days was a huge fire of wood collected from the local woods and lanes as we walked home from either school or church. We had an old fashioned fireplace, usually burning Llay Hall Queen coal, at a shilling for a hundredweight bag. (Llay Hall colliery, near Cefn-y-bedd, has been closed for nearly 45 years).

Everything was cooked on that grate, and water was boiled in the side boiler, filled, when empty, with a spouted pail out of the tubs which caught the rainwater off the roofs. It had a brass tap all polished up, and a large shiny fender. The oven, on the opposite side to the boiler, made all the best dishes in the world – delicious beasting from the farm during the calving season, rice puddings with always a scraping of nutmeg on the top, bread and butter puddings, and *'ponsh-maipe"* (a dish mum made from turnips, spuds and something else, which I can't recall).

Both my parents were excellent cooks and, although we were poor, we had fantastic meals. I remember the butcher calling on a Friday night, often with a piece of brisket, at a shilling a pound. We would have about a pound and a half (there were seven of us), and we still had enough to make a meal for Monday.

I can always remember the place we called home – the kettle shining, steaming on the hob, and boiling its bum away. Many a good meal was cooked on that fire, and I will give my mum full marks for the way she looked after us, feeding us out of what was a mere pittance on which to live. She would buy all the cheap cuts. A big pan was required – as I've said, there were five hungry mouths besides Mum and Dad. One of my most treasured memories was Sunday dinner. Mum would call us in and tell us to wash our hands, all of us in the same water.

Inside the house there was only one door. Behind it was a high screen consisting of a long bench and a high back which kept the draught off when you were sitting there. When we were eating, the table was pulled to the screen to seat three of us – with Dad at the head of the table facing the fire and Mum with her back to the kitchen to enable her to get there to serve the meals.

There was no water in the house, only what we collected from our rain barrel or carried from the Ffrwd about a mile away, so there was no tap to turn on, and no sink to drain water away after washing up. It all had to be taken away in buckets and thrown in the nettles at the rear of the house.

The floors of the house were covered with the old twelve-inch square tiles. My mum used to get on her mat and scrub them, with the aid of 'Aunt Sally', which was a liquid soap and very searching to the hands. She'd go through the house and do the front step with a yellowstone to make it look nice and clean. She would shake the rag rug, which we'd all had a hand in making. We'd all sat in a circle with our own peg and got cracking, poking three-inch lengths of material through the fabric of a hessian sack. The fender had to be cleaned. If there wasn't any Brasso, you used the dust out of the ashes and the old 'spit and polish'.

On Sunday, the Sabbath Day, everyone had to go to church. I was under five years old when I became a member of the choir in the Cymau Mission Church. Mr R Mayfield Jones, who lived in Hope Village, conducted most of the services. He walked from his home to Cymau twice on Sunday. He was qualified in all aspects of music and taught me to read music. He offered to teach me and train me at sixpence a lesson, but my parents couldn't afford it. I have regretted it ever since.

The evensong service was never missed by any of the family, unless through illness. It was a ritual every Sunday. My dad was a church warden. There was always a meeting outside the church afterwards and then the usual evening walk of about four miles or so, down to Ffrith, along the Ffrwd Road and up the Barracks Hill. During the long summer evenings the whole family would walk through Cymau, along Bryn Yorkin farm road, up through the farmyard, up on to Mount Horeb and on to the rocks. There must be hundreds of initials carved on those rocks. This spot gives a beautiful view over the Dee and the Mersey estuaries. On a clear day you can see Liverpool Cathedral. We would walk almost as far as the Chapel Horeb to listen to the late evening singing.

Dad had a wonderful voice. He sang falsetto and bass as well as anyone. It was nothing for us to sing together on the way home via The Forlace crossroads back down the Barracks Road, passing Lord Derby's farm on our left. When we arrived home we would have some kind of butty, a drink and go off to bed.

Mother was born in the last grey cottage before you reach the River Alyn down Fagl Lane in Hope. The cottage belonged to Pont-y-derlyn Farm on the main Mold to Wrexham road. She was my gran's firstborn and, in her early teens, went to live on Mount Horeb with her gran, Mrs Griffiths, my great-gran, whom I remember quite well. She must have been about eighty and she lived in a small white cottage, just below Lake Horeb. There she took in laundry for most of the 'toffs', such as Plas Teg Hall, Bryntirion, Pont-y-derlyn and Celyn Hall, near Caergwrle. My mum used to collect the laundry and deliver it on a small pony and trap. She called the pony 'Dobbin', and she told me quite a few episodes of her life with that pony. Washing was their 'bread and butter'. A shirt would cost a penny. If it had a starched collar it was 1½d. If it had starched cuffs it was ½d extra. A dress was 1d.

There was very little profit in it unless you did large amounts. Great Gran had a large tall stove with bars all round to hold about twenty irons for pressing the clothes. As one cooled off she would replace it and someone had to keep the fire going with something burnable – bark, coke, coal, sticks, gorse, peat – anything! The ironing took the time. It was all neatly folded in little wicker baskets with the name and the price on it. Probably four or five baskets would be put into the cart and off they'd go down to the village – with maybe 10 shillings' worth of clean clothes after two or three days' work, or more if it was wet and the laundry took longer to dry.

All this practice made Mum a good washerwoman. She had no boiler to boil clothes. She used a galvanised tub, a dolly peg, plenty of elbow grease and had an aching back. Washing day was on a Monday, *if* there was any water in the tubs from roofs of the houses. Even the gutters were segregated to save neighbours squabbling over the water. If there was no water in the tubs, it was the duty of all the family to fetch the water from the Ffrwd. This was a mile away, but what made matters worse was that it was down a steep hill with a gradient of about 1 in 8. Two people took a galvanised bath and each had a bucket. Opposite the Old Red Lion in the Ffrwd was an old cast-iron pipe stuck into the bank, with a continual flow of spring water. It was like champagne! You had to fill the buckets and then empty them into the bath. Here came the crunch – carrying it up the hill, one each side of the bath. You got to know every stone on that hill. It was originally a cart track, with a grassy centre of the track for the horse to grip, which could be really dug up if it was used a lot. You seldom see it today. We carried on together until the tubs were full and the baths and buckets were full. The family worked together, ate together, sang together and played together.

I was five in the February just before the Easter break and it was nearly time for me to go to school. I had an uncle in Saltney, a sergeant in the police force. He gave my mum a policeman's cape and she made me a suit out of it for my first day at school. I think it lasted twenty-five years! I tried all ways to wreck it but couldn't.

At Easter 1927 I started school, aged five years and two months. I walked more than three miles to Abermorddu School, which is now no longer there. It was opposite the bottom of the Cymau Hill. A Miss Jones came to speak to me, and my sisters, Stella and Hope, left me quite comfortable in Miss Jones's capable hands. I soon settled down for my short stay in the 'infants'. Miss Silver, two Miss Shorts and a Mrs Roberts were the teachers and Mr Rogers was the headmaster.

It was a long walk back home from school, uphill whichever way you went. We could walk through to Cefn-y-bedd, up Lord Derby's drive, along Hilda's footpath, up the bank on Plas Maen, over the stile and into the yard by the houses.

After I had been in school for about six months or so my dad took ill. It was something to do with his work. I was much too young to know anything about it. He was in bed for months.

I can remember him taking to his bed and he didn't work again to my knowledge. This made us poorer. Dad had a small insurance pay-out of 7/6d per week, and that is all we had, so we were brought up on parish relief. God knows what my mum had – I will never know.

Eventually Dad's health improved and he was up and about again. Instead of us taking sandwiches to school, he used to meet us outside with our food. This was probably chips and something. We all sat on the logs at the bottom of the Cymau Hill to eat them. Dad used to smoke, although his doctor – Dr Crookes from Caergwrle – told him he shouldn't. He smoked Woodbines and the price was then 2d a packet for five. I think he met us almost every day carrying a Buckley mug full of hot chips and a stone bottle full of hot tea. We couldn't afford pop. We may have had an orange drink, but I cannot remember. Sometimes after we had eaten he would walk to our grocery supplier at Abermorddu. The shopping was always heavy, so after school we all had to go to the shop to collect it and carry it the three miles home. There were no buses. It was the only way to get your shopping. The only deliveries were coal, greens and pots for rags. The only mechanised transport was provided by Reg the butcher with an old chain driven Trojan; all the others were horse-drawn. I think a bus service started up to Cymau when I was about twelve. It was an old

Tilley Stephenson, with gate change gears, rear brakes only, a mag drive, hand starter and no lights – only an old carbide lamp in the front.

We all met our friends from school. One family was from the Ffrwd, the Pughs. They were all lads, Roland, Sydney and Tom (in seniority). They lived in the Rock Cottage on the top of the bank, opposite the Red Lion. We have remained friends to this day. The nearest shop to us was in the Ffrwd, about a mile away. It was owned by a 'Mrs Lucky' – or was that her nickname? Anyway, she was related to the Pryderch family who also had a hand in the shop. We very seldom had money to spend so we had to use it wisely. The best buy of the day was a sugar mouse, which cost ½d. If you were very careful, it could last two or three days, if your brother or sister didn't get at it. I think we had about ½d a fortnight, unless one of our relatives gave us something. If they did, we would forfeit it to our mum, who was always short of money. She must have schemed for fifteen years to try to feed and clothe us – a wonderful woman, my mum.

Dad must have been feeling his feet by now, probably fed up because there was no way he could ever work again. He had a terrible temper. I will never forget walking home passing Mr Powell's cottage, which was situated on the road between The Barracks and The Forlace (this was the junction on the Cymau Hill). Mr Powell passed me, with my dad at the rear. When he spoke to me, I replied politely. I was about six or seven. My dad came behind me and he belted hell out of me. Can you guess why? It was for not touching my hat to the man. Mr Powell was the *head cowman* at Lord Derby's farm. That's all. *The good old days!* Ha!

When you were leathered by Dad, you were 'leathered', I can tell you. It lasted for days. You couldn't sit down for a day or so. It is not allowed today, but who is right? They were our parents, after all. Beatings were commonplace, even in school. My brother George, two years my senior, had a hell of a hiding one day. My dad brought a melodeon home. He gave it to me, as I was the more musical. I managed to get a tune out of it. I suppose George was jealous, so he took the melodeon onto the midden wall and smashed it to pieces with a ball paign hammer. I had nothing to

10

do with it. I think this caused ill feeling for the rest of our lives. He was hammered – poor lad. I felt sorry for him, but if we other children had said anything we would have been dealt with in the same way.

The midden wall was the part of the large yard where everyone emptied their ashes from the fire grates. These were eventually spread over the yard and the layer would harden. This is what the whole yard was made of. It never flooded and we all played there – skipping, cat and kinney, 'all in together girls', sardines, hide and seek, hopscotch and clock scotch. It went on for hours after school. There were very few arguments. It wasn't very often the parents 'fell out' either. It was a close-knit community. Ethel, Rosy, Fendolene, Connie, Beth, Bobby, Jimmy, Hope, George, Stella, Betty, me, Maggy, Wilson and I can't remember Wilson's sister's name – I think it was 'Elsie' after her mum ('treacle butty Elsie').

We had very hot summers in those days. We would head for the shade and go under the hawthorn bush in the corner of the estate, by the gardens, as you walked down to the Ffrwd. We liked to play 'babby house'. My brother was the doctor, Roly Pugh was the vicar, Maggy was the mother, Hope was the granny, Betty and I were the babies. We were quite serious about it too. All broken pots were taken there, and sticks for knives and forks. Everything represented a teapot or some domestic utensil.

We amused ourselves with all sorts of things. I could make a good bow and arrow when I was eight, a whistle, a catapult – it was easy – and we knew how to use them too. We would 'pinch' the netting wire out of the fencing and wrap it round the flights of the arrows to give them a better flight. We knew all the answers. Opposite the entrance to the yard there was a set of high railings. We kept all the jars, turned them upside down on the top spike of the railings, and competed as to who could break the most. This was for boys only. After the game was over we had to clean up all the glass, as there were always cattle in the field. We had tree tents and dens everywhere. We knew every inch of the land and where the squirrels hid their nuts.

As I grew older I was expected to do some chores around the place, as I was always active and willing to please. I got pleasure out of helping others.

When we were outside the square we were more or less on trust, but inside the square there was always someone watching. You had to behave. Inside The Barracks square the ground was holy. There was a small gap of about three feet, with a stile, between the houses in the L-shape, through which to get a barrow – I'll tell you why in a moment. The stile gave access to the rear gardens where the toilets were situated. These were earth toilets, whereby every day someone had to go round with ashes from the fire to cover the day's 'output'. They were about 150 yards from the stile.When they were full we had to contact a scavenger to come to empty them. The stile was removed and an old solid wooden wheelbarrow was used to empty the toilets. A horse and cart would be backed up to the stile, the stile taken down, planks put up to the cart, the 'night soil' loaded into the barrow and pushed into the cart. This stile was right outside our front door and the stench was vile, 200 times worse than any cesspool. Mum always tried to take us out when this was being done. It seemed to linger for days. White live lime was spread throughout the toilet afterwards.

We all had to use these closets in the middle of the night. If it was cold or not you had to go out with a candle in a jam jar to light your path. Many a time I went on my own in the early hours of the morning and got belted for singing at that unearthly hour. There were several families to one toilet and not a week went by without one family or another meeting on the path. The only alternative to this was a 'goes-under', but they weren't very hygienic. We did have one, but only for emergencies or illness.

I mentioned earlier Hilda Powell's cottage. Hilda was the wife of Arthur, a brother of Billy Powell. Billy was herdsman and Arthur was head horseman. The Hall had a large herd of cattle. Hilda and Arthur had one son and I often went down the bank to play with him. The cottage was just over the railings, looking down into the beautiful valley towards Cefn-y-bedd. It was a further walk round to get down to the cottage, up the lane, over the stile, across a small path and a sheer drop. The path down was two yards wide and, because it was so wet, it would freeze in the winter. We all had 'high jinks' in the winter going to school as we often went that way to Cefn-y-bedd. There was quite a gang of us and when the bank froze over you would each find a flat stone, about six inches square, set the stone under your bum and, if you could keep it there while you slid down, you had done your quarter mile to school in record time. If you didn't, you had a wet backside all day! Now, large stones were hard to get hold of so one year someone had a brainwave – why not bury the stones until next year? And so off we went for the garden spade to bury them. We each had a turn at digging and carefully removed about an inch of turf to suit our individual stone and buried it. We buried 14 stones altogether and knew exactly where we had put them, but we never found those stones again. We must have excavated half the field to no avail. One of the mysteries of life, I suppose!

From Hilda Powell's cottage you could turn right to go to the Ffrwd, along a beautiful little coppice. This was the area of an old mine works. To the right was the bank sloping up to The Barracks, which was wooded and the most beautiful place in the world to me. It has everything Mother Nature intended. Every Spring it was, and still is, covered with a carpet of yellow primroses. A month later, nearer to the cottage, is a blue blanket of bluebells.

Further towards the Ffrwd, in the glade, was the wooden bungalow of the Davies family. Mrs Davies always welcomed me when I called to see David who, incidentally, was killed at Dunkirk. Walking the opposite way from Hilda's cottage was a wet muddy path with stepping stones, until you reached the tarmac of Lord Derby's drive. Half way down the drive were big white gates, then it was a short walk on to the Corwen/Ffrwd Road by a bungalow where a Mr A Wright lived. He worked for the Electricity Company. Another 100 yards and you were on the main Wrexham Road called Hollybush. The first house on the right, just under the bridge, was a Mrs Edwards'. It was here, I understand, that the great Emlyn Williams wrote his famous play *Night must Fall*. Not many people know this. I actually met him, not knowing who he was at the time. I was told some time after he had left.

Turning back along the Ffrwd Road was the post office, then the Old Mill House where the Davies family lived. There were two sons about my age. The mill was running at that time, which

I visited often. It was a water mill run by water from the River Cegidog, a tributary of the River Alyn at Llay Hall. When the mill was running on full water it was fast and I found it frightening to walk round when it was at high revs. All the workings were of wood. I can still see the flour being ground, then fed into sacks which were stitched up after weighing, and then transported by horse and cart. I believe the mill is a relic today and the water gates are still by the causeway.

Chapter 2

'THE RUNNING FIELD'

My standard of education was only elementary and, although I passed examinations for the grammar school, I was unable to attend Hawarden Grammar School as we were not in a financial position to afford the books or uniform (I had never even had a new pair of shoes by this time let alone a uniform). Then there was also the train fare at 6d per day return. It would have deprived the rest of my family. I think people offered to help, but there was no way. It might have been all right for the first year, but what about the second and third years and further education? My education didn't suffer for the disappointment – I was never brilliant, just a good second or third.

Our family was now growing up. We were all nearing puberty. Indeed, Hope, my eldest sister, was past this and she had to go to live with Great Gran on Horeb. She was Gran's 'eyes' as she was getting blind. There were only two bedrooms in our house, so it was Mum and Dad in one double room, partitioned to take Betty and Stella too, and George and myself in the back room. The whole place was infested with fleas and Mum had a difficult job trying to keep them down. She lifted floorboards and used all kinds of disinfectant to try to get rid of them. I now know all the cottages were the same. Mum was doing her best to find another home. As fleas bite normally during the night, not many kids went to school without them.

As Dad's health had improved we all started to do things together in the garden. We had about half an acre of virgin ground to cultivate. The grass was long so that we burned it where we could. We used pick-axes to break up the heavy clods, gathered them up and made compost heaps. Even my mum and the girls helped. We formed beds with paths between them and had every vegetable imaginable. Seeds were going in by the dozen the first year. We kept two rabbits in a hutch which we'd made out of orange boxes. We also had a Chinchilla and an Angora and, as I was only eight, I didn't know there was a difference. We did get the sex right – one was a buck and the other a doe. They did breed and were very funny.

The first vegetables were excellent – a first year 'success.' I'm sure the potatoes were like huge turnips, beautiful and white. The whole crop was very good, including the flowers. We manured the ground and were looking forward to another early Spring. This paid dividends. The spuds lasted right through the Winter, apart from what we sold to friends – everyone was pleased. It gave us an incentive to do well the next year!

Dad was still on the sick, but as I mentioned earlier, he had a small insurance of 7/6d per week – I think it was a trade union insurance he had through his brother, Bert, who lived in Sandycroft. Uncle Bert was a great gentleman and worked at the steelworks in Shotton.

Because of our plight we were granted a certificate to enable us to obtain shoes through the parish relief, but to get them we had to go to Penymynydd. This meant walking from Cymau to Penymynydd, along Barracks Lane, across the field to Bryn Yorkin woods into Caergwrle, down over the Sarn Bridge, up through Hope, through to Penyffordd and up the back lane to Penymynydd. My brother and I usually had clogs, or I would finish off a pair belonging to him and he would have the new pair. He was ill one time so Dad went to ask for the shoes and took the old pair with him. Although the cobbler was selling the shoes he refused to let Dad have them without first seeing the child. There were no fittings in those days, so it wasn't because of that – he was afraid of someone reporting him and losing his licence. I would have liked to have got a strap and chased him back to Cymau to see how he liked walking all that way for a free pair of boots. We felt like telling him to 'stick' his boots. Dad felt most indignant about it and told him so. I knew he was upset as we walked home in the dark. It was a long trek, especially up through the woods in the dark. You never knew where the bull was in the field and we had many a scare.

As I mentioned before, Dad had a very bad temper. If you

didn't behave you got it – and I mean 'got it'.

Our back bedroom window was about a twelve-foot drop into a bunch of nettles about three feet high and six feet wide. There was a clear field when you got out of the nettles and we christened it 'The Running Field' because this is where you went if Dad was after you with the strap. I had received my warning and if I could see Dad's belt coming off, I was up the stairs and through the window before he could catch me. I hoofed it across The Running Field and stayed out until dark. My mum would come to the fence and call me in and Dad would just clip my ear as I walked past him for my cheese butty before going up the 'wooden hills' to bed.

The Running Field separated our hamlet from Pant Hyfryd. It had three cottages all in one row: Edwards at No. 3, Thomases at No.2, and I'm not sure who lived at No.1. Iorweth Edwards and Emerys Thomas were our friends and Emerys had a sister Glenys, who was senior to me by five years and, as her education was by far superior to mine, I was jealous of her. Iorweth, Emerys and Glenys all attended Hawarden Grammar School. Glenys was a very good friend to me. Her mother was excellent to me also. I did a lot for her and she paid me well. They had a lot of ground and Glenys had incubators for breeding chickens. Anyway she asked me to help with the chicks and, as they were in their hundreds, we had our work cut out when those eggshells started to crack. I was interested in that sort of thing by now and found it very rewarding. I would clean out the hatched shells, and keep the incubation area warm and as clean as I could. Glenys was studying for university so she couldn't spare as much time as me, but she always fed the chicks.

Emerys and Glenys had an uncle who kept a tobacco shop in Wrexham. Emerys went there every Saturday until the afternoon, when he would come home with enough cigarettes to give us all a packet each! We smoked ourselves to death, especially after Sunday school. Opposite Emerys' house was an old smithy with a balcony. If we had any cigarettes left we would hide them in the holes in the walls. How our parents never found out I'll never know, as we must have smelled of cigarette smoke. I now wish they had and had stopped us, because we all became addicted – I was only nine years old and knew what a Gold Flake was. We were never discovered.

We were all growing fast. Mum was concerned about the girls not having their own rooms. She was always looking for a bigger house.

Entertainment was very sparse. I will never know where the money came from, but Dad took us all to Brymbo pictures, not far from the steelworks where Green Bros have their yard today. Of course we had to walk it – down the Ffrwd Hill, over the River Cegidog, through the Ffrwd up to Brymbo. We all sat in the fourpennies. One film was about Dick Turpin. It was a silent film and during the interval Mrs Gittins from the Ffrwd played the piano and the reading came on to describe the film.

I can remember a cowboy riding his horse in the clouds, bringing a cigarette out of a case, trying to light it with a match, losing the match and then grabbing a star out of the sky to light it. I can also recall Mum and Dad trying to explain to me how he kept his horse in the air without wings!

My grandmother, originally Mrs Jones, lived in Rhosddu. She had remarried and my then step-granddad, Mr Tom Roden, was an engine driver with the railway running from Wrexham to Seacombe. The number of his engine was 5193 and I used to wave to him going over the bridge at Hollybush as he went past slowly to stop at Cefn-y-bedd station. Mother used to visit Gran a lot. The fare was 3½d from Cefn-y-bedd and she walked from Gwersyllt to Rhosddu, caught the quarter to six train from Gwersyllt and we would meet her. It was often dark so to get through the wood by Hilda's cottage we always took the candle in a jam jar. There were no torches in those days and if there had been we wouldn't have been able to afford one. Maybe carbide lamps were available where you placed lumps of carbide in a base container with a trickle of water, giving off a controlled gas, and 'Bob's your uncle' you got a light, boy! But we never had one.

It was difficult at night walking through the maze of stepping stones to save getting your feet wet. It was all right when you reached the cottage – you had to climb up the 1 in 7 bank to the top of the field (the one we used to slide down for school) and then you were home.

Around this time there was a coal strike but we managed to keep some kind of fire. We always had a spence (the space under the stairs) full of logs, slack or what was known as 'kennel coal', which we picked from the slag banks of the pits or the old colliery workings between Hilda Powell's and Davy Davies' bungalows. There were three pit shafts. If you cleared the turf off you found slag that was burnable. We picked this for months on end and walked it to Llay main colliery bank pushing a wheeled box made from an old pram. We must have pushed that for miles. My mum would come with us to Llay. We would pick about six bags and push them to the railway siding. Uncle George was an engine driver and he'd pick them up for us and take them to Cefn-y-bedd station. We pushed the empty truck to go to collect them. Instead of going up Lord Derby's drive we had to go via Ffrwd because we couldn't get up Hilda Powell's bank to our house. We had to have ropes on the truck to get up the Barracks Hill. We all took a turn at pulling, even the girls. Five or six bags of coal made a difference to the coalhouse or the spence. Bryn Yorkin wood was the next call for firewood. We took a rope with us and any rotten branches were loosened, pulled down, broken up and put into the cart. We stocked up well for the winter.

Thinking of winter reminds me of Christmas and Christmas means toys. What were toys? They too were very sparse. We didn't take our socks or stockings to bed. We pegged them out on the line over the mantelshelf and, of course, in seniority too. Dad, Mum, Hope, as she would be home for Christmas, George, Stella, me and Betty. Father Christmas would come and our sock's contents would consist of an apple, a tangerine, an orange, a bar of chocolate and a ½p mouse. I was lucky – one year I had a mouth organ. Maybe my Gran had sent it. She was ever so good to us, especially to me. Each year we all took turns at having a 'booby', when your sock was full of cinders. I don't know whose joke it was, but it made me cry when it happened to me. I suppose our parents did their best – we had an occasional toy, whether it was second-hand or not. Food came first and we all had a good Christmas dinner. We knew there were always 3d bits in the pudding, with white sauce. We made our own decorations from tissue paper, sometimes in school, but we never bought any. Holly was always prominent and to this day I love to see holly at Christmas.

Milk was collected from Lord Derby's Farm every evening. Someone in the square would call out "Milk!" and all the kids responsible that week for the milk would go out and walk together to the farm with quart-sized galvanised cans. At Christmas the Derbys invited all the kids to the hall and we gathered around the door and sang a few carols. We were presented with a shilling and an Eccles cake. This meant that every year my family would receive five shillings, which was an absolute boon – what my mum could do with five shillings!

At times there was beasting (colostrum – the first milk from a cow after her calf is born) to be had. This was free and it was delicious if cooked properly. Don't forget – Dad was a baker and he was also a good cook. When he made a pudding in the oven it was perfection. I don't think it is served to the public today. I have never seen any. We collected the beasting in a pail and it would last a week. Mind you, you did get fed up with it in the end.

Christmas meant carol singing. We went down to the Red Lion, Ffrwd to sing carols. We sang outside the pub and there was complete silence – you could hear a pin drop. We were all good singers: Bobby, Edith, Ethel, Eric and Dorothy Rowlands, Rosy and Fendolene Roberts, George, Stella, Betty and me from the Hughes family, Roly, Syd and Tom Pugh, maybe Noel and Dennis Wright. We went round with a hat and collected 37/6d, which was a lot of money. It was the only money we ever had to give to our parents. On Christmas night we all went to the Hall again to sing more carols. Standing outside the door were the butler and staff, together with Lord and Lady Derby. We all sang our hearts out for another shilling and an Eccles cake. I don't know why we had Eccles cakes. Perhaps Lord Derby had an interest in the business! This ritual continued year after year and kids we didn't know were there too, they had just come for half a pint of milk in order to qualify for a shilling.

Dad had an old gramophone given to him. It was an HMV and played the old '78s – *Soldiers' Chorus, The Village Blacksmith*, John McCormick, Will Fife, Gracie Fields and George Formby. This got us all singing for Christmas. We were together as a family.

When Christmas was over it was time to get ready for the new year at school. All the kids showed off their presents – dolls, prams, skipping ropes, tops and whips, home-made cat and kinney sticks painted up. One lad came with a leg off a sofa and a four feet stick with a good strong cord attached as a whip. If you haven't seen one I must explain. The bottom of a sofa leg is cut off about eight inches long and a good solid pin is driven into the end so it spins like a top. You grind a bit of the belly out of it so you can wrap the cord around it and put a flat-headed pin on the top to hold it lightly with your foot to the floor. Then you pull the cord and give it a whack – just see it fly in the air, it will spin for ages. As there was very little traffic on the main road at that time, you followed it to school, whacking it all the way, with a good audience following you. In 1928 and 1929 there were very few cars on the road and those that were went very slowly so you had plenty of time to move out of the way after you heard the klaxon horn or the tube horn. We tried to make one but the balance was out because you really needed a lathe to do it, so I had to be content with fag cards or marbles.

The only person in our community who owned a car other than the landowners was Tom Roberts at No. 2. He had a Model T Ford. He didn't drive it much – he probably couldn't afford to run it. Petrol was 11½d a gallon. I can remember Tom starting it up. He jacked up the back wheel to start it, or so I thought. It had a cloth hood covering a metal frame. The two doors opened, but one had a spare wheel attached to it. I can't remember seeing a starting handle anywhere. When it did go out it chugged away nicely. Its top speed was 20-25mph. The law had long been rescinded whereby you had to walk in front with a red flag but I remember Lord Derby's Armstrong being driven and the attendant carrying and waving his red flag. I found out later that it was going to the Carnival at Caergwrle. Most of the transportation was horse-drawn. There were a few charabancs on the road – and maybe a few cloth-covered buses around Wrexham. 'Gentry transport' was by pony and trap. One gent, Mr Gittins, had a Raleigh bicycle. It was about the first one with the two wheels the same size, and was very well made.

Wintertime and dark nights were not for us as we liked to stay out until eight o'clock or so. I hated walking home from school and when it was very bad we went through the Ffrwd. I was frightened as a child. The traction steam engines carried slag from the slag banks opposite the Bridge Inn, Ffrwd. It always upset me as they went past and yet I was nosy. One driver, Jack Taylor, grabbed hold of me, lifted me into the stoking cab where the roaring fire was and got hold of me by my neck and pants. He pretended to throw me into the fire. I can remember screaming. I don't know why he did this because I know I was not cheeky to him nor did I aggravate him. He was nuts. I had the pleasure of meeting him some 32 years later to tell him so. I had nightmares over that and used to scream in my sleep. I even told my mum about it years later. Then she knew why I'd had the bad dreams.

The Barracks Road walk from The Forlace junction must have been one of the most beautiful walks in the area for watching birds, plant life, lizards and grass snakes. They were all there if you kept quiet. I knew all the plants: garlic on the stream, the golden water marshmallows, buttercups, catkins, willow and hazel, primroses, cowslips, celandines, bluebells, violets, harebells, red raddle, cow parsley, deadly nightshade, nettles, dead nettles, dog roses, pink campions, dandelions, and honeysuckle in the hedgerows, which you could guarantee the birds used for their nests. The birds would return each year if their nests were not robbed either by the cuckoo or by man. I knew where to look the following years, to find the same species, if not the same bird. The kingfisher used the same nest for years on Jacks Corner along the Ffrwd Road. I have watched it dive and get a trout many a score of times. A small tawny owl swooped down on our cat one night when we were late bringing water from the hole in the bank at Ffrwd. Pudge was about two years old and followed us about. He was quick and like a tiger. We heard such a noise and scuffle – the owl was on the cat's back. The owl must have seen his eyes shining in the moonlight. Pudge had a good bunch of hairs missing off his neck when we arrived home and examined him – but I think he won.

A little Jenny Wren or one of her fledglings nested for five years on the trot in the same nest. I have seen many a cuckoo's egg in a blackbird's, starling's or thrush's nest. But remember, never interfere with nature. Stupid people, feeling sorry for the nest

22

owner, sometimes removed the egg but if that had happened too often we would have had no cuckoos. I've watched a hatched cuckoo throw an egg out of a blackbird's nest.

I have walked this lane since and the whole hedge has been taken away and a new road built. "Where have all the little birds gone, long time passing?" I ask myself. Even the high bank on The Forlace has been dug out, with all the wild flowers. How we saw them in their turn coming into bloom at the respective times of year. You could rely on that bank to show off its foliage right through the Spring and Summer. A stone wall has now been built to save the bank slipping on to the road.

The road from The Forlace down to the hamlet was only a cart track really. I don't think it was filled in with tarmac – not while we were there. All the road holes were filled in with chipping stones thrown by hand from a horse and cart.

School was beginning to mean something to me and as I moved up my classes I lost the help I had received from Miss Jones. She was a super teacher. The headmaster turned out to be a pig. We had a long walk to school and I think some sympathy should have been shown to us. Everyone who registered late in the morning was caned. There was no messing – you got it. What good it did under these circumstances I have yet to find out. It made your writing hand so sore you couldn't write, which in my opinion impeded your education. I remember my sister, Hope, being knocked all round the classroom with the large register. She had helped us all to get ready for school, made herself late and knew what to expect when she got there. She didn't let us down. She would usher us into our prayer-rooms, be late herself and get caned for it. Caning was allowed in my school days, but in my opinion this man was a real 'capital B'.

I moved up with the rest of my classmates, but had to go into standard four for singing lessons because there were so many classes combined. There were several spare teachers and they walked around the assembled children. No teacher was without a stick. I was too interested in singing to get into lumber.

Once when I was about eight years old there was a commotion half way down the class where I was sitting. I was singled out and hit across the buttocks with a thick stick. When I reached home

23

my brother told my mum and I was examined. I had three very severe welts on my bum and could hardly walk. My dad and mum took me to see Dr Dalling in Caergwrle (what a walk that was, along to The Forlace, down the Cymau Hill, to the first stile, over Bryn Yorkin fields, through the woods, down Plas-yn-Bwll, into the doctor's at Castle Street). I was examined and given some kind of ointment and bandages. The weals had swollen and bled. They were too high up the thigh to bandage and adhesive plaster was not on the market at that time. The doctor asked me who the teacher was – it was a probationer. The doctor took out a case against her and she was sacked. She was very wrong for branding me – I should not have been chastised. I was off school for a month and had to visit the doctor's to go in front of a board. The weals turned septic and I was in a mess. My mum cured it and I was a lad again.

On the way home from the doctor's one day, there was only Mum and me and it was dusk, the night being frosty and bright with a good moon so that we were able to see well. We walked through the woods which never bothered us. I feel more scared today than then. There was generally a bull in the field, but this one was a bastard. As you came out of the woods there was a short field of about 50 yards and then a stile – and over that stile was the bull. Well, we waited to see if the damn thing would go but it wouldn't budge. Mum had her brolly with her and it wasn't just a short one, it was very old and long. Mum hooked the crook of her brolly in the ring through the bull's nose and held it. She told me to go and get over the stile and proceeded to walk the full length of that field with the bull hooked to the brolly. I then had to hold the brolly and the bull until Mum got over the stile. She had a problem trying to unhook the brolly but when she did the bull let hell loose. I knew my mum was a country girl and she knew a little about bulls. We continued our journey for another mile and then Mum said to me "he was very calm" – meaning the bull. Dad went mad and Mum said she wasn't walking round Bryn Yorkin at that time of night again!

Chapter 3
GROWING UP

Just before Christmas 1930 my mum and brother George were disappearing quite often in the mornings. George was missing school and Mum was walking round the house with a new bucket. What was going on? I had no idea. It seemed Mum had got a job somewhere and was taking her own tools. George was missing when we were ready for school. There was something afoot because they were not getting back to the house until after dark. I arrived home early one day and to my surprise there was no one at home, which had never happened before. This state of affairs carried on for a week or more and I was very suspicious. We then broke up for the Christmas holidays and I really smelled a rat. Mum was yanking everything out of the cupboards and bedrooms – and when the coal was being loaded into sacks from under the stairs I knew something was about to happen.

Sam Lawrence, a little fat man who was the coalman-cum-carter, had a fleet of transport (not lorries, but donkeys!). He lived in a straw-thatched cottage next to the Chapel between Cymau and Pistyll Lane. All types of machinery were in his yard, some for repair and some for sale. This man did, knew and had everything. He was OK – a very sound character – and Dad knew him well.

Sam had two donkeys and carts pulled up outside our front and only door and everyone started to carry what bit of furniture we had out to the carts. The first cart was loaded and roped up – and we were on the move. Honestly, I only knew we were moving when Mum walked out with Stella, Betty and me. She told us on the way we were not going back to that house again. Mum knew she had done the right thing for us all and everybody was jumping for joy because now we could get rid of the fleas. This was the most exciting moment of my life and I had not seen the house I was going to live in yet!

The house was called 'Sunny Cote' and was in the village of Hope along Stryt Isa. We arrived well before the first donkey, which gave me time to scrutinise the place. It was *everything*. A flush toilet at the top of the garden, a slopstone and a proper tap you turned on for proper water, drains, a reasonably well kept garden back and front and over the front gate was a laburnum arch. It was absolutely Heaven. No carrying water, no walking up the Cymau Hill from school. Five minutes to the village shop and a beautiful view of Mount Horeb. There were solid roads to walk on, no puddles to splash in. In the dark I noticed there were lights around although there were none in our house. The first donkey cart arrived. My dad was on it with most of the bulky furniture. The cart was unloaded and just moved away to let the other one unload. We were now living in Hope!

The two carts left together in good time to get up to Cymau before darkness fell. Soon a good fire was burning in a much larger grate. Everyone was doing something to get settled in. Dad told me to sort out the paraffin lamps, find the glasses and clean them ready for lighting. There were three altogether. The glasses were always highly polished, the wicks cut straight and cleaned, so I had little to do but to fill them with paraffin and get Dad to light them. I did upset my dad – I asked him if he realised he had carried the paraffin all the way up to The Barracks for the donkeys to bring it down again. Struggling up the hill with our stuff was an absolute pain that we got rid of the day we moved.

One of our uncles called to see us that evening. Mum was wondering what to have for a meal so Jack took Stella and Betty to the village to bring back fish and chips. I was nearly ten and it was the first time I had eaten fish and chips. They were from Bill Davies opposite Arthur the Blacksmith's shop. They were delicious – a taste I will always relish. We were all busy doing something useful. It was a thrill to go to the toilet and pull the chain, watch the water go down the pan, and only have to walk twenty yards. What a treat to go to the tap to get a drink of water and it was nice water too, although the tap only had an old slopstone (no more having to keep buckets of water covered up for drinking). My mum was thrilled to bits not having to carry every drop of water.

Tomorrow was a new day and a new kind of living. Not so

many hardships. A new school and social background, new kids to meet, and even to find the Pughs, who had already moved to Hope. We were a few days off Christmas 1930 and a bit behind with our festive decorating, but knowing Mum and Dad they soon got that right. We had two days to make what decorations we could. All the old stuff had been thrown out at No.3 Plas Maen, The Barracks. Never mind Christmas – what a relief to go down the road 200 yards for a shop! We bought crêpe paper, found the edging off the wallpaper Mum and George had dumped and we made chains with this. All the printing on the edging made it look like the real McCoy. There was holly on the picture frames and a little piece of mistletoe over the adjoining door to 'the parlour'. In those days we had nothing much in it, but it was our 'parlour' and it was almost as sacred as our church – you behaved yourself in the parlour.

It had started to snow. Mum was hanging the last of the curtains and there was a tap on the door. It was the Rev R Theo Jones, the Rector of Hope Church. He was a bit upset. Every year we received a parcel from the local Parish Council and the Rev Theo had been all the way up to The Barracks with the parcel. He said to my mum: "I find you here on the doorstep. You should have told me you were moving. I'm annoyed with you."

He owned a Morris 10/4, which had no heater and he was starved to death, although he was only 300 yards from the Rectory. He saw the fire grate, fell in love with it and was there for an hour. My dad found him a drop of tiddly and Mum managed to calm him down. He was so good to us, but he was also a gentleman to everyone. I will never forget him or any of his family. As he left he shook hands with my parents, telling them he wanted to see me in the church choir the following Sunday morning. Mrs Theo Jones fitted me out with a cassock and surplice. I was a chorister there for 19 years (if you include my Army service in the 1939 – 1945 War).

Christmas came and went once again. At last there was light at the end of the tunnel for us as a family. School was on all our minds. It was to start on the 8th January. I was still in short pants although I was tall. Because I was wearing home-made clothes my knees were up round my hips somewhere. I was clean and tidy and afraid of no-one as I went to Hope Elementary School for the first time. I had left Abermorddu in Standard 3 – Miss Roberts' class. Where I was going now I did not know. I walked into class and was introduced as "the new one from Abermorddu, his name is Austin and he lives along the Post Office Road." Everybody looked at me – have you ever tried to remember names? I felt dejected. Then I saw a face at the back of the class beaming at me. It was Syd Pugh from Rock Cottages in Ffrwd. Was I pleased to see him! I sat as near to him as I could and a teacher came to tell me to go to the headmaster's office. She pointed out the way and off I went. My brother and three sisters were there too, although Hope only had to attend until Easter, when she was leaving for service, in Rhyl of all places. I was given a quick test and soon returned to the class I had left. It was Standard 4 – Miss Silver. As I am left-handed, one of the first upsets I experienced was that I was made to write with my right hand. I was buckled over with this and it showed for a few months ahead. Naturally I thought I would never master this and it put me back quite a bit. It was proved as at the end of the term I had fallen back, half way down the class, but I moved up with the rest after the Summer holidays.

Our new house was going a treat. Mother thought it was marvellous putting the kettle under the tap to fill it (and I thought it was bloody marvellous that we didn't have to carry the bloody water). No fetching milk from Lord Derby's. No walking miles to school. A better bedroom. Although it was only a two bedroomed house, Dad had already put a separation in the bedroom for the girls. George and I had a nice room in the back with a good view over the top road looking over the damson tree, the 'goosegogs' and the strawberries all in the back garden. I was looking forward to the Summer – I was always interested in the garden.

The Winter was quite a severe one and we noticed the difference. It was so much easier here. The roads were tarmacked and cleared or made passable. We'd had to dig our way to school at The Barracks and into the bargain we were caned if we were late. If you didn't get the big shovel out you starved as there was no way to the shops for food. The snow was much thicker too up in the hills.

I had settled in at school. I met Eric and got friendly with all the Garners, two girls and Eric. Connie was the eldest, a year older than me, but Mary was my only schoolgirl sweetheart. They were a smashing family. I also met Mum and Dad Garner. They kept a farm along Stryt Isa Road. Connie was 12, Mary 11 and Eric a bit younger than I at 9½ years old. I went to the farm as often as I could to play and skate on one of the ponds that had frozen over wearing a pair of clogs belonging to George. We would skate for hours. I'm sure my mum thought I had started courting or something! Mary called for me every morning to go to school. Mum even spoke to my dad about me seeing so much of her. It seemed so different going to a house that had everything and meeting people who my mum thought of as 'posh people.'

"Why are they posh people, Mum?" I asked.

"Because Mrs Garner is a sister to Fred Whittingham, and Fred is a 'millionaire'. And you shouldn't go there – they are the family your Great Gran did the washing for when I lived up the mountain," she answered. My mum was really old fashioned and very proud at times – and nothing would alter her, either.

I got on well with the teachers at school and moved to Standard 5. A Mr Norman Baker (later to become head at Elfed School, Buckley), was sports mad and we all had to do it. I was not very good at sport other than football, but I could run a bit (which I had to do, living with my dad, or you received the 'buckle end'). The classes were split up into teams. I was in 'Castle', along with some good sportsmen. One such footballer was Roy Connah. He was a schoolboy international. Roy played for Wales a few times, but this got him a very bad injury which finished his football career for the rest of his life. Les Speed, a Wrexham player, was in the school team too. As I say, I was to be included in the Castle team and I played my first game at right-half against Saltney. We were top of the league. I was dithering. I scored my first goal ever and it took me five minutes to get out of the crowd of players – it was painful. I certainly wasn't used to all this fuss. The team never lived it down as I scored the winner. I never lived it down either!

I moved up to Standard 6 where Mr John Gladstone Jones was my teacher. In that class the girls and boys were mixed in their seats. I don't know why. I had a girl named Phyllis Downing at my desk. I have a feeling this was to get us used to mixing with each other, probably an experiment. I was never behind in my work and it never worried me either. One day Mr Jones was marking our work when he called me out to him. He asked me if I had been copying Phyllis's work. I proved to him I hadn't, so he moved her. She had been copying mine. I knew she was doing it, but I wouldn't tell.

We did gardening in the sixth form. We had our own plots. Mine was always one of the best so I was singled out to show everyone how to get the most out of their efforts. Mr Jones thought I was good, so he asked me to go to do some work in his own garden for him. I had to be careful as I had a paper round to do for Mrs Shone at the Post Office. The two jobs were not spread out much so if I got stuck I could ask my dad to do them for me after I had picked the papers up from the Station. So in the long summer nights I could be at it until dark. They both paid me well, and it was money going into the house. Mrs Jones was good to me. She knew I had newspapers to do so she made sandwiches and a pint mug of tea so that I didn't have to go home to eat, but could go straight on the papers after I finished there. I did mostly all of Mr Jones' gardening by this time. He had a cork leg and, of course, his nickname was 'Corky'. Woe betide anyone he heard calling him that name. He had a very bad temper, but none to compare with Mr Rogers at Abermorddu. Norman Baker was a 'temper' man too, but the head of Hope School was very placid – Mr Emerys Davies who lived at the end of Fagl Lane in the big red house.

Opposite the school was 'The Willow', where we had high jinks. This was where you met your sweetheart, if you had one, at the far end. It had a tip where everybody threw their old mat-tresses or bike frames, anything that was not required was tipped in The Willow. I wanted to try to make a bicycle of sorts so I'd go down to The Willow, pick what I could and hoped it looked like a bike. It did resemble a bike, but that was all. I couldn't find a chain or front spindle. I put the wheel into the forks and bent a six inch nail to make a spindle. It was a bit wobbly, but it moved when I pushed it, so I went up the Church Hill towards the crossroads by Hooley's Garage (it wasn't there at that time but has been built since). There were no tyres or brakes. I had no sense – but try and tell me that then! I turned it round and started down the hill, went to turn into Post Office Road and went smack against the stone wall as I turned in doing 15 mph. The brake lever attached to the handlebars stuck in my neck. Mr Welch came to my aid and I managed to pick myself up and push my pride and joy home to Sunny Cote. I also had a belting into the bargain. I suppose they couldn't see I was mechanically minded and they should have known that there's 'nowt queerer than folk.'

The Willow was for everything. Every dinner time at school we had our sandwiches and went off to pick groundnuts, play 'footy' or meet the girls. We all flocked there. We had a whale of a time. We tried to sell the nuts to the girls and if they had no money they had to forfeit something. One girl, Daisy Grandy, lived in the house by The Willow. She used to go home for money and would never come back to save paying the forfeit. We got wise to this and if she messed us about we used to stuff her knickers with grass, one of us collecting the grass, two holding her down and another stuffing the grass in her knickers through the leg. She was always late for school and would be reprimanded. Daisy, although she was in a bad state, with grass all over her, never told on us, not a dicky bird to anyone. She was a great girl. When she arrived home her mum, who had been watching her through the bedroom window, would belt her. Our names were mud, that is Roy Cliff, Georgie Jones, Vernon Lewis and me. Daisy's mum would meet us as we came out of the school yard and chase the hell out of us – and us being choir boys too! She complained to the Rector and when he saw us on the Sunday he used to laugh his head off.

"You've been at it again, you lads!" he'd say.

Where did I find the time to do all this? I was a paper boy, a bellringer, troop leader in the Scouts, I did Mr Jones' garden, and had bell practice twice a week. Saturday was reserved for the Cymau to help Glenys. She had given me 24 chicks to have for myself. I had a proper bike by now and I gave her the full day to clean everything away from the incubators. She was always pleased to know I had been up and done so much of the work. I whitewashed all the interior and dug nettles from outside. Mrs Thomas came up with a jug of tea and sandwiches and I was paid well for doing it, together with a dozen eggs to take home – and they were eggs too!

Trippers from Merseyside came to Caergwrle every Sunday. The return fare was 1/6d. They crossed from Liverpool to Seacombe, then took the Wrexham train to Caergwrle. When the trains came in the lads were like vultures. The Castle was always the venue and there were hundreds of them there. It took all sorts to make Caergwrle.

I became friendly with Ivor Moore – we did Scouts, choir and bellringing together. Ivor was a great friend. He died very young. I really missed him when he died as we were inseparable. We never went out without each other. Ivor lived by the school and he seldom came to my house and when he did never came inside. I often went to call for him but never went inside his house either. His mother was very reserved, very nice but stand-offish. Every Sunday morning after Matins we would walk round Caergwrle. Ivor had a girlfriend. I think she was Gwyneth Edwards who lived in the house up the drive by the Glynne Arms where the traction engines were kept which Jack Taylor used to drive. I hadn't been friends with Ivor for long when his dad died. He had been ill for some time. I remember Ivor going to his funeral and us having to go in the choir for the service. We had special time off from school. It was a sad day for Ivor and his family. It left Mrs Moore with a teenage daughter Glenys, Billy, who was Ivor's senior by five years, and Ivor.

As time went by we went through the same ritual every Sunday. A walk through Caergwrle, up past the Castle High Street, down Fellows Lane and along the Sarn and over the bridge. Ivor brought me out quite a bit, in style of clothing, how to look as though you owned yourself, not dirty or scruffy. I was earning money here and there and I gave it up at home. Even when George started to work the parish relief took their share out of it. It turned out we got nothing more. It did help a bit when Stella started to work. She had to give Mum 2/6d a week and she lived out at Meadowslea Hospital. George was in a quarry on 4½d an hour, approximately £2 a week or less by the time the stoppages were taken out. Everything we earned we had to tell the authorities about and they stopped money from us. George was only gaining 7/6d per week after his hard work. You can guess why I was still in home-made clothes. I was always clean, but could never look smart. I was hoping by the time I started to work the system would change, but it didn't.

I was spending a lot of time at my Gran's in Rhosddu. Every Saturday I caught the 8.20am train from Hope Station to Gwersyllt, and either walked or got a Price's bus from Badrocks corner to West View in Rhosddu. The train fair was 4½d to Gwersyllt and a penny return ticket on the bus and it dropped you by the door, too. There were no bus stops. I used to scrub out for Gran. I started on the red tiles by the front gate, worked my way through the passage, washed around the block of carpet in the parlour and the fireplace, then went on into the kitchen, did the whole of the kitchen and finished in the scullery – all on my hands and knees. I would clean out the fire grate and the brasses, go out into the yard and swill that, and then Grandad would be due home and I'd have a bloody good dinner. After dinner I cleaned the shoes belonging to Grandad, Jack, Sam, Trevor, Albert, Aunty Nancy, Dolly and Ethel. They were all put on the stairs in seniority. Before any of them picked up their shoes they had to pay me 6d for cleaning them. Gran saw to this. She kept a wonderful house. There was never an argument or an ill word from any of them. If I cleaned two pairs of shoes, I had a shilling. I used to have about six shillings altogether at the end of the day. Gran gave me 2/6d and we always went to Wrexham to get the margarine from The Maypole in Regent Street. I always got seven lbs and it would cost near enough 2/3d. The grocer used to parcel it up in brown paper and string it so it hung on your fingers to save it melting in your hands. Gran and I would catch the bus after she did her shopping and she would say her goodbyes on the bus as she got off and I continued to Badrocks Corner to catch the train home. I had 3d change out of the margarine (which lasted us all week) and six bob to give to my mum.

With me being such a big churchman, it was time for me to become confirmed by the Bishop of St Asaph. I had to have a new suit for this and let me tell you it was the greatest thrill of my life to be able to go into long trousers. I was sure everyone would laugh at me when they saw me and I felt very embarrassed when

I put them on for the first time on the Sunday to go to church. The first two people I saw were my friends Dorothy Lloyd and Hazel Underwood. "Oh, don't you look funny in long trousers?" they cried. I suppose I ran like hell. Someone in the choir had seen me and they were waiting for me as I walked in through the vestry door. They all whistled. I remember Mr Wykes, the Curate, saying how smart I looked.

My Gran had promised me this a long time ago so she took me to Burtons in Wrexham. Uncle Sam worked there and it was he who kitted me out. Long trousers, brown tweed suit. Not only had I not had a new suit, I had never had long trousers. Friends passed me in the street because they didn't recognise me.

The world was changing for me. I was just 14 years old and I was confirmed at Hope Parish Church at Easter 1936. I was also due to leave school that Summer. You couldn't leave at Easter.

That year we moved from Sunny Cote to Inglewood Villas. Mum met a school friend from Pont-y-derlyn. She had a three bedroomed house and gave Mum first choice of it. It was in the centre of the village just behind the Red Lion towards the cemetery. It was Sam Lawrence who moved us once more. By this time he also had moved to Hope into a thatched cottage in Fagl Lane where the new school is now right opposite Ted Hill's shop. His donkeys were still in the yard, but he also boasted two lorries, a Reo and a Chevrolet. This meant that the donkeys were on their way out for haulage purposes. He used the Reo to move us.

When we moved it was a long trek down the single path to the backs of the houses. It must have been at least 350 yards to carry the furniture. A big consolation prize was at the end of our flit we had our own bed. Our sisters had a separate room and Mum and Dad had their own room. We still had to manage with paraffin lamps as no houses had electricity as yet (I think it was on the agenda), so it was still candles in jam jars for bed, although we all had our own little lamps for our bedsides. We met our new neighbours – the Lewis family – Tom, Charlie, Lena, Barbara and Beth. We all got on well together. We soon became a part of village life and I made lots of friends outside school, most of whom were in the church choir. There was Ivor, Les, Philip Price, Vernon Lewis, and Kenny just over the hedge. To our amazement, the Pugh family had moved to the top of the entry right by us. It seemed we couldn't get away from them, not that we wanted to, but we seemed to follow each other around – Syd, Tom and Rowland, who was a friend of my brother George.

It wasn't long before I was a member of the North Wales bellringers' association, eventually ringing in almost every church in the area of North Wales – Hope, Buckley, Mold, Northop, and the great peel at Gresford, where the Randles almost had a full team. They were all cousins of mine. I can still remember the peels: Plain Hunt, Bob Major, Bob Minor, Grandsire and, as usual, the call changes. Ivor, who was also a bellringer, was a King's Scout and Troop Leader. I, compared to Ivor, was a tenderfoot, and had just become Patrol Leader of the Peewits.

Ivor was a little bit older than me and had already been on a Jamboree. There was another one shortly after at Abergele Castle and the Troop was run by George Evans from Vounog, Penyffordd, who became District Commissioner in 1938. The whole Troop was learning semaphore as often as we could, as our task at the Jamboree was to build a signalling tower at either end of the camp and send and receive a clear message in semaphore. Ivor lived nearer the school than I did and we met for a bike ride before we went to the meetings. He would drag me along to his girlfriend's home in Caergwrle. I would buzz off and leave them. Her surname was Edwards, and lived in the greystone building just past the bottom of the Gwalia. I would nip up the Gwalia to see my Aunt Kate and Polly, while Ivor did his little bit of courting. I often pinched his bike before he was ready to go to the meeting held at the Church Institute in Caergwrle. I wanted money for my uniform and to be able to go to the Camp at Llandulas, so I took a job delivering papers, again for Mrs Shone at Hope Post Office. I was earning 2/6d a week. I gave it to my mother and didn't get much out of it.

The world Jamboree was held the following year at Abergele Castle. The Chief Scout, Lord Baden Powell, was present. Once again, our task was to build a signalling tower out of Scout poles for sending the semaphore messages to another one built half a mile away. It was 35 feet high, with a 6ft x 6ft platform, and safety rails all round the top. The whole structure was held together with rope. It was quite solid and Syd Bellis from Rhyddyn Hill was the Semaphore Signalman for the Peewit Patrol of which I was Patrol Leader. We won our heat of the day and the troop was presented to the Chief for congratulations. We were there for four days. The weather was beautiful. We had a good camp.

The following year I went to Llandulas to a fortnight's camp. Ivor and I had worked hard for this for six months. Most of the tents and equipment were from the Scout Headquarters and were transported direct to the camp right on the sea front – Jones' Farm under the railway bridge. The weather was good and everyone expected a good holiday. This was the first holiday I had ever had and it turned out a semi-disaster for a few of us. It concerned Syd Bellis, his brother, Jess, John Griffiths from Caergwrle and myself. Most of the Senior Scouts were out at Rhyl and we had the youngsters down for the night. We were all sitting around the campfire singing, eating cheese dreams and drinking cocoa, and thought nothing of it. We all went to bed and I heard the Seniors coming in and told them that everything was OK. I tried to go off to sleep, but couldn't as I had pains in my tummy. I got up to go to the latrine and there I stayed for most of the night. It felt like dysentery or something. I was ill and ended up at Rhyl hospital. It turned out I had been dosed with 'castertabs' in my cocoa. I was in a very bad way. This was a lesson to most of the company. Two Scouts admitted they had dosed me and they were expelled from the camp and sent home. It upset a lot of people. I was ill for the rest of the camp and a further week. The only thing they could give me was chalk. I was on this for three or four days.

My pal Ivor was not feeling very well before the camp and arranged to follow on at a later date. He didn't arrive so the first thing I wanted to know was how he was. I went to see his mother, who told me he had been to see a doctor and that he was very ill. We were inseparable, both being in the choir which meant being in church three times on a Sunday. Every Sunday morning we took a walk into Caergwrle, back home for dinner, out for Sunday School, a walk round Caergwrle again, Evensong at 6.30pm then, if it was nice, a walk round the village again. I suppose were were getting to be interested in the girls. We both had bikes, so we would bike to Llay, Cefn-y-bedd and back through

Caergwrle. We knew everyone and everyone knew us. Ivor was always whistling. He picked up a song as soon as it was out but, of course, he had a radio. We didn't have one. I wondered at times what he was singing as he knew every song. I was miles behind him. He was always making dates with girls and he seemed to be too forward and I was trying to catch up with him. He passed for Grammar School so I didn't see him at school. That was the only time we were not together.

Ivor was a real mod of the day. As soon as a tune came into the radio chart he had it – all the tunes of the day. Anything that came out he knew it. As we didn't have a radio, I picked up tunes from Ivor. We cycled for miles and he never stopped whistling. He was also a dance 'tanner hop' lad. Never missed a dance at The Institute. It was sixpence entrance fee and good modern ballroom dances. If you saw Roy Cliff and Margaret Grindle dancing a 'tango' you saw dancing. Although I never went on a dance floor, I knew what a dance was. Ivor had lots of girlfriends. They even came to church to meet him afterwards. I usually tagged along with whoever's friend turned up as there was no one special in my life then.

I was always interested in transport and spent a lot of time at Sam Lawrence's yard which, by this time, had moved down the Sarn Road. The old straw-thatched cottage had been condemned, and it was now derelict. Sam had quite a fleet by now. He had four sons and a daughter, so had plenty of young help. They carried coal, milk, anything for a profit. I would be up early to go for a ride round the farms, meet in the yard at 8.00am and off to Liverpool to Hansons. The Mersey Tunnel was not open at this time so we had to take ferries, Runcorn, Wallasey, Woodside. Any of them – I have crossed them all. The one at Runcorn was chain driven. It was weird. I never felt safe on it as the chain rattled like mad and it frightened you. Driving on and off was as bad too. We were also held up at Queensferry. At that time shipping was on the move on the River Dee. Most of the ships were owned by Coppacks of Connah's Quay. The old blue bridge used to split in the centre and raise upwards to let the shipping go through and it could be a good half hour before we were on our way again. You could then wait for the ferries for anything up to an hour.

Old Sam was a learned man. He did most of the repairs. He even smelted his own white metal for the mains and big ends. I watched him for hours, so I got to know all the family – Sammy, Stan, Jimmo, and Dorothy, the village 'bombshell'. I suppose they all had to live off the profit. I was gradually learning to drive and I backed into something. Sam kicked my backside off the yard. We were friends later as my dad was his pal. Incidentally, my dad was the first person to give Sam a banana. He had never seen one before. He had plenty of new custom, doing crankshafts and smelting big ends for engines.

The Mersey Tunnel was about to open. This would save hours off transport runs – no more waiting at the ferries. I went through the Tunnel in about 1934 at a cost of a shilling. I can't remember exactly when it opened, but I'm sure we were some of the first to go through.

At last our home was to have electricity installed. A man came with a bag of tools, drilled holes in walls, pushed and poked wire through, connected round switches to the wire, dug up the entry path and connected wires into the house at the front door. He spoke to me and told me I could switch it on. Hurray, no more bloody paraffin lamps! No more candles in jam-jars! This was living!

The house was beautifully situated. The view up over Mount Horeb was stunning. We were also handy for the shops. Ted Hill's, Shone's, The Post Office and Madley's Chip shop were only a stone's throw away. The station for a train to Wrexham was nearby too – we were in clover.

I was lying in bed one morning when I felt a disruption. It shook the house and the surroundings. I went into my dad's room. He was sleeping on his own because he was ill again.

"What was that, Dad"? I asked.

"God knows, maybe an earthquake!" he replied.

It was terrific. It was an eruption all right – the Gresford Pit Disaster, where over 200 men died and are still buried underground. This is the price men paid for digging coal for us and nobody cares. I think it was about 11 o'clock in the morning. Please don't quote me on the time, but I know I was in bed and felt it shake the room.

My dad became ill again. Mother was concerned, so she had the doctor to him. He came and took samples of his sputum, analysed it and found the complaint from which he was suffering. He still smoked Woodbines and I'm sure these were killing him. Why I started smoking I will never know. Dad was sixty-two.

Dad improved in health and we seemed to be a little closer. We did things together more. The doctor ordered him out more so he took over the paper round. He met the trains in the morning, took the papers to the Post Office and helped to sort them out and get ready for delivery. I think the money had gone up to 7/6d a week by now, because it was a big round, all along Stryt Isa, down to the school, as far as the bridge on Fagl Lane, up to Nelly Walton's in Caer Estyn, Hope Hall, all Station Road. The papers had to be collected three times from the Post Office. This was all done in my name, otherwise Dad would have lost his insurance.

After we left Sunny Cote, my sister Hope moved from Rhyl to Meadowslea Hospital. Stella already worked there. I used to go up to take a dress or something that mother had washed. Mum was 'wash mad' – if there is such an expression. She started to do some washing for Mrs Shone at the Post Office, who paid her well.

The Pughs were up the entry and Mrs Pugh was like Mrs Prydderch from the Barracks, always a welcome, and a treacle butty if you wanted one. We didn't possess a radio. When Tommy Farr was fighting Joe Louis in Las Vegas (I think) my dad, George, Tom next door, Syd, Tom, Roly, Dad Pugh and me met at three in the morning to listen to the fight. The youngsters had pop and butties, while the men had beer. It was a full house. The reception faded every now and again as the sets were powered by dry and wet accumulators. I think Farr won. There were more fights which came over the ocean by cable.

The Scouts were having a celebration to commemorate the 1st Hope Church Scout Troop. The Guides were led by Miss Theo Jones, assisted by Bunty Stennett from Pennyffordd. This coincided with Caergwrle Carnival. We had been planning for months. We were able to tell people about the underground passages between Bryn-y-Gar, Caergwrle Castle and Bryn Yorkin Farm. We had discovered the tunnel at the Castle. We found the entrance at the farm in the cellar in Bryn Yorkin and had excavated a tunnel part way up to the road to Caer-Estyn. We did well with this and I think it went on record for 'Travels in the Wirral'.

My brother George had started to work at the brickworks, hoping he would be better off, but it was piece-work. The oil from the bricks and the pressings left a smell on his clothes. He worked too hard for what he was paid. This is where Rowland Pugh and he met up again. The brickworks (Drury Works) was run by Johnny Thompson. George wasn't there for long as he moved to a quarry at Gwersyllt working for Alun Edwards. He then moved to the quarry at Caer-Estyn which was nearer home.

I remember Mother making sandwiches for him and she tasted the salmon out of a tin. Apparently the tin was 'blown' and they were both poisoned. I had to call home from work to try and do something for them. It was terrible to see them, both Mum and George, they were so sick and also had diarrhoea. All the bed sheets were dirty. I had to use the sheets off the girls' beds and try to get some warm water to wash the dirty ones. Drying them was the worst part. We had no heat, only the fire – not even a side boiler in this house. There was a washing boiler in the kitchen and a proper bath under the window. This was covered with a worktop and a slopstone in the corner with a drain. I got the boiler going. You had to transfer the water to the bath by bucket, so I filled it, dumped everything in and put the sheets on the line to dry. The doctor made a formal claim on some insurance and Mum received some compensation.

The verger's job had become vacant at Hope Church. This entailed a lot of cleaning and the Rector came to see us to ask if our family could do it between them. It meant the job would be in my name, again because if it had been put in Dad's name, he would have lost his insurance.

Anyway, I was now parish clerk and verger of the parish church. I also blew the organ for about six years. This didn't stop me being a member of the choir too. We had to see to christenings, weddings and funerals and also to make sure that the church was locked at a certain time of night, keep the central heating going through the Winter, order coke, clinker and clean the huge boiler, bleed all the radiators, keep the church clean, lock and look after the belfry. One did a lot for one's money, but I enjoyed every minute of it.

My dad never had any money to gamble with, but he was always on the look out for £1. There was a man named Bellis who was a bookie. It appeared Dad did a bit of running for him and some stupid idiot reported this to the police. The police went to the Rectory to ask for the keys of the belfry to view the bells. They must have had spying glasses with them because they told my dad they saw him pass betting slips to Bellis. My dad, who had never been involved with the police before, fell for it, and after being summonsed to appear at the Magistrates' Court, pleaded guilty and was fined ten shillings: it was his first offence and the only one ever. After the case, the Sergeant gave Dad the ten shillings back. Dad asked him if he could also give him back his character. Bellis was fined heavily as he had a lot of cash on him and they proved my dad had passed the slips. They were written in red pencil which they found on my dad. If he had thrown it away they couldn't have proved a thing as we knew it was impossible for them to see from the belfry. The Rector found out about this and I know he really went for the Sergeant. I had never heard him swear before, but he cursed him good and proper.

Ivor, Les, Dorothy and Hazel – great friends of mine through attendance at Church – were among the select few to have the privilege of the use of the tennis courts at the Rectory. In return we kept the courts in playable condition, mowed them and marked them out with the lime marker. This pleased 'his lordship', especially when they had guests at the Rectory. It was appreciated that we kept it nice. We met as often as we could to play tennis. I was the only one who hadn't played before. All the others had played at school as they all went to Grammar School. I didn't know what a racquet was or how to use it. I lost and lost and lost. No-one wanted me for a partner. Anyway I improved and caught up, and began to know what an 'ace' was. I was also left-handed so it suited when we played doubles. I began to win games. We alternated partners. Not all of us could be there together all the time, so it would be Hazel and Ivor playing Dorothy and me.

Let me explain – Les and Dorothy (brother and sister) went to Hawarden Grammar School, Hazel went to Grove Park, Wrexham and Ivor to Hawarden Grammar School. Les was a slim nine stone, very agile, a Rugby lad at school, Dorothy was 9½ stone, with a heavy frame, but very agile and smart, a very good looking girl. Hazel was about 7½ stone, just like a gypsy's whippet, a beautiful looking girl. We all got on well together as we were about the same age, Ivor was the senior. He was puny, underweight in fact, but he had packs of energy. I was about 11 stone at the time, always active and agile, but not the Rugby type. I was friendly with Hazel's parents. Her dad had a lorry so I suppose that was the attraction – it was on wheels and moved! Hazel's mum was very reserved, although she was all right with me whenever we met. She appeared to be shy. I never saw her out. Hazel told me later her mum had a limp and it was getting worse. That was as much as she told me. (I learned much later that Hazel and her mother thought I was the cat's whiskers!). After the war I called to see her, but she was working abroad with the British Embassy in India. I think she now lives as a spinster in a bungalow at Hope.

Chapter 4

FIRST JOBS

I was 14 years old and found my first job as an apprentice fitter with Alf Davies at Padeswood in his new garage. Herbert Evans got me the job at 7/6d per week. I needed tools and overalls. I was very excited at this and was looking forward to starting to work. I was bitterly disappointed because I never started. Someone had informed my dad that R Newbrook wanted a lad to learn horticulture. It meant digging yourself to death. The wage was ten shillings per week and I had to take it because it was 2/6d a week more than serving an apprenticeship.

There are things I will never forgive my parents for and this was one of them. I was 14 and I cried for days over it. Not only that, I had let Herbert down. That to me was as important as losing a chance in a lifetime – to get to use tools.

It didn't take me long to find out how to double dig. I dug about 100 yards by 25 yards and this took me about three to four months. What bothered me was that it was never used afterwards. A fisherman friend living next door to the land told me it was never used for growth, only to be grown over with vegetation. What a waste of energy and the talent that I had with a spanner in my hand – which I will prove later on. I packed this job in and went to another market gardener – Halls in Penyffordd. I stayed there for only a few months because I found a better job as an errand boy for a butcher, Reg Buckley. He was a proper butcher who knew his trade. We killed our own animals and Reg could side a beast with the next man. It paid ten shillings per week, plus my food and was only a quarter of a mile from home. The food was out of this world and I had never tasted food like it, although my mum was a good cook! We had the best of all the offal, lambs' fries, sweetbread, liver, kidney, self-cured tongue, oxtail soups, everything, and his wife was a good cook too. She was Olwyn – a Williamson from Cymau. Her father was still alive and he helped me with the pressed meat, pies and sausages which I decided to make ourselves as Reg was buying them in. My job was also to keep the place clean, wire brush the blocks, clean and sawdust the floors, clean the runners from the sheeps' offal to make skins for sausages, cut up the meat from the sheep and beasts' heads, the pigs' heads, everything that was good enough to eat. I made certain to put only the best in my sausages – consequently the sales went up after I had been at it a few weeks. Everyone was after my sausages!

Reg and I got on well together and I liked the job, but he had a filthy temper. One instance in particular: he bought a new set of scales costing £40. He had only had them a few weeks when I had done something to upset Mrs Buckley. He came out of the house in a foul temper and eventually threw the cleaver at me. Had it hit me it could have marked me for life. Instead I ducked and it hit the scales and smashed them. That is the kind of person he was. Another instance we went to collect sheep from Caer-cloggyn which is near to Cymau. By this time he had a new chain-driven Trojan, and it got bogged down in the mud. He got in a filthy temper and threw a brick through the windscreen. We eventually got away, but we were late for slaughtering at Dawsons in Kinnerton, where we did all our killing. Every week it was a beast, two sheep and maybe two pigs. The meat was hung till Tuesday, cut up and we were on our rounds by Tuesday afternoons. We did a good area – Hope, Llay, Caergwrle, Penyffordd, Broughton and I did a lot of locals on my bike. I used to handle a lot of money. I wanted 1½d for something, so I diddled my sister, who worked for a lady at Hope Hall, out of this by putting it on her bill. The family were very well off anyway, so they wouldn't have missed it. My sister found out, told Reg and I was sacked. I was sacked for 1½d.But I was only sacked for two days – Reg came for me and I went back for 12/6d a week. I had half a crown rise for pinching 1½d! This is quite true and I have regretted it ever since.

Reg said to me: "Come and ask for it next time."

It was a good job in that I could get away in the summer nights to play tennis at the Rectory. Les, Dot and Hazel were still at school, so they were already playing as I reached there. Fair play, they always stopped when I arrived to make up the double team.

Doubles were more interesting. We played most nights of the week. Bellringing and Scouts were only on Wednesdays and Thursday and we had the place most Saturdays too.

It was getting near to Christmas again, and we had a lot of killing to do at Dawson's Slaughterhouse. Reg liked his noggin of whisky, and this particular Christmas Dawson called him in for a drink. We had a beast, two ewes and two pigs to kill. We arrived there at about 2.30pm. Reg went in for a drink while I got the boilers going for dressing the pigs. He hadn't shown at five o'clock so I decided to kill and dress the two ewes. I had kept the water boiling for two hours and was fed up. I had dressed the two sheep when Reg came out and really blew his top. He threw everything at me and a beast's foot hit me on the side of the ear. I flew out of the yard, by which time it was dark. I ran almost all the way home up the Kinnerton switchback. I went in, told my mum and dad, and in a few minutes Reg was by the back door wanting me to go to help him kill the beast and the two pigs. I, like a fool, went. I stuck it for another few months.

I had applied for a job on the Railway as a trainee porter. This could be at any station between Hawarden and Wrexham. I had no way of getting there even if I got the job, so I had already started saving a deposit on a new bicycle from Walter Roberts' of Wrexham. It was 7/6d as a deposit, and 2/6d a week thereafter. I think the bike cost £4.7s.6d plus the hire purchase charge. Anyway I bought a brand new Raleigh sports model, with dropped handlebars, caliper brakes and a hub dynamo. It was the gear! Eventually my job came through to join the Railway. It was 14/- a week at Gwersyllt Station, starting at 4.20 am. It had taken me a long time to get this job. I had only myself to thank for it. I had references from Mr R Theo Jones, Mr Emrys Williams, my old headmaster, and one from Mr Gladstone Jones. I still have one of these references. It was very complimentary and, at that time, I suppose it must have been deserved. Anyway, it got me the job. I was doing 'great guns.' I could work out a good career for myself, so I was happy.

I was up early, about 3.30 am, so as to give me time to get to Gwersyllt by 4.10am. I could do it comfortably. I was cycling down Llay Hall by the Holly Bush behind a lorry load of bricks, or what looked like bricks, when one dropped off in front of me and I hit it. Over the handlebars I went and damaged myself and the bike. Eventually I was taken to Dr Clark's in Abermorddu. I had clips and stitches and was told to go home, leaving my bike at Mrs Davies' sweet shop in Cefn-y-bedd. I don't know what happened, but I went to work the next day and was told I was sacked and I would be getting my notice through the post. I got it and finished.

My next employment was as delivery boy at Ledgards' in Abermorddu. I stuck at that until I was old enough to go driving. At 17 I applied for a licence and took a driving job with Bill Hughes at Penyffordd. This was to be £3 per week on the coal wagon, filling bags with coal for delivery around the area. We had a large area to cover. When I first started we went to Llay Hall to the sidings for it. The wagon was a three-ton Morris Commercial. We carried 50 sacks and every sack had to be weighed, so it was a job for two people. Bill handled the sacks and I used the shovel. It took a few hours to load. I had no idea about driving on the road. I can't remember starting this job, although it was the best one I ever had up to this time. The first day I wanted to see how Bill drove the wagon. I know now he wasn't a good driver. He had no 'go' in him. Anyway, he had just married Betty Hall, who was Guide Mistress at Hope. I knew her fairly well. I had to meet her a lot so it was as well we got on together. Bill gave me a go. I didn't have to be taught a lot and soon picked it up, so off we went to Llay Hall, bags and shovel ready. I took over the driving and was going through Caergwrle to Cefn-y-bedd. I came to the fork in the road by Ledgards', lost control of the vehicle, everything went blank and I lost control of myself as well. I got out and refused to get back in. Bill calmed me down and in I got and did very well after that. It is best for a learner to do this, so long as he doesn't damage anything. You realise after that sort of shock that you must keep control of the vehicle.

I started this job in the Spring so I had the Summer to look forward to. My routine was: finish dead on time, bike home, wash and go out for tennis with my friends. Wednesday – Scouts. Thursday – bell practice. I followed Caerestyn Wanderers football club. For a few seasons they were top of the league. They beat everyone in their stride. I took up amateur refereeing, but packed it in to concentrate on scouting and became a King's Scout at the end of it all.

Les, my pal, came to see me to tell me he was leaving Grammar School at the end of the term to go on a course and start a job with the Railway in the London headquarters. According to how he progressed would decide his future. He was therefore away from the tennis so I had no help with the lawns. I was working away, grass cutting, and I saw someone pushing the barrow. It seemed Dorothy and Hazel had been watching me with the motor mower for a long time. After that I showed them what to do. I would often arrive there to find the grass cut and one of them starting to mark the court out, so long as I left some lime in the marker. They said Les and I had done so well keeping it nice that they had to offer to help. This is the kind of girls they were. Although we missed Les, we still managed to play quite a lot.

Summertime was near, and the coal business gets a bit slack then, so we had to find other work to keep us going. We would shift hay, furniture, anything to keep the wheels turning. Bill asked me to help in the garden. "OK, Bill!" I said, so it was spades out and get digging. We were putting spuds in when one of our best customers, a Deacon, came past. I say 'best' because he bought all his coal in the Summer. We filled his coalhouse full to the brim and we only called to see if he was all right afterwards. This type is a good customer. Anyway, he walked past and said: "Hello Bill, putting tatters in?."

"Aye" said Bill.

"What sort are they, King Edwards?"

"No" says Bill, "Presperterians."

"What sort's them, Bill?."

"Those big hollow buggers," Bill replied.

No need to say we lost the order for his coal!

If we ordered Haydock coal it always came in at Penyffordd Station in a railway wagon, and we filled bags the same as at Llay or Llay Hall, but we had to wait until it came in, so any day we could be busy from 8.30am. The trains were running to Mold at that time from Central Station, Chester. It was a very busy line. Every morning there were 20 or 30 passengers from Penyffordd to

Chester. Three or four girls were customers of ours, Mary Davies, Joyce Bellis, Margaret Fox and probably some I didn't notice. Oh, and Bunty Stennett, the new Akela, the daughter of Colonel Stennett from Hope Road. The Colonel was a veteran of the 1914-18 War and of the Boer War. Bunty was the cat's whiskers, a beautiful brunette who was noticed by everyone, but well out of my class. She walked with a wiggle. She did the 'Tennessee wigg-walk' for everyone. I am dwelling on Bunty because I met her in the Forces during the War on more than one occasion.

I was just turned 17 by now and had not been out with a girl. I was getting interested, so while we were loading in Penyffordd I was all eyes as either Joyce, Mary or Bunty would come for the train. I was more sweet on Mary than anyone because I thought she was on my level. Her dad was a railwayman, and we always passed the time of day with each other. Her mum was nice too. I was just interested, that's all. Then Joyce would walk down, give a half wave because Bill was there, and on to the platform for the train. When we were loaded we went up to Bill's house for a break – tea, biscuits or a sandwich. There was always something. One particular morning we went for our break and I was introduced to a girl who was there. She was quite attractive. Her name was Ivy and she lived in Pontblyddyn. We seemed to hit it off together so we dated. We went to the Regal Cinema in Chester, the tanner hops in Pontblyddyn, the Majestic in Wrexham. Where else to go round the area?

I was also friendly with the maid from the Rectory at Hope – Vola Hopwood. She was a very attractive girl, although she was courting and much my senior. She asked if I would mind meeting her off her bus at Pont-y-derlyn crossroads at 9.30 pm. It was a lonely walk to the Rectory at Hope on the dark nights. There was never anything between us, but we were good friends. I went with Ivy to the tanner hops at Ponblyddyn one night and Vola was there. She came to speak to me and dragged me onto the dance floor. I couldn't dance, neither could anyone teach me as I had two left feet. Ivy took exception to this as she knew I was meeting Vola off her bus at night because I had told her so. I don't think things were quite the same after that, and there was nothing in it at all. In fact the Rector asked me to meet Vola to save him going with the car.

Easter Sunday 1939 was a beautiful sunny morning. There was a stranger in the front pew of the church. We, as choirboys, had a full view of the congregation and knew who were strangers to the church. The stranger was a girl, with slightly sandy coloured hair, big light blue eyes and aged about 17. I casually took particulars, sang and then walked down the aisle back to the vestry – nothing unusual in that.

"What a gorgeous smile," I thought, so it was off with my surplice and cassock, out of the vestry door, down the steps to where the organist, Mr Herbert Evans, William Pritchard, Mrs Clark and daughter Ann were always talking. We had a meeting every Sunday after Church. The girl in the pew was also there. Mrs Clark introduced her to me as Alice Cooke. She was from Blackburn, Lancashire. When the meeting broke up I walked with Alice to Caergwrle and found she was a cousin of one of my school pals, John Thomas, from the corner shop in the High Street. We hit it off, and arranged to meet that night after evensong. She was in church and we met for the ritual afterwards and walked our way to her aunt's in Caergwrle. We told her aunt, whom I knew, that we were going for a walk. We went to Fagl Lane and over the stone bridge, along the River Alyn, back to Sarn Bridge and then up through the bottom street into High Street to her aunt's house. She was staying for two weeks, so I would be able to see her again in the week and I invited her to the Rectory for a game of tennis. There was no doubt she was a dresser and she looked great in her golden slacks and black sweater – very 'tennisy' indeed. Hazel and Dorothy were pleased to see she knew how to play, so we played doubles for a change. It was better than one sitting out now Les was not there. After tennis I walked home for my bike to save walking from Caergwrle after seeing Alice home.

49

Chapter 5

THE WAR STARTS

Everyone was edgy just before the War, which we all knew was inevitable the way things were going, as Hitler had invaded his adjoining countries and was about to invade Poland. Our family was concerned about my brother, George. He had already been notified of his eligibility to be called up for service because his job was not a reserved occupation. He could receive his call-up papers any day.

I was still with Billy Hughes and concerned about what would happen to our family if George had to go and I had to follow, with Dad being as he was. I made discreet enquiries from a cousin, Syd Bellis, who worked for Alun Edwards. He couldn't promise anything, but tried to find me a job with them, hoping I could be employed in a reserved occupation. It was not that I had any inclination not to be called up, but I looked at it from my mum's point of view, and I said nothing at home.

There were rumours everywhere. According to the newspapers the Territorial Armies were mobilising. Hitler's name was beginning to ring in the ears of the youngsters. Earl Belisha was forming an army. Some men were joining as Bevan boys for work in the pits. Industry was flat out, with Shotton Steelworks going crazy.

Our family was all working, except for Betty, who was on her last term at school. She was to finish in the following August. Dad's health had deteriorated again and he was more in bed than out. I went in to see him and could hardly get in the room for smoke from his Woodbines.

War was declared in September 1939. I was still with Billy and didn't want to leave him, as he was so good to me. Coal was to be rationed, but we were still busy, if not busier. With everyone claiming their ration, it made more business for us. People were putting coal everywhere. War was gaining momentum. Our forces were pushed back and France was almost occupied. Then came Dunkirk, but I am not well read enough to dwell on this aspect of it, I only know we lost a lot of young men.

By now 'Jerry' was making raids on our islands. Bill and I were filling bags at Llay when we stopped for a smoke and to stretch our backs. I lit up and heard an aircraft. I said to Bill: "Look Bill, a Jerry!" The markings on the plane were clear. It swept over the pithead and out towards Caer Estyn. As it went we heard three thuds – and they were thuds – three bombs were dropped in the field as you left the colliery on the right-hand side. There is a bungalow in the field and the craters are still there opposite to Sharp's factory.

Jerry did a few raids over our area. Caergwrle had it. One night a bomb hit the rocks at Plas-yn-Bwll. It shattered every window in the village. Another few craters were opposite the Smithy on the Penyffordd to Pontblyddyn Road. These craters are still there to this day. Sergeant Hassall, who was retired from the Police Force and a Chief Air Raid Warden, was on duty one night switching the decoy lights on around the Pulford Marshes, when he got blown up and they have never found his helmet to this day. Guns brought by A.T.S. girls were used by Hooley's Garage in Hope one night, and there were also W.A.A.F.s with searchlights mounted on transport lorry flats. There was a terrific raid over Liverpool that night. They all seemed to attack from over the mountains.

By this time my brother George had been called up to the 13th Battalion, The Royal Welsh Fusiliers. He went to Wrexham for his square bashing, where he found the discipline hard. He came home for an evening after passing out and tried to explain it to us, but we wouldn't listen. After passing out he was posted to Burnham-on-Sea, in Somerset. Dad was on the danger list when George went back and I think he asked for compassionate leave, but was refused. The next day he had to return home as Dad died on the morning he got back to his camp and George came home for his funeral. Dad is buried in Hope Cemetery, grave No. 58, by the dividing wall by the council houses.

I did my best now to get deferred from being called up. I didn't want to leave Bill, but I had to for my mum's sake. As the War was going we would all have to go, so I went to Alun Edwards to drive a Dennis. Again I said nothing at home. I was as fit as a fiddle on the coal; I did get black, but it was an enjoyable job. The new job wasn't as dirty and eventually my mum asked me why I was as clean as I was! I had to tell her and why.

The job entailed getting to the yard for 7.00am, going on the round to pick up the men and take them to their respective jobs at Saltney, Lache and Flint School. The lorry was a 2½-ton Dennis which still had solid tyres on the rear. It had just been in to have pneumatics fitted on the front and was a gate change with the handbrake lever next to it. This took all the room by the driver's door so one entered the seat by the left-hand side of the lorry. On the gearshift lever there was a diagram like the letter 'H' and an extra leg for the reverse action, you lifted a little peg on the gate change lever. The clutch was the same as those of today but not hydraulic. Brakes were rear wheels only – hand and foot. No fronts. It was mag dynamo, starting with a cranking handle at the front. I had had no experience with breakdowns so I hoped for the best if anything did happen.

After I delivered the men, my job was to keep them supplied with bricks, mortar, sand, lime, slates, timber – anything to keep them working. Once a plasterer got going it took you all your time to keep him in materials. Although you had to load yourself it was cleaner than the coal. Mum noticed this with my clothes.

One thing a driver must not do is to be late to pick up the men at night, especially on a Friday night – pay night. I didn't get over-time, so it was up to me to get the men home as soon as I could then drive back to the yard and bike home. It was always nice on a Friday night to hear the men singing on the way back. There was a canopy lift on the rear of the lorry, dropped off at the last drop and picked up at night for travelling home. I always had a full load. After a few weeks driving I had the misfortune of my lorry breaking down between Northop and Flint, on the dip before Flint Mountain. I don't know what it was, but it stopped and I tried to fix it by checking the fuel, spark, anything I could think of, which was the worst thing I could have done.

Never play with anything you know nothing about.

I took the plug leads off and mixed them up. I think I cured the problem, but I mixed the leads up so was worse off than before. I scratched my head a few times, trying not to get anyone out to me, but it didn't work. I was getting panic-stricken, as I didn't want to be late for the men. I stopped a vehicle, asked if the driver could call at the school and tell the men I had broken down and to try and make their way towards home. This they did – apparently one of the other lorries had picked them up – and I was told to telephone for assistance. I got through to Jack Slater, which cost me 2d. It was expensive then for a 'phone call. I did eventually get it back from Syd at the office. Jack Slater came out to me and asked what the trouble was.

"Have you had the plugs out or the leads off?" he asked.

I was too frightened to say "Yes."

I think he would have belted me. Anyway we got back to the yard late that night and Jack worked on it on the Saturday. When I got in on the Monday he went spare with me. He told me that if I had told him I had had the plug leads off he could have fixed it in two minutes. I almost got sacked. This taught me a lesson. He lectured me on how important it was to tell the truth. He had taken the cylinder head off for nothing. I learned to leave things alone unless I knew what I was doing.

Now, this job was important to me to try to get deferred from call-up. Jack Slater was working and driving a dumper at Mickle Trafford. A store was being built (and it is still there today) by the railway siding for the Ministry of Food by Alun Edwards for William Moss, Liverpool. Jack asked me if I would swap jobs with him, me to go on the dumper and he to drive the lorry. Jack was getting on – 50ish – so we officially swapped through the office. I had no reason to smell a rat, but I smelled one after I found out they had put one of their fogies on the lorry to keep him out of the forces. As it turned out it was a good move as I gained in the end.

I started on the dumper on the site. There was a 10 R.B. working on skimmer, a brand new D.6 Caterpillar which had come into the country just that month. The cost would have been in the region of approximately £4,000.

At this point I must tell my readers, whether you are interested or not, or if you know anything about them or not, bulldozers are going to

53

dominate my story for a few years to come. Sorry about that, but they were my interest and my life for a long time and by the time I have finished, you will know what they were for!

I was young and wild-headed and I drove the little Muirhill dumper like a madman. Everyone just got out of my way. The 10 R.B. was digging out and loading the dumper, and I had to tip it at the top of the railway bank, which meant me going on to the main road. Although I was mad, I was still capable and cared what I did. I got on with everyone, even the bosses. The foreman was pleased with my work because it was a muck-shifting job and you did it as quickly as you could, for while I was not under the digger, it was standing and that was no good if you worked out the cost. As soft as I was, I realised this and was up and down that bank like a rally driver. Dinner break was half an hour. Both the machines were left running, so nosy parker me got on the dozer, lifted the blade, let the clutch out, put it in gear and moved it forward, then backward, lifted the blade again and was quite enjoying myself until William Moss himself came and caught me. I was in the doghouse with him, I can tell you.

"Four thousand pounds for a machine for you to play on! I'll kick your backside if I catch you again," he said.

The operator was a friendly lad and as helpful as he could be, encouraging me to take it up. It is a most complicated thing to start up in the mornings. It has two engines – a small donkey engine and the main one. The donkey engine is started; two small levers are on the side to engage the gear onto the flywheel to turn the big engine over. The hot air from the donkey engine heats the air to flow to the main engine on half compression, you throw in the lever for full compression, while checking on the oil pressure gauge. If it is OK, you open the throttle and it should now start. Then you leave it to warm up for a few minutes and it is ready for a day's work. But the machine is only as good as its operator. This is where I come in.

Jerry was over from Liverpool night after night. The bombers would try to hit anything with a light on it. They would fly over the top of Hope Mountain. The drone seemed to go on forever. Everything by this time was on rations. We had 2ozs butter and cheese, and 1lb of sugar to last a week. Clothing was on coupons; furniture on tokens. Everyone had to cope.

I came home from Mickle Trafford to find my friend, Ivor, had been taken ill and he was admitted to Meadowslea Hospital. He hadn't been well for a while, and it was finally confirmed that he had TB. I went to see him only to find he had been moved to a hospital called Llangwyfan, near Denbigh. He was not there for long and, sadly for his mother and everyone, he died. It sent a shock throughout the village. Everyone knew him and he was very well respected by all. I had wondered why he had not been liable for call-up. Now it was obvious he hadn't been fit enough.

The funeral was at Hope Church. It was the full choir. We as bellringers, rang the muffled peal. The Church was packed – I think everyone was there. The cortege to the cemetery stretched from the church to the cemetery gates. Although only a youth when he died, he was an example to everyone. Ivor gained a posthumous award for his courage during his illness and his devotion to the Scout Movement. He died young and I would love to be able to relate to him my experiences of my lifetime. We were really good buddies.

I called a few times to see his mother, but she said very little and I'm sure she was upset every time she saw me. For months after his funeral his girlfriend took flowers to his grave every week. She came to church and said a prayer. I always had a talk with her and accompanied her to the cemetery. It was so upsetting that I stopped going in the end.

Evacuation from the cities had started and we had a visit from the Property Inspector. Eventually we had to take someone in although mother wasn't very pleased.

"I don't want strangers in my house," she said.

She tried her hardest not to take anyone, but I knew it would be company for her because, as the war was going, I was the next on the list for call-up even though I was in a reserved occupation.

I noticed a couple walking up from the station one Sunday morning and they had a little boy with them. They asked me directions to Inglewood Villas. They had asked the right person: they were the Jones family, our evacuees, from Birkenhead. Their home had gone. They had some of their possessions with them, and some at their relatives to be collected later. Anyway they took the two front rooms. As there was only Mother, Betty and me it worked out all right. Little did we know that we were never going to live all together again.

Mr and Mrs Jones, and Bill their son, lived with Mum for three or four years. Thank goodness they got on well together. They were clean and most helpful to Mum. Fred, as I knew him, was given a job at Llay main colliery.

I had kept in touch with Alice from Blackburn. I met her again in Caergwrle and she went to the church when she came over. We always met afterwards and I walked with her to Caergwrle. John Davies, her cousin, would always call me in for a cup of tea and a natter and I probably arranged to see her at night for the same ritual.

Alice was quite a poet. She wrote some beautiful poems and in a way it was Alice who got me interested in poetry. It was on this visit that I showed her a piece of poetry I had found in my dad's wallet after he died. Don't ask me the title or who wrote it, as I have never been able to find out. It is as follows:

Something tells me you're unhappy
That life has dealt a blow
You want one to comfort,
And understand, I know.

I'd like to send a present,
Or think out a surprise, so fine,
That it would banish
The sorrow from your eyes.

This folks has gone beyond me,
So I will do my part,
By sending loving thoughts out,
To heal a wounded heart.

I showed it to Alice. She took it and copied it so that she could try and find the author. This happened over 50 years ago now and I am still none the wiser. I'm wondering whether my dad wrote it himself. He never appeared poetic to me.

Alice had poems published in 'Poems of the Year' in 1938. She showed me copies of these on a later visit. We walked in the country, mostly along the River Alyn. There was nowhere more pretty than the walk along the River Alyn, and the walk from the Fagl Lane bridge to the Sarn footbridge. It was along here I learned to swim. Stan Lawrence threw me in the deep end when I was 12. I did the doggy paddle and got out. I had been on the bank long enough anyway. I learned to swim and I thank him for it.

I wanted to go to see Alice in Blackburn. I had no transport and no idea how to get there by train. I didn't want to ask her, because I wanted to surprise her and to find out if we had anything going for us apart from real friendship. I was almost certain it was the latter. Herbert Evans, the organist at the Church, had a car – a three-wheeled Morgan. It was in beautiful condition and I didn't know how to ask him if I could borrow it to go up to Blackburn. We were outside the Church one Sunday morning as usual. Alice came up in the conversation so I plucked up courage and asked him if I could borrow his car and, to my surprise, he agreed. He said he was going to London for three days for his music exams and provided I took him to Chester station and met him on his return, I could have it. That is what we did.

Herbert was a professional musician. He had rows of letters after his name and he went about teaching everywhere. I accompanied him on many occasions and used to drive his three wheeler very well. I picked him up at his home in New Broughton, took him to Chester and off I went to Blackburn at 4.30pm. I knew I might have to stop the night somewhere, so I telephoned from Chester station to tell Alice I was paying her a surprise visit. She was due to come to Caegwrle that evening for the week-end and if I didn't mind driving in the dark in the 'black-out' she would be agreeable to travel with me, so off I went to Blackburn to pick her up. Her address was 118 London Road. I found it fairly easily and I also passed one of her shops. She was running three shops, one a hairdressers, but I didn't know what the other two were. I went in to meet her mother and they were identical except for their ages. I could see where Alice got her good looks from and she was also like her aunt in Caegwrle too. We had a cup of tea together and then set off for the drive through Liverpool, hopefully through the Tunnel.

It was a dark night and searchlights were all over Liverpool. Jerry bombed the hell out of it – there was never a night without a raid.

All car headlamps with domed glasses had to be replaced with flat glasses and tin shades with louvered openings about a quarter of an inch apart half way down the shade. The shade also had a helmet around it to save the light showing through the fins and only allowing it to shine on the ground – very effective! The only trouble was that the driver had to guess where he was going and I must have been good – I never hit anything. The L.D.V. stopped us around about Gladstone Docks.

He said: "I shouldn't go any further, sir, if I were you. There's a terrific raid on and it will be dangerous for you to continue."

Searchlights were at full swing and most of these were mounted by W.A.A.F.s – and what a brilliant job they did for us. Three or four would concentrate on an area, meet up in the middle, keep a plane in the dazzling position and the ack-ack guns, again mounted by our wonderful A.T.S. girls, would have a go. They were terrific getting Jerry to go for a swim in the Mersey and the noise when they scored a hit – one of them caught a barrage balloon. All of these girls were superb.

Anyway, we wanted to get to the other side of the water.

"It has gone a bit quieter now, sir, maybe you can venture on now," he said.

Off we went along the dock road towards the Gas Works. We could see something on the road shining and runny. A bomb had hit the Gas Works; the contents were sprayed over the road and we were sliding in it. I stopped and Alice opened the door and put her foot out. It was slimy tar. She lifted her foot up, but left her shoe where it was. Her foot was covered in tar. Instead of her keeping still she had it all over the car mats and on her clothes. She was crying and someone shouted: "Get the hell out of there!"

The front wheels did about 200 mph! We spun all over the place. There was a loud explosion and we saw a body float in mid-air, through the searchlights. A man passed the car headless and dropped ten yards away. Alice just screamed and went silent. I was shocked and did not stop the car – I was petrified. Eventually we cleared the area and stopped to speak to the guards on the Tunnel entrance to tell them what we had seen. They seemed unimpressed because it would have been the same story from everyone. In complete silence we headed for home and were glad to get into the Tunnel for a break. God knows what we were to face the other side. I spoke to a Tunnel policeman before we left the area. He said the 'All Clear' had just sounded and we were free to go ahead. It was still a half an hour run home and we were both pleased to see the blackout of Caergwrle. We related our experiences to Alice's aunt – her cousin was not there as he had been called up.

We said goodnight and off I went home. My mother was anxious, but pleased to see me. We learned the next day that RAF Sealand had shot down seven aircraft that night.

RAF Sealand was amalgamated with Hawarden Air Station. Some of the planes were on standby and scrambled from there. The actual perimeter for Sealand is where I used to live, the part of the airfield where the bonfire was held each year. The deep shelters were right alongside the conifer hedge I owned. These deep shelters were for the protection of the crews.

I went to Church on the Sunday morning and it was nice to see Alice in her usual place when I looked through the corner of my eye as I walked down the aisle to the Choir. We met afterwards for the usual ritual.

I said goodbye to Alice after the Sunday night service and she told me she had no idea when she would see me again, so off I went in the black-out along the river and home.

The only lights to be seen at night were the searchlights. These were a very powerful spotlamp. Any aircraft spotted in that beam was attacked from the mobile guns from the ground. The guns sounded and you could hear the retort in the mountains. Some of the guns were carried behind lorries and were completely mobile. Many raids occurred. We were very lucky living where we did. The docks were the target as quite a number of ships were always there. At that time Cammel Laird were flat out making Corvettes, submarines etc. People were too busy working to worry about houses being blown out of the ground. Complete rows would disappear overnight. There were Anderson shelters. Some people slept under the stairs and some were there the next day and some had gone forever. Guns were out, mobile guns, along the hedges. Hooleys Corner in Hope was a favourite spot. When the gun fired it would jump right up into the air. A.T.S. girls usually commanded these. All the men had been called up.

I was still at Mickle Trafford and was caught again on the bulldozer. I was reprimanded and told I would be sacked next time.

It's funny how things work out. The boss was back the next day asking me if I was interested in going on a course at Hatfield, to Jack Oldings, the Caterpillar people. It was only a six weeks' course to learn how to operate, service and properly adjust the machine.

"See your parents when you get home and tell me tomorrow if you can go," he said.

Without any consultation, I told him I could go and to arrange it as soon as he wished. I told my mother when I got home what I was doing as I hoped it might get me a further deferment.

I went by train to Seacombe, and crossed the ferry to be picked up at Liverpool. I then went to Hatfield by road, arriving some four and a half hours later. I was put into the Rockstone Hotel and started the course after documentation the next morning. I will not dwell too much on the course because it will be boring to you, but it was extremely interesting to me. We sat in the cinema for two weeks just watching the machinery working: what it was used for, what it could do and how it was done. This included all the oil changes, the adjustments, everything you should know. I was tested at the end of the course and came out with flying colours. I was very satisfied and returned to my home life again. Life had been too hectic there. I did not know what it was like to go into a hotel until I went to Hatfield and even when I left, I still hadn't tasted a pint of beer.

I returned to work and, as the job was almost finished, Alun Edwards told me I was no longer on their books as I had broken my contract by going to Hatfield. I was transferred to Southport to do the same type of job as we did at Mickle Trafford. I was a bulldozer operator and not a common dumper driver. I enjoyed the work. My money was £2 per week more, which was the whole point of my mission in the first place.

Mum was very pleased with me. I was able to escape call-up too, but don't think I was shirking my responsibilities. I thought my duty was to my mother first and not to my country. This is what I thought, but not what the country thought. I arrived home one day from work and Mum literally met me by the door.

"What are the R.E.s, Austin?" she asked.

She had been crying and she didn't know how to tell me. In the end she said: "Your papers have come! You're going into the Royal Engineers and you have to go to Newark."

October 1940 – this was the dreaded moment of my life.

Why should I have to leave my mother to go and fight for my country?

Chapter 6

THE SAPPER DRIVER

I was to pack my bags and leave home. What was happening? Did everyone else feel the same way as me? I had to leave my mother alone. We had a good talk and I tried to encourage her to pack in her work in the community and to get a job in the factory. No way would she do that. She could have earned a fair wage and lived a less lonely life. She was only young – in her forties – and she sat there for five years waiting for us to return home.

I was to catch the 11.20am train to Chester. I had a voucher for the journey: the route was to change at Chester, Crewe, Nottingham and then up to Newark.

Anyway, I had bought a small case for my belongings. I was told what to take. I said goodbye to my mother and off I went down the station road. I saw a lot of people. I don't think I spoke to anyone. I walked around the corner of the building and was skidded off my feet by a kid riding a four-wheeled truck. He carried me ten yards in to the muddy ditch. The lad's name was Austin Griffiths (I met him again 14 years later).

I eventually got on the train and I was bound for nowhere. I sat dumbfounded wondering what, where, how and why? I changed at Chester and Crewe and had a long wait at Nottingham. I sat and wrote a letter to Alice, as I hadn't seen her for over three months. I finished the letter on the train and posted it at Newark Station with a penny stamp.

When I arrived at the station I was met with a greeting: "Do you want a cup of tea"?

I said: "Yes, please."

It was an A.T.S. girl controlled by the R.T.O..

"Are you going to Bowbridge Road Camp?"

"Yes, I am."

"After your tea follow the crowd and me to a coach outside."

I sat for a good ten minutes smoking and supping the last of the tea.

"Fall in outside!"

What did "fall-in" mean? They soon showed me what "fall-in" meant.

We were hustled into a bus and all the windows were covered. It was well lit inside, but why the covers?

"To save you finding your way back to the station, young man!" I was told.

There were about 30 of us. We were ushered out of the coach and into what I know now was the Quartermaster's stores. First a pillowcase, boots, shirt, P.T. shorts, socks, vests, battledress, denim boiler suit, Glengarry hat, belt, full kit-bag, small pack, messing tins, knife, fork, spoon, mug, two plates, shoe brushes, lanyard and knife, plimsolls, cap badge, puttees and finally a bayonet, scabbard and a P50 rifle. Bath towels, toothbrush, toothpaste and a bar of stinky soap.

From there we were ushered across a yard to a huge building. Inside was a massive stock of straw.

"Fill your palliasse with that and your pillow and go back across the road to a hut," we were told.

It was hut 42. This was my home for the next three months and what a gang of soldiers! There were all sorts – hooligans more like – and yet lads I will never forget as long as I live. Some I saw die, some I would like to see again and some I wouldn't.

When I got inside the door it must have been half full. It consisted of 46 double bunk beds. The door was central and had two steps up to it and also central was a 'tortoise' stove for heating. There was a left and right-hand and the beds were neatly placed. On the extreme right was the N.C.O.'s room. All latrines were outside in a block used by our huts. I bagged a bottom bunk and threw my kit onto it. There was no one on the top bunk as yet. We all grabbed our eating irons and grouped outside to go for a meal. It was a set menu. I had bubble and squeak and rice pudding for afters, plus a full pint mug of good Sgt. Major's tea, and came out very satisfied. The next hour or so was spent meeting one's comrades, and there were all sorts – Cockneys, Scroungers, Taffies,

Geordies, Scots. One lad I made a friend of was from Southampton – he was known as 'Lofty New'. I met him all over the world. He was a mate. Anyway we were in this together and we had to get on with it.

I made my bed down, which you were not allowed to do before 6pm, starting from the next day. I filled my locker with my gear and put the rest under my bed. I can never remember what happened to my civilian clothes because it was cold and we dressed in our new suits to go out to the N.A.A.F.I. Although we had just left home, we knew we had to get stuck in or our lives could have been hell. So, the N.A.A.F.I. it was. Lofty tried to persuade me to have a pint of beer, but I thought: "No way, man."

I had tea and a wad. The N.A.A.F.I. was vast – big stage, long counter, plenty of girls serving behind the bar, and a grand piano at the foot of the stage being played by a lad in overalls, which was very pleasant to listen to.

'Lights out' was at 10pm, so until we found our way round we got in early. The beds in the hut were almost full now. I got into my sleeping clothes, which was P.T. shorts and a vest like all the others. You didn't have to ask, you followed the leader. Although a few of the beds were empty and people were still coming in, the lights were put out, all except the one by the door. We all tried to sleep – but you must be joking! You never heard such a row in your life. A Cockney – Harrison – by the door, started to cry like a baby. It kept us in uproar for ages. He must have been one of the best Cockneys I have ever met. Later on, he kept us all alive.

In the end, I saw a tall man walk out of the end room. He went to the switch, turned the light on and told us to pay attention.

"I am your N.C.O.: your mother, your dad and your superior officer. I have had to leave it until now to introduce myself, as there were people late in. My name is Corporal Hunt. You address me as 'Sir' and you stand to attention when you speak to me. I am God and whatever I say you all do. You will call me a bastard and on parade I will be one. When you get to know me I'm sure you will all respect me. I will not be a bastard off parade and anyone can come to me at any time if they are doubtful of anything. Goodnight to you all. P.T. is at 6am. Don't forget to read daily orders on the company's notice board. It may concern you. If you don't, you can and will be charged with neglect of duty."

I am sure we all tried to get to sleep. Can you imagine going from a comfortable home to a mattress and pillow stuffed with straw, and someone on the bunk above you waddling about? You felt every movement. Then Harrison, the baby crier. As soon as you thought you were away, that fool would start, funny as it was. I got to sleep at last, but awoke to find something dripping on my bedclothes. It was the lad above me who had wet the bed.

I had never lived with other people except my family before. I didn't know what to do or how to tackle it. I waited for a while and then saw the Corporal go through to what I supposed was the latrine. I followed him and told him what had happened. He said to leave it with him and he would deal with it and I was to get as comfortable as I could. I chose another bed close by and the next thing I heard was the 'Reveille'. Some lads were already up. I was in my P.T. kit with my trousers on smoking at the side of my bed.

Everyone went out for P.T., and we all sort of lined up and made what one may call an effort. The Corporal was there and he took us on a run for the first morning. After P.T. we had an hour before breakfast and after that we all went down for documentation. As we were Engineers, we were trade graded as soon as we went in. I was given a rank, name and number. From now on I would be known by that name. I was 'Sapper Hughes', not 'Mr Hughes', No. 2153373. I was first given a grade as 'Pioneer E3'. I brought to their notice that I had a bulldozing grade, was told to report to the grading office and was then re-mustered to 'Operator Excavator B3'. This made a difference of 1/9d per day, over ten shillings per week, so I made a voluntary contribution to my mother of the ten bob a week.

The next month must have been the hardest of my life. I'm not saying I didn't enjoy it, I did, but what a grueller. Every day on the Square, the holy ground. You were not allowed to breathe on the Square unless an officer told you to. Our section was B Section, our Corporal was Corporal Hunt, and the section Sergeant was Smithy. He was a bastard too on the Square, but after we finished our training he too was a fine fellow. We did what was known as a line of communication training. We did everything – full rifle, sten guns, bren guns, all types of explosives, gun cotton, gelignite, all types of detonation. How to put it to explode and how to defuse it too. Clock timing devices, fused times. We had to learn everything on a full scale. We did bridge building and blew up bridges. I did really well on my trade test to blow a railway line out of the ground with gun cotton. We did trench revetting, land-mining, built the Ingloes bridge and also the famous Bailey Bridge. We blew rocks in mountains and dug underwater tunnels. We learned semaphore and Morse codes, mapping, aircraft recognition and had to be able to defuse both landmines and bombs, which were unexploded when dropped.

When I look back on it I think we must have been a carefully selected group, because everyone did a fine job of their training. You had to rely on your mates and do it the correct way. We all passed with flying colours and we were called Sappers. We now knew what discipline was. We also knew what bullshit was, comradeship too, and gave our all on our passing-out parade.

A party had been arranged at the New White Hart in Newark. Almost all the lads, instructors and officers in charge were at the party. I had *never* had a pint of beer before in my life. There was a big fat mamma playing the piano. I drank seven pints of beer that night. I suppose some drank a lot more than I did. I know I was singing, and what the hell – we might not be here tomorrow. The next day was a rest day when we did nothing.

What was the next part of our lifeline? Await a posting, further training, join a unit, go on a course, become a batman? Not on your nellie.

I had few problems with my hut mates, except one. I couldn't stick him. He was a crafty Cockney bastard. Cyril, one of the lads in his group, came and asked me to lend him some fags until the next day, so I went up to his side of the hut. Cyril seemed a nice sort of a fellow. Don't forget, I had come from a very straight-laced community. He was from Northampton, a city dweller, so we didn't talk the same language. We got on OK, but I couldn't bear Cyril's mate. He always tried to take me for a ride. In other words, 'extract the urine'. You did get them and I would never stand for it.

Cyril asked me to lend him a shoe brush, which I did, and it appeared he lent it to the crafty Cockney. I asked for it back and he went to his mate, who said he didn't have my ****** shoe brush, but I spotted it in his locker. We were to report anyone pinching, but I wouldn't. If there was a kit inspection I was the loser. I let it lie. I knew he had it so it was up to me now to get it from him. We passed each other on the steps and I asked him for it.

He said: "I haven't got your ******** brush, and if you can prove otherwise, do so."

I had marked all my equipment long ago, so I could prove it. I went over with the rest of my belongings and the Corporal was sitting on one of the beds. I went to the Cockney to show him my markings, and asked him to show me the brush in his locker. He told me to go away, or words to that effect! The Corporal butted in to sort it out. He examined the locker and took the brush off him, gave it to me, told me to keep my own counsel about it and he would keep him under surveillance. He said the Commanding Officer was looking for troublemakers.

I had never been in a fight in my life, but this devil kept on at me. He challenged me to go outside and I told him we could both be charged for fighting, so to pack it in. I had my towel to go to the ablutions and as I went out of the door, he hit me on the back of the neck. As he came down the step I hit him under the chin. Consequently he hit his head on the step and flaked out. I thought I was now in dire trouble.

The Corporal came out of his den and told me not to worry as he had told his Sergeant about what was going on.

He said: "You will automatically be on a 252 charge, but I will see to it that it is dismissed before it goes to Company Office. We get these cases and they are best dealt with locally."

I thanked him for being so wide-awake on my behalf and that was the end of it. However, there was the crafty Cockney to think about too, so later I plucked up courage to go to the medical quarters to see how he was. He had a lump on his head, but seemed to bear no malice. The next day he came over and shook my hand. He explained that everyone his side thought I wouldn't retaliate and that it was his fault and to forget it. We met again in various places, including abroad, and we ended up the best of pals.

Postings and courses were on company orders for the next day and I was on an Advanced Military Transport course at Halifax.

We arrived at Halifax Station on the Friday morning and were met by drivers to take us to Thorp Mills, about two or three miles from Hebden Bridge, a small place called Triangle. I was to do a Driver Mechanics course. It was an old mill and, to top it all, I was on the top storey of this mill. Every time we moved to go anywhere we had to go up and down 92 steps. Eventually you got wise! I counted the times I went up and down each day: ablutions, P.T, breakfast, first parade, then to get your gear on for work – 460 steps to climb and 460 steps to come down – that was without going to the toilet. I managed to acquire a tool bag for myself, and put my day's clobber in it, including my knife, fork and spoon. I cut my wear and tear by half.

I was stupid at Halifax, for within three days I had passed my driving test. I was also on a Mechanics course, but I couldn't start that for another five weeks. They trade tested you first, then decided what level of course to put you on. A few others and myself did the driving test and we got through it within a few days. How daft can you get? There was no further need for us to continue in the workshops. We were all put on fatigues! The weather was not that good, so I sloped my way into the cookhouse, where I was working with the girls. Instead of driving round Thorp Mills like the other lads, sitting in the back of a three tonner smoking, calling at transport cafés, eating wads and drinking tea, I was working like a fool. Each driver did a stint at the wheel and, as he got proficient, he was tested. If he passed he went ahead on his Mechanics course, but everyone had to be through within six weeks, so I had about five weeks to do in the cookhouse.

I thought I had dropped a clanger until the guard duty roster came out. Those who had passed and were ready to return to Bowbridge Road were not on the guard list of duties.

I had a good time at Thorp Mills. I finished my work early. I was spud bashing really, but the kitchen had all modern facilities and most of my time was spent loading the peeling machine and keeping it clean, swilling the veg room, playing cards, having a smoke, and chasing the A.T.S. girls with a handful of spud bashings.

I applied for a weekend pass, which you were entitled to do if you passed your course, and I tried to hitchhike from Triangle. I had no idea which way to go, but my pal Howarth was going to Rochdale, so we hitched together and I went on to Oldham from there. I headed to Piccadilly, Manchester and had more trouble getting through Manchester than all the rest of the way home. Anyway, I saw a bus going to Sale, jumped on it and went to give my fare. The conductor said it was free to the forces throughout the area. I thought this was great as I could use the concession when I returned. I got to Sale, and hitched a lift to Bowden Lights on the A556 to Chester. It was dark at Bowden and I tried in vain for quite a while to hitch another lift – I must have been there for two hours. It was now 8 o'clock and my chances were slim. A car stopped, but the driver was only going to Sandiway. I waited there for about one more minute and was picked up by a lady in a sports car going to Vicars Cross. I walked it towards Chester, a taxi driver took me to Bridge Street and I walked home to Hope from there. I got to Hooleys Garage when a car stopped, asking if I was going far. I said I lived in the village and had hitched from Halifax. He said he had just come from Altrincham. It was the local Curate, Mr Wykes, in his M.G.

It was after midnight when I got home. The back door was unlocked and there was a light on. There was a helmet and a res-pirator on the mangle as I walked in through the back door – George was home. What a coincidence! I hadn't seen him for 12 months. I walked round the door and up the passage, to see him spread out on the settee. He got up and we shook hands, said something we shouldn't and I gave Mum a hug and a kiss. She was ever so pleased to see us together. The last time had been when Dad had died. Unfortunately we didn't have much time together as George had to start back for Burnham-on-Sea on the Sunday afternoon by train, via Chester, Crewe, Birmingham and Bristol. Once again we three said our goodbyes and had no idea when we might meet again. It was more sad for Mother than for us as we did have adventures in front of us and the company that went with it, whether we liked it or not. Mum had only memories.

I had to be back for the Monday morning, so George and I went together to Chester. We had a pint, I saw him to his train and then headed for the Manchester Road via Vicars Cross. It was about 4pm when I reached the lights on the Manchester Road. A shooting brake picked me up, and the driver said he was going to pick up swill in and around Altrincham. I was delighted even though the vehicle stank of pigmeal. I could get a free bus to Piccadilly and now I knew I could also get as far as Oldham. Oldham to Rochdale was easy, so I was doing better than my homeward journey. I was going to be in Triangle before midnight. I had a lift outside Rochdale on the Halifax Road and a staff car picked me up. I was dropped at Hebden Bridge and was able to have a cup of tea and a wad before going in to camp. I wasn't due in until 23.59 hours anyway.

The course soon finished. Some failed and some would never make drivers as long as they were in the forces. I did well, got my M.T. wings and felt as proud as punch. My uniform was beginning to take shape now and I felt proud of it. I was an awkward size, so I had a Canadian battledress. It was better material than ours and looked a lot smarter. I had a shoulder lanyard, a jack-knife, a beautiful white belt (whitened with toothpaste), lead weights hanging over my puttees, spit and polished toe-caps, a polished cap badge, and a creased pleated blouse with weights (not allowed!) to keep the blouse in shape at the back. With the R.E. flash on my shoulders, I was the 'kiddy'.

First parade was 7 o'clock now the course was finished. We went on parade and the transfer postings were read out. I was posted to Mechanical Equipment R.E. Castle Barracks, Newark. I arrived there the following day and was told not to get settled as I might be going off to Scotland that afternoon. It was true – later I was on a train for Edinburgh. We arrived at the station and were transported to the Greyhound Stadium at Portobello just outside Edinburgh. We were ushered into the rooms above the spectators' seats and this is where we slept for a few nights. All we had were blankets. There were no beds, nothing between the wood and me.

There was an officer, two sergeants, two corporals and ten men. I was selected duty driver for the three days I was there. The first job on the list was collecting rations, which I picked up from Penicuik. The officer, Captain Martin, went with me. He was a fine fellow. I looked after him and he looked after us. As we returned to the dog track we came through the city so that he could show me around in the daylight. He gave me instructions that I was to take him to the 'Palais de danse' that night and to pick him up in the early hours of the morning. The vehicle was a little Standard Ten Four, very new and nice to drive, but in those days there were no heaters in them and you got cold. I dropped him off as arranged, went back to Portobello and, unusually for me, went out with the lads for a pint. I had to be careful, as I didn't want to upset my Captain.

I had stacks of time on my hands, so I walked back to the dog track and then back to the corner pub. There were some Canadians in the pub and as usual, plenty of girls with them. I had a half and made off out from there as I could see trouble brewing. It was just about dark. I walked about ten paces to the corner and a girl was going mad with a lamppost. Someone had dosed her in the pub. I saw a Red Cap, asked him if he knew about her and he came over and examined her. He asked me where my base was and I pointed to it. He asked if I had any transport. I replied that I had and he said he would come with me to the hospital. He said someone had doped this girl with Spanish Fly and if she was not treated soon she would go mental. I did as he said. We lifted her in to the back and I drove off to the hospital.

I got a notification to report to her Commanding Officer. Apparently they had pumped her out and she was all right the next day. I was to be thanked for saving the girl's life. How true this was I don't know, but my Commanding Officer sent for me to tell me about it.

The same day I was to go to her camp, I was posted up to Penicuik into civvy digs. Penicuik had a huge A.T.S. camp, where girls did their training, and also a transport training school. There were thousands of girls there, all billeted in Nissen huts. These were vulnerable to air raid attacks in that a bomb by the door would block their entry, so the Pioneer Corps were filling four-gallon benzine tins with the slag we were to carry from the slagheaps about a mile away. They were also filling sandbags and building them around the entrances to prevent the problem or at least reduce the risk and, of course, to eliminate the light for the blackout. The Engineers were responsible for getting the slag to the site. We had three large Muirhill Dumpers, an A19 R.B.

71

Dragline, a 2/10 Smith Skimmer, a D4 Dozer and two Dennis Tippers. As I was already an Op.Ex.B3, I was expected to drive or operate any of them. I had a go on everything and eventually opted for the Dennis Tipper to get me out of the way for a spell. It was just a nice run to the camp from the slagheap, which was an old colliery working.

On about my fourth load I stopped for a break and asked one of the A.T.S. Sergeants where I could get a cup of char and a wad. She pointed out that we were not allowed to use the girls' canteen but they had opened the Sergeants' canteen for us to use while we were working. The girl I spoke to sounded Welsh, so I asked her where she came from and she said Wrexham. As it happened, she was from Rhosddu and lived two doors away from my Gran! She looked after me from then onwards. I had my tea in her office. She was a C.Q.M.S. – Company Quarter Masters' Sergeant. She was quite a few years older than me.

When we moved from the dog track we went straight to the slag-bank and left our personal kit there until we had finished that night. We were all billeted out and I went with Howarth – the lad I went home with on leave to Rochdale. We were with a lady about as old as my mum, and we had good food. I had never had porridge with salt before and I left mine on the table. I told the lady I didn't like it with salt, and she said I should have told her and that I would have sugar in future.

They were excellent digs, but we weren't there long enough to get to know anyone. We completed the job, cleaned the place up and put the plant ready for transportation back to Newark. We all went by train back to the bullshit of H.Q.. I didn't manage to settle in there long, either. My name was on Company's orders for the next day to be posted to Jack Oldings, Hatfield. I was to be prepared to be picked up to catch the ten o'clock train arriving at Hatfield at 4.30 pm. I would be met off the train and taken to the same hotel that I was in when I did the civilian course 12 months previously. The Rockstone had not altered. I mentioned to no-one that I had been there before. I was interested in all I saw, and met some of the lads from Bowbridge Road Camp. The crafty Cockey was there, Harrison the crying baby, Farrieman, Lofty New and lads whose names I didn't know. We had a couple of drinks at the bar and went then off to bed. What a difference! A bed to sleep in. The place was really comfortable.

Parade was at seven o'clock and I had to go for documentation. Nobody seemed to recognise me, so I pretended not to recognise them. I remembered what happened at Triangle through knowing too much, so I kept mum.

"We don't know what you can do so we will put you in the school along with the rest. We'll keep an eye on you and give you a test if we think it necessary."

"Yes, sir."

I saluted and went off out.

I went with the school to the cinema for the first three days. Although I had seen it all before, it was still very interesting to me. One of the lecturers kept looking at me very hard and often, and I wondered how long I could go without being recognised. I didn't push my luck too much, but had to take the course as it came. I was OK until I went into the field operating. There was a new D7 working on angle-dozing. Someone asked who could operate it and I had to say I could. I got up on the seat and revved up, pushed the clutch out, selected the appropriate gear and must have made one of the best cuts I've ever made. I got off and the instructor asked if I'd had any previous experience on the Cats. I couldn't tell lies, so I fluffed my way out of it. I still didn't say I had been there before. I think he knew, and he took me to one side and told me that he remembered me. He said he could soon find out, so I had to admit I had done the course before. Sure enough, I was on company orders to report to the Chief Instructor at nine o'clock. When I got to his office he already had my military papers out and the information from the previous course. I was told I was going to be trade tested and that if I was the person they thought I was, I should have told them. I was asked if I had attended a course as a civilian. I said I had and had a reasonable excuse for not telling anyone – nobody had asked me.

I don't think I should have done that!

He gave me my past record of the course and told me that it was men like me they were looking for to train the others to get machinery moving. I was told I would be trade tested to see if I was as efficient as when I was there last. If I passed anywhere near as well, I would be recommended for promotion to instructor, and while I was at Hatfield I would be formally made up to Corporal Instructor with another £1.10.0. a week.

"Re-mustered to Op.Ex.B2 as from today and your duty will begin now. How do you feel about that?" he asked.

I was made up. It seemed funny everyone congratulating me and eating with the Corporals – great. The C.O. was a Captain Bradbury, and he lived on the site where we trained. The road or track to his house was always messed up, and one of us had to clean it up for the weekend so he could get his car out, otherwise it was like big molehills. My mate, Taffy from South Wales, said he would do it, and I forgot to remind him about it. I walked over to the factory gates to see some of the drivers who were transporting fuselages from the local Vickers Armstrong factory to Broughton, Chester, which was near my home. I knew quite a few of them and, in fact, I spoke to Teddy Moss.

He said: "If you want to go home any weekend, just come across. We go straight home."

I had received a letter telling me that Alice was going to be in Caergwrle that particular weekend. I decided on the spur of the moment to go home. I went back to see Taff, who had already gone to his second home in Hatfield. I wrote a note and put it in his pint mug where he was sure to see it Saturday morning, telling him I had gone home for the weekend and would see him on Sunday and to be prepared to level up for Captain Bradbury if he called. I met Teddy Moss at the gates of Armstrong Siddleys at six o'clock and was on my way home for the weekend on French leave. I got back about two o'clock on Saturday morning. I managed a few rations from my friend in the cookhouse. Mum was pleased and I enjoyed the weekend.

You don't yet know what it cost me! I met Teddy at the Broughton Gates and drove for most of the way. I got off the wagon by the hotel and changed into my overalls for the first parade at seven o'clock. I met Taffy and he told me the bad news – I had dropped a clanger. Taffy was away on Saturday afternoon, and when Captain Bradbury had called for a bulldozer to clear his way out for Church on Sunday morning, I wasn't there. They looked for me and couldn't find me, so when they called my name on parade I was to report to the office.

I never thought I would be put under close arrest. I was put in a little hut and they took away all my laces, braces, cigarettes, matches, money – everything. All my kit was confiscated, the lot. I was charged with being absent without leave. While I was in the hut, all the lads came to see me. They brought me cigs and matches, and I was smoking in the hut. They could see the smoke coming out of the knotholes and thought it was on fire!

I went up before the 'old man' and was charged.

Asked what I had to say for myself, I said: "Nothing, sir."

He said: "This is too serious a case for me to deal with and you will be referred to H.Q. at Newark."

I travelled to Newark 'under close arrest.' They were two of my mates – I had no problems with them. I was allowed to smoke and they gave me my money back in case I had my case dismissed. At Newark I found it very hard going. I was in the main guardroom. I was charged the next day and got 68 hours' detention.

Before anyone can do any punishment in the forces you have to have a medical. After doing 'jankers', scrubbing and re-scrubbing the steps of the building, I was sent to Bowbridge Road Hospital and I was kept in with piles. That was my detention over! I was in for a week. I got back to the Castle and saw some of the lads doing their detention. They would have killed me to do that.

I kept my nose clean afterwards I can tell you. It was all over.

The 'old man' sent for me the next day. I was posted back to Hatfield and within the week I was made up to my old rank again and told that next time I wasn't to be so stupid. I would have been given a pass if I had asked. I was informed that from my records I was due for leave, to take my week's leave and come back in a better mood.

I had a good leave and returned to Jack Oldings to continue my work. Altogether we must have trained 50 'passes' every eight weeks. I really enjoyed my work and I only went home because it was so easy to get there and back. The wagons were back and to, all the while, with aircraft wings and bodies.

I lectured on diesel and how it works on the Cats, and that is when I was given the nickname I still have – "Diesel Taff".

Chapter 7

BOMB DISPOSAL

Our armies were pushed back in the desert. Rommel had counter-attacked and pushed them back as far as Kilo 200, what we now know as the Half Way Café. This meant that reinforcements were bound to be mustered for desert service. I, of course, was in that category. I think our instructing job was declining in volume. We had trained quite a good team of men to spread around the world who were able to operate the machines. My name was on orders for posting. To my surprise I didn't get a posting for Halifax, or abroad, because that is where all our despatches went. I was posted to London!

I lived at a house in Balham, No. 20 Thornton Road. It was huge, with probably 20 or so rooms. I was on the second floor with about 12 men. A new company was being formed to go abroad eventually – 871 Mechanical Equipment Co. R.E.. Our first priority was to build a new workshop and when I arrived everyone was busy doing this. Two diggers were doing the excavation and four tippers were carrying from them, tipping and bringing ashes back from the Kennington Gas Works. It was at this time that 39 Mechanical Equipment Pltn. R.E. was formed and I was the only driver in the platoon holding what was known as a T.P.T. Class 1A. This was for a driver to be able to go out with a lowloader to transport plant and be able to load and unload it. He had to have knowledge of the plant, trailer work and driving.

I was in London during the early part of the Blitz and we were expected to go anywhere and be capable of driving any type of mechanical plant. I was based at Thornton Road, but I was also attached to Bomb Disposal. My job was to operate a small mobile crane known as a 'Jones Mobile' which was used for lifting bombs out of bomb holes or craters. The members of the team also had to be capable of doing what everyone else did – defusing and displacing bombs. I was responsible for lifting quite a few bombs out, particularly in the East End.

One night, there was a raid on the Docks where a whole consignment of Caterpillar plant had arrived from America.

An order was received to scarper immediately to Wapping Docks, start any piece of equipment up and move it anywhere out of the way of the docks. At that time Caterpillars were imported in large boxes or crates. The yoke, or blade holder, was fixed, the blade was under the belly and the rest of its components were sided away. Under normal circumstances the crate would be opened and the Caterpillar taken out neatly, but there was no time for this. It was a raid. Aircraft were everywhere, people were running, and there was no time to open wooden crates. So, with a jemmy bar, we opened the top off the crate, prised enough room to get to the donkey engine, started it up and drove straight out through the wooden crate.

I was moving a D7 Cat. weighing about 19 tons. It was on crawler cleats. Normally you had to fit these cleats with pads for tarmac protection, but there was no time for that either. I just had to get the hell out of there. I didn't give it a thought. I slewed round to turn into a narrow cul-de-sac and dump it there. I was on a wooden block street. The corner of the cleat dug into the blocks. I must have ripped about 30 square feet of road. It was no use trying to do anything about it. It was about 10pm and the raid was at full swing.

I walked back to the docks to select another machine – this time it was a new D2 Cat. I had difficulty putting a drop of petrol in the donkey engine, but a searchlight lit the place up just enough for me to find the spout. I spilled most of it, but managed to choke it enough to start it up. You have to leave it running for a while because it heats the air passing the exhaust of the donkey engine to help the combustion of the main engine before you put it on full compression to fire. When this happens you can switch off the donkey and there is peace again. I broke through the crate front and drove off out of the dock area, aiming anywhere just to get out. Altogether we moved 24 machines at an average price then of £6,000-£8,000 each. We saved a little bit of money for Mr Churchill. If you were on night duty you did anything you were asked to do.

The 'All Clear' was sounded and I managed to get hold of a senior A.R.P. warden to notify him what had happened to the street. He sat on a lump of rubble and laughed his head off. There was still good humour even though we were half-asleep, as some of us had not had any sleep for two or three nights for quite a few weeks. You could be out of bed for three or four days at a time.

On one occasion, a bomb had been dropped between two buildings at Streatham Hill, near Tooting Bec Common, a hundred yards or so from Drewstead Hospital. It was lying at 45 degrees and unexploded. I was a member of the bomb disposal team and duty plant man for the week. We'd had it quiet for two nights on the run. Captain McKellar called for me to go on to Tooting with the mobile to lift the bomb out. I had no lights. I don't suppose you have seen one of these things – a Mobile has got four-wheel drive and each wheel wants to go its own way. I was going down Thornton Road and by Kings Avenue all I saw was a flash. It felt as if it had lit London up. I heard splintered glass dropping on top of the cab. It was like thunder. My wheels still wanted to go their own way and I put the bloody thing into top gear and scarpered at about three miles per hour, towards the hospital. But I couldn't go far that way – the road had gone and the gas main, too. I turned back and went down Criffel Avenue into Killessa Avenue to get through. I found the men at the site and they showed me where I was supposed to go – with a four-wheel drive crane that wanted to do its own thing all the time! I measured the gap and I could just get through. There was nothing to spare.

I had to see the Commander and tell him there was no way out for the men if the machine was brought in at this point. It was best to leave it until they wanted a lift, then bring the crane in. This we did and fortunately the detonator was the right way up for a change. As a rule they are 'detonator down' and have to be turned before the team goes in to defuse the bomb.

The team is run strictly by the leader. Each man has his own element to deal with and when you have done your part you move very slowly out of the way to a marshalling area. This is to be able to 'call the roll' as it were. No-one is allowed in or out of the checkpoint. You record everything you do to your element and you shout 'out' when you have finished your task. This can go on for hours, and you can hear a pin drop. Eventually the detonator is out and until the bomb is to be lifted, no one can breathe. It is obvious you can't use anything other than a silk sling. No metal whatsoever. This might cause a spark and up the bomb can go even after it has been defused.

They called the crane in and off I went. The two slingers were waiting for me to lower my jib, hook it on to the silk rope, and hoist away. When you lift you have to be careful that the bomb doesn't sway and hit something. We hoped that the weight was not too heavy to make me alter my jib. I hoisted carefully and out the bomb came. It had to be lifted on to a vehicle with a crib to take the cushion of the transit.

I never went to a bomb dump, so I don't know what they did with them. I think they were vacuumed out. Some had to be steamed out, others were separated to save one liquid running into the other and igniting in a similar way to a twin fire extinguisher.

The danger was over for another day and we could relax. We did relax too. We had the best of everything. Because we were attached to Command Royal Engineers (C.R.E.), we had a proper mess, and wine with our food. We had a wonderful house to live in, a superb cook and were waited on with our meals. We were also allowed a ration of spirits, a room orderly, and white sheets on our beds. We lived a life of luxury while we were on bomb duty. You were only allowed a six months tour of duty and sometimes less if Jerry had been very busy.

I don't want to dwell on the London bombing too much, only to say I did have a stint of duty there. I got to know London well. All the commons were equipped with some sort of equipment, guns, and barrage balloons. It was wonderful to see the girls going into action – A.T.S. and W.A.A.F.s. There were no men manning the guns. I was friendly with one of the W.A.A.F.s. She was a tall blonde, my age, but there was nothing between us. We were just very good friends. She was on the barrage balloons. You should have seen those girls going to town, putting a balloon where Jerry didn't want it. They did a wonderful job. When I was off duty I always went to see Jessie. If she wasn't on duty I knew she would be in the W.A.A.F.s Club at Tooting Broadway. I called in to see her one night and she was missing. There had been a raid and I found her down one of the shelters nursing an old lady she had found lying in the street. She had thought the woman was drunk at first, but she had been blown off her feet by the blast of the bomb. She was with her almost all night and the old lady died in the early hours of the morning. These are the things that stay in your mind forever.

Our leisure hours were spent mostly in the forces' clubs. Theatres were still going and I went to see Will Fyffe and the Dagenham Girl Pipers at Streatham Hill Theatre. I still think it was one of the best shows I have seen in England. There was always a nice welcome in the canteens run by the Salvation Army, Toch H and the W.V.S.. There were lots of them. You were never on your own in London during the war.

Thank goodness I was on normal duty for a week. It was nice just jumping in the lorry and going for a load of ashes to the gas works. We were so busy the day went quickly. It was time for our dinner at night before we knew it. The food was good and there was no bullshit.

We worked hard and well. The workshop was well on its way to being completed. The brickies had finished and, best of all, the outside walls were done. The 'old man', Major Jacobs, was happy and it was time to apply for leave again.

Mail from home was very sparse. Mother did write, probably once a month or so. Anyway she knew I was going home and I suppose it was the same routine in the village. I came home by train and it was only five and half hours from London. Balham wasn't far from the tube, and it was easy to get to the depot from there. It took longer to get from Chester to home than from London to Chester. The first thing was to go to see cook in the basement for something to take home with me. He was always more than generous. Don't forget, everything was rationed. He gave me tea, sugar, butter, cooking fat and dried egg. Mum was ever so pleased. I don't know how she and other people kept alive with what they were expected to live on. She was full of joy when I arrived home. She asked why George couldn't bring anything. All he brought was his week's ration card. She said George gave her the ration card and then expected her to buy the food when she hadn't any money, so that when he went back she had a bill she couldn't afford to pay.

I got home about two o'clock and walked through the back door, went to put my respirator and cheese cutter hat on the mangle and a cat landed on my chest. I heard the remark: "Get out of it, you bugger!" I thought my mum was talking to me, but it was the cat she had ousted out from under the stairs where there was a mouse. She threw the cat out for not catching the mouse and put the kitten in its place. I got the cat. She threw it in mid air.

I had a good leave. I went to Church on the Sunday morning. I was in uniform. No one knew me, not even the Curate, the Rev D Saunders Davies. When people realised who I was they all gave me a welcome home. They couldn't believe how I had altered and how smart I looked in my best battledress with all my proficiency badges – lanyard, jack-knife, M.T. wings, bomb disposal badge, two tapes and my service chevrons.

I met all my friends that week – Dorothy, Hazel, Phyllis, Herbert, C W Pritchard, Ann Clark, her mother, the Rector, the boys from the choir, most of the bellringers, all the church wardens and the people who knew me.

Dorothy had told me that Les had joined the Air Force. She gave me a photograph of him in uniform. I still have that to this day, but I have not seen Les since I was called up. I believe he went to Canada to train for the Air Force and that was the last I heard.

I saw Ivy in Pontblyddyn. I saw Vola at the Rectory. I went to Meadowslea to see my sisters, Stella, Betty and Hope. I had to return by 23.59 hrs on the Sunday night. There was no point getting in late as there no doubt would be an air raid, so I got back about 6.30pm. I took my small valise up to my room and went to see if there was any tea. I had a cheese fritter because there was one left, my usual pint of Sgt. Major's tea and a small portion of rice pudding, once again because there was some left and cook's rice pud was as nice as my dad's used to be.

I didn't go out that night for I needed to sort my bedclothes out as you had to strip your bed when you went on leave, then the orderly knew you were away. When I went to look at my bed area, there was kit missing. I found the orderly and asked him if he had seen any of my kit. He said he hadn't. I got a bit worried as my boots, blankets, pillow, shoe brushes, battledress, a new pair of denim overalls – a Canadian pair too – my working leather belt, my Glengarry hat, knife, fork, spoon, the mirror I used when combing my hair, two favourite pin-ups and my mattress had been swiped.

I found the Corporal I/C stores and reported them missing. He told me to leave it until the morning and then see the C.Q.M.S. and Jaco, our C.O., to see what he said. There was a lot of pilfering going on in the section. I went in to see Jaco the next day and he told me to leave it for a time to see what happened. He confirmed that there was a lot of kit missing. He said I wasn't the only one to lose stuff and that, so far, I wouldn't be charged. He told me to keep it under my hat for now, as they had their scouts out, and to carry on as normal.

They wanted me to concentrate on the ashes from the gas works and to take a new corporal with me and show him the ropes. Corporal Hutchinson jumped in as I was turning in the yard. Some had already gone to the gas works. He asked my name and I told him "Hughes" but that my mates called me "Diesel."

We were just about to turn in to the gas works off the High Street and I told him that the landmark for turning was just this side of the gents' toilets. We reached the security gate and I spotted one of the men from the unit with my boots in one hand, receiving money in his other hand. He was handing my boots over to the security man.

I said: "Hey, they're my bloody boots he's flogging there!"

Hutchinson said: "How do you know they're your boots?"

I said I'd used a bayonet to mark my initials on the insteps.

Hutchinson jumped out, grabbed the bloke and put him under close arrest. I went for a load and picked him up with Scotty, one of the lads from the billet. He knew me, but I didn't know his name. I found out later that he was called Thompson and came from Scotland.

I have no idea what transpired. I had to write a statement. This corporal was from the S.I.B., and someone must have confessed to a multitude of thieving. A gang was on the loose everywhere in the capital. Little did I know, but it was my boots that clobbered them. Seven men were arrested, charged and taken into custody and the pilfering died a natural death for some time.

I was friendly with a lance corporal, Arnold, and he asked me to go for a bevvy with him to a pub in Tooting. I went and he seemed to be pushing me on to a girl present in the company. She was too pretty to be left on the shelf and she even bought me a pint. I was getting a bit tipsy and thought I'd better control my drinking as I never ever got drunk. I knew I'd had only three pints. I certainly wasn't drunk, but I felt tipsy. I had been doped. It was a Mickey Finn maybe – I don't know. Anyway, this girl was hanging on and it was time to go. We walked out and I was attacked from behind. There were about six of them and I managed to crawl under a car and stop there. God knows who the girl was or where she went. I don't suppose I will ever find out. I discovered later that she was a decoy and the gang which had been arrested was responsible for my battering.

Eventually, I managed to board a bus back to Thornton Road. Corporal Cuncliff met me as I climbed the steps to the front entrance to the house. He wanted to know what had happened. My ear and nose were cut and my eyes bashed, the skin was cut everywhere. I went to the local hospital to have my wounds dressed and nursed them for a week or so.

I had to go in front of Jaco again and he quizzed me to try and find out what had happened. Arnold was hauled over the coals to answer for me being lured out. Someone had bribed him to get me out. The bastards.

I had my next week's time of duty attached to bomb disposal. The mechanical equipment section was responsible for the plant for lifting. Jerry, by this time, was dropping land mines by parachute. The warning had gone well before I had finished my tea. The aircraft seemed heavier than usual and the searchlights were on the ball. Landmines were being dropped and if a gun could hit one before it got too close to the ground, it was a bonus to the gunners. This didn't happen very often. The gun was only as good as the searchlights would allow. This particular night they must have been given extra generated power from somewhere. They played their part well and if anyone deserved medals those girls did. They were one move ahead of Jerry each time.

We had a call to go to Kennington. The gas works had been hit and there were unexploded landmines in and near the gasometers. When we arrived we could see one of these damn things hanging over the side of the storage tank. There was too much gas in the tank to attempt any removal. The gas works turned all the feed off the one tank to bring it down as near the ground as possible, with safety, so we could get round it to defuse it. We all scarpered for two hours or more while they did this. Rather than risk leaving gas in the tank to maintain the height, they managed to put blocks in to prevent the mine touching the floor, then they withdrew the gas from it and we had a go when light dawned. On examination it was found the detonator was the wrong way round and would have to be turned. The only way to turn it was to put a silk rope round it tautly about ten times, allowing enough rope at each end to revolve round the mine when we pulled the rope one end and fed it the other. This had to be very well controlled and we managed it.

I went in with the Jones Mobile at about eleven o'clock to have a bash at lifting the mine for the team to try to remove the detonator. We found this was a different type and we had to resort to our training books to find out how it was done. It wasn't in the book, so we had a problem! We sent for the Chief. I hoisted the mine and left it suspended with the bottom trailing the ground, and left the site for safety until the Chief arrived. We had a break. There was always a mobile canteen in touch with us wherever we were working and they were a godsend. We just had a char and a wad – and they were always good brews, too.

Eventually the Chief came with his briefcase, examined the mine and compared it with the types we knew of. The bottom had to be screwed off as the detonator was in the base. It was no larger than most bombs. We laid it flat and I hoisted it onto two trestles. Unscrewing was no problem, but it was different all right. The usual procedure was observed, and you got out when you had done your thing. I kept well clear until the Chief called me to load the mine on the crib. It was all done – thank God for that. There was only one thing wrong. There was another one round the back of the next gasometer; all in all we did three that day.

Although you got used to the job, it still gave you the jitters. As far as I can remember, we only lost one man, and he had not observed the rules because he had been drinking. If a man had been on the 'pop' and was called out, his first job was to tell the Chief so that he could be excused and this was a must. You needed every ounce of nerve and concentration in your body.

We arrived back at about 6.30p.m. We had a meal and a shower and went to bed with a bottle of brown ale and a book. The billet was quiet, and I woke next day at 11am. I was off duty now for two days. I trudged downstairs to see if there was any tea in the cook's pot. I had a cup, got changed and went out to Tooting to see if I could find Jessie. I called on the Common first and she was on duty. We nattered for a minute and arranged to meet in the forces club for a game of table tennis. Neither of us drank much so it was soda for her and a pint of Three Star for me. That did us all night. We would have a game of chess or cards and a walk along the Common before going home to sleep.

This was my routine for months.

The war in the desert was to and fro and it was on the cards that we would soon be off. Eventually 39 Pltn only were given embarkation leave, so it looked as though we were going on our own. I only had four days' leave and had to report back to Halifax.

We had to go to a Chapel in the centre of Halifax – Ebenezer Chapel, it was called. I was starting off in the right place if God was going to be on my side, wasn't I? We were bundled in the chapel, anywhere in the pews. I managed to get on the top storey and was right in the front row overlooking the balcony. There was Lofty New, Cyril Merryfield and Hank Bowen Gittins. These were my immediate mates. We were allowed out, and to stay out all night if we wanted to.

Everyone except us knew where we were going. The girls in the town knew more than we did. We went boozing as usual, got with a gang of girls and sang all night. We arrived back at about 2am and at 4am it was 'everybody out', with full pack, everything. Thank God, no rifles. Every man was loaded. We marched to Halifax station and then caught a train to somewhere!

No one told us a bloody thing. The only thing we knew was that we were off. All the girls we had seen the night before knew. We had to pass the early shift at the Mill to get to the station. They had hung their knickers up on one line, from a window one end of the factory to the other. Every girl must have been minus her knickers! As the column moved past the Mill, we were halted and fell out. This must have been a ritual for every despatch. Every window in the factory was open, and we were cheered to the station. They were adorable screams that we might never hear again. We hadn't a clue what was going to happen next.

We all had a fag on the train. "Never mind where you're going, have a fag," was the routine. The train stopped in Liverpool. We all alighted. It was a case of "full kit, march in three ranks and sing you bastards, sing." The film, 'The Shores of Tripoli', had just been shown and, wherever we marched, we sang or whistled the theme tune. Little did I know that I would get to Tripoli one day.

Morale was as high as it could be. We hoofed it to the docks, where there was a bloody big ship, the *Athlone Castle*. We were sailing on that. What a ship – 36,000 tonner, with what we knew afterwards to be 6,500 troops on board. We went on, in our turn, and were put on C Deck on the water level. It was a massive ship, they said it was about a mile and a quarter to walk all round her.

We were loaded, heard a fog horn and then we were moving. The tugs were busy pulling and pushing us out. The roar of the main engines, or turbines, was noisy, and we sped out into the mouth of the Mersey. It was foggy and we appeared to slow down again. Eventually we stopped and I heard such a clatter. It was the anchor being lowered. We were there for three days, possibly waiting for the fog to lift. The hills where I was born were tantalisingly close. I wondered where I was going, how long for and when would I see those hills again.

I joined the lads on our mess deck. The cards were already out. It was to be our first taste of food on ship and we organised our mess rota. This was going to be nothing like the C.R.E's mess facilities, I knew. The meals were collected from the galley. Two men each day were on mess detail. We wondered what the first meal was going to be like. It smelled OK and up it came. There were 20 men to a deck table so imagine 12 tables in a row along the starboard side. There were seats down both sides of the tables, 10 men on each side, four lengths of tables across to the other side portside. There were 960 men in the space we were allocated. There was plenty of fresh air from the air-ducting overhead, and I noted hooks on the steel structured beams. What were they for? Anyway the meal arrived – white bread, best butter, an urn of tea and fish, which was very nice too. The bread was the best I have ever tasted, the tea was good and we had apricot jam for afters spread on the beautiful white bread. It was scrumptious. Everything went smoothly. We all had enough to eat and were quite happy.

Mealtime was a major part of our life for the next three months, and I wouldn't have missed the experience. This was when you got all the wit – it was enough just to sit back and shut up. You could write a book on the sarcasm. Jocks, Cockneys, Taffies, Spud Bashers from Bungey, Yorkies, Lancashire lads, Scousers, 'Down Sowf' men, Somerset lads... All types of men together. We were like sardines. We would have had more room in a tin!

After tea the tables were cleared and the beer flowed. The canteen opened and you were allowed to drink on your mess deck. We played cards, chess, dominoes, Chinese checkers – and smoked. I think everyone found that smoking was best done on the open deck. Nevertheless, it took us a quite long while to get adapted to life on board.

Anyway, from the very beginning the food was excellent and we had everything we needed, except for knowing where we were heading. We hadn't moved yet.

On the third day the turbos started up. We were off, lads! And so we sailed out of the Mersey Estuary late in the evening in October 1941. We sailed through the Irish Sea. It was rough and waves were pounding high up the side of the ship. We were allowed almost everywhere, except the female section of the ship. I knew I had to go and have my last look at Blighty before it was too late. I walked up the stairway to go onto the open deck. It was blowing a gale, dark and everywhere was blacked out. There was a glimmer of light over Greenock as we passed the Scottish coast with a raging sea ahead.

I was parallel with the bridge, when suddenly a big wave broke over the side from starboard, picked me up and smashed me against the bridge wall. I was sure I'd left the imprint of my body on the white painted background. I lost something there – my whole life was completely altered from that moment on. I felt as if my life rested on the whim of Fate: and I just let the future take its course. I didn't know what was happening, or where I was going.

There were other ships about and the turbos were thrashing through the white-topped waves. It was very cold in the gale force wind. I was clad in my overcoat, Glengarry, balaclava, scarf and gloves. I saw the last of Scotland fade out of sight.

Chapter 8

LIFE AT SEA

I went down to the mess deck. Some of the lads had fixed their hammocks up on the hooks I was wondering about earlier. All the hammocks were in rotation. There was room for everyone if you wanted to sleep below decks and everyone did the first few nights.

The next day we had slipped down the Irish Coast to rendezvous with a convoy leaving the Bristol Channel. Altogether there were 30 or so ships in the convoy – *Athlone Castle, Sterling Castle, Largs Bay, Empress of France, Empress of Japan* (now renamed and known as the *Empress of Scotland*), four Corvettes, two battleships, a cruiser, the captain of the convoy, *Empress Battleaxe*, and the *Volendam*. I can't remember any more. There were ships galore and we were heading west-south-west, towards the Tropics. A convoy sailing during the War never sailed in any particular fashion. It zig-zagged all over the place. This gave the enemy no indication of its direction.

There was no doubt that there was danger in the Atlantic. At that time I was scared: the convoy was on its way, we didn't know where to and if you didn't like it you couldn't turn back!

The climate began to get warmer and we started sitting outside. When you went to the open deck you had to slide your way in between your mates if you were lucky. The sun was nice and the nights were shorter, so we were eating, sitting, sleeping, reading, lying in the sun, writing letters, yapping, doing anything to pass the day along.

We had deck drill and emergency drill. Everyone had a life jacket. That was your passport to survival. If you didn't carry it at all times you were on a 252 before you knew it.

They organised all kinds of pastimes. I went to the library for the first book I ever read, apart from schoolbooks. It was a love story called 'Blame it on the Moon'. Can you remember the first real book you read? I will never forget mine.

Some of the passengers were seasick for the first few days and my mate Geordie had a horrible set of false teeth. I asked him why he didn't do something about those bloody teeth.

He asked: "How do you mean, man?"

I replied: "Can't you be sick over the side and lose them?"

He thanked me and said it was a good idea. He pulled them out and away over the side they went. He went on sick parade next morning and finished up with a lovely set of teeth from the ship's dentist. Nobody asked any questions.

Then everyone started to run to the toilet with violent diarrhoea, even me. Have you seen the toilets on board a troopship? Imagine a long pipe, 18ins in diameter, cut across to form a trough 14 or 15 yards long with some kind of covering. Everyone sat on a plank of wood, which was clean, disinfected, warm and comfortable. It was dry and you could speak to your mate while you were 'draining', because that's what we thought we were doing with this wretched diarrhoea. You left your throne and you knew you shouldn't have given it up, because you wanted it back again right away.

On one of these trips to the toilet, I ran up the stairs again, keeping to the code of being on the right, and bumped into someone. He swore at me and I swore back.

"Will you come out into the light? I'm sure I know that voice! You're from round Wrexham somewhere," said the voice.

He was a lad from the Church choir, Ray Evans, from the bottom street in Caergwrle. He was in the South Wales Borderers going to the Far East. I asked him how he knew this because we Engineers hadn't a clue where we were going. The two of us met regularly after that, and reminisced about the past.

I managed to make the toilet and sat there for ages.

The medical orderlies came round the next day and told everyone what to do. The outbreak of violent diarrhoea was soon under control and we got back to normal.

Under normal circumstances life on the ocean wave was quite nice, but we all knew of the risk we were under. There were German U-boats in the vicinity; the convoy's escort was bouncing about all the time, and you could smell trouble. Every nautical mile or so the convoy altered course, turning in all directions, north, south, east and west. This was to try to baffle the enemy as much as possible.

A convoy always had to travel to the speed of the slowest vessel and the *Largs Bay* was the slowest in ours, which brought us down to approximately seven knots. This was very slow for the Castle liners. Our ships could do anything up to 38 knots, so life was very tiresome. The ship's company did all they could to try and amuse us all, but it got very boring. A draw was organised for the distance the boat travelled each day. I think it was 6d a try and the nearest to the distance won. I could never get it right because I couldn't convert nautical miles into ordinary miles. It's surprising what you learn as you get older. I know how to do it now. The only way you could calculate was on time, you had no chance on distance because of the zigzagging. We must have done a terrific amount of extra miles.

'Action Stations' was a frightening experience, because we knew that if it was for real it would be catastrophic. It was not hard to work out that there were too many of us for the lifeboats. Anyway, we had to go to our stations every time we did the exercise. We were supposed to get to know what to do in the event of an emergency, and how to save ourselves. We were brainwashed, really, that everything would be all right, but we knew in our heart of hearts that it wouldn't.

We were heading for tropical waters. Life down below was good and the air wasn't as bad as you might think. There was probably an air duct for each hammock. I never felt I was without fresh air, although we could take our bedding and sleep on deck now the weather was warmer, and we did. We spent all our time sitting around talking, writing or reading, telling jokes, singing and smoking. Funnily enough we all seemed to keep to our own places too. We met the same lads each day and got friendly with men from other units. One day I was looking over the shoulder of a man in the Royal Welsh Fusiliers. He was showing photographs to his mates and I asked if I could have a look at one of them. He gave it to me and I said: "Do you know him?" He said he did. I told him it was my brother George. This was the lad whose sister was engaged to my brother! She was from Burnham-on-Sea. This coincidence was one of quite a few to come in my travels around the world.

We were due to see 'Lord Neptune' the next day. Have you any idea what this is like? I can tell you it's weird. I crossed the Equator three times and found it strange each time. You could almost see the bloody man with his trident and shield! The sea was like glass, and as the *Athlone* splashed along, she brought beautiful colours out of the waters, ploughing her way to I don't know where.

An alert was sounded on the *Empress of France*. She answered a distress signal from the destroyer forward, port side. Although I could read a little Morse, I was broadside before I could get the message or part of it.

'Action Stations' was sounded and, without panic, everyone went to their stations. We were slightly aft, above us was an 8-inch gun, manned by the crew. The ships' hooters were sounding, as there was something amiss. We heard the gun above me open fire, but saw no aircraft. I was in shorts and felt the elimination singe the hairs on my legs and the retort from the gun rattled in our ears for ages afterwards. We saw the defence ships move into action. They put many depth charges out. These were exploding deep in the water and caused a wave to come up from the explosion. There was something afoot. Jerry was there all right.

It was in the early afternoon. I think everyone was scared, as we were miles from anywhere. Someone spotted a movement in the water and a fin on it like a shark. It was heading for our ship. I have no idea if the hierarchy saw it, or if they did, whether they could have done anything about dodging it. It was a torpedo, heading straight for us. It struck on the water level and the ship did not budge. We heard a terrific thud and waited for the explosion. It never came. The torpedo ripped a hole in the starboard side of the ship. There was a certain amount of panic, mostly from the crew, not so much by us, because we knew nothing.

The torpedo sizzled through the ducting and the caged-in wiring of the ship's signal systems. It pushed along the deck and folded into the swimming pool, which was approximately 12ft square. The three-quarter steel plate was shattered like soft tin; the force or the speed must have been the reason it penetrated so deeply. We were all astounded to hear that the torpedo that hit us had not exploded. That part of the ship was evacuated, the holds shut and it was marvellous to see the naval crew now handling their responsibilities so efficiently.

How lucky can you be?

It was not over yet as the ships were still dropping charges and we saw oil appear on the surface of the water. Had we got the bastard U-boat? We tried to work out what was going on. No-one told us anything. Where the torpedo penetrated was the recreation area. We didn't even have to move our stuff and everything calmed down. The convoy didn't wander from its position. All the ships were in the same place, and because of the zigzagging, no-one knew which way we were moving.

The evening came on us quickly. As darkness fell we were all concerned and waited for the news from the ship's radio. We usually had five minutes' news of the day's log, how far we had travelled and what the weather would be like the next day. That night it was a rather longer news bulletin than usual because of the seriousness of what had happened. They were telling us the facts for a change about the day's events. Then we were plugged into the World News of the B.B.C. and the armed forces' network.

What we heard read was something like as follows: "The *Athlone Castle*, carrying British Troops east, was sunk in the mid-Atlantic. Our U-boats had a direct hit and she sank."

This was outrageous. It was Lord Haw-Haw, peddling his hateful German propaganda.

We were still sailing, but we had a big hole in our starboard side and the torpedo to deal with. All the Royal Engineers aboard were asked to report to the Captain's office by 9am the following morning. I reported with the rest and they led us into a dining room or mess. Captain Bradbury was our Officer in Charge. He knew most of us, although we had come out on a draft number. They wanted volunteers from the bomb disposal lads to help defuse the detonator of the torpedo. International law did not allow one to just drop the damn thing over the side. It had to be defused. Twelve were selected. I was number nine, which meant I was to control the lifting and take the times down on record. The crew engineers had already cut the steel floor out and it was thick steel too. This allowed the derricks to be lowered to the lift. The torpedo was still in the pool, which was now drained. As soon as the detonator was out we could breathe. Screws, circlip, plastic padding, all had to be removed, then the touchiest part of the job – the detonator.

"I've got it. Hurrah!"

The derrick lifted the torpedo out to the side of the ship, a time fuse was installed, it was let go with a sway over the side and *thud* – off it went.

We were steaming south, still within reach of the enemy. We still didn't know where we were or where we were going, but we were in tropical waters. We were at sea for 18 more days and there was no sign of land. We were sleeping out on the open deck and only went down for meals and our free rations. We were given 50 cigarettes a week and these were the best cigs I had the whole time I was overseas. They were Waverley's 50 tins and they were like smoking silk. We played cards for them, lost some, gained some, borrowed some, gave some away... But we were with our buddies and you always had a half of what was theirs.

We noticed the deck hands getting the decks cleaned up so everyone was all agog that we were nearing land. I awoke to find myself living through my wildest dream. We had hit land overnight. We were outside the Bay of Bahia in Brazil.

What a sight! I awoke from my sleep on deck, lying on my hammock, with my head on the pullover and buoyancy safety pads I used for a pillow. It was something I do not think anyone can describe. It was so beautiful!

As you looked towards land, it was as if someone had painted the side of the hillside with different colours, vivid colours, purple, bright blue, vivid green, white, red, every colour of the rainbow. They were in layers like wide ribbons on a wall. As we moved closer, we could see houses in rows, one behind the other, rising from the quayside to the top of the bank about three hundred feet up at an angle of 45 degrees, rows and rows of coloured houses, not brick built like ours, but wooden structures – and very well kept.

We eventually entered the harbour. The quay was tidy and little boats were scampering round us trying to sell their wares in baskets hoisted onto the side of the ship. You put your money in the basket first, shouted what you wanted, and let the basket down on the rope. Bananas, oranges, mangoes, pineapples, coconuts, cigarettes and tobacco were all for sale. Anything you wanted, all for a silver sixpence.

We were the first British troops to go ashore there. Eventually, we did a parade through the town. We were given the freedom of the town and what a time we had! Do you know what the freedom of the town was? It meant you could have practically anything you wanted free, for example, beer, cinema, shows, anything, so long as you don't break the law.

We were ordered to parade at 2pm, in best K.D.. You should have seen the shape of some of the uniforms, they were terrible. The issue from this country for tropical wear ought to have been thrown in the bin. Although a British soldier takes great pride in being smart on parade, you simply never could look smart in that tropical outfit.

Anyway, we paraded and marched around the town. Everyone was out in force to greet us, as we were the first troops to disembark in Brazil. We marched to the top of the coloured houses I had seen from the harbour, but to get to there you had to walk about three miles round, so this was just like a route march. You could get to the top by escalator, run on a one up, one down, system. There were a few of these along the way.

As we marched we were cheered by the inhabitants. It was a real rousing cheer, so they must have liked what they saw. The temperature was in the 90s, and we were certainly ready for the fall-out order that came after we hit the summit, before the march past the City Hall, with what may have been their equivalent of a Lord Mayor. The parade lasted three hours, we had a lecture about conduct and were told that we were ambassadors of the United Kingdom and to behave ourselves. We were dismissed and rested under the shade of the palm trees. The grass was much longer than in Britain, the blades were wider and not as well knitted as ours. Round each palm was a circular table for the refreshments we bought from a huge square of shops around the beautiful park.

There were people everywhere just looking at us. Children,

youths, girls and boys – just staring. They couldn't understand the language or our presence, and yet they were so friendly towards us.

Lofty New was flicking a sixpence on his thumb and tossing it in the air. One of the beautiful girls out of a group standing by us grabbed it and ran off. We by this time were sitting around the tree table. Some of the other girls followed her to the ice cream parlour. After a while they came back with refreshments we had never seen before. Talk about a cocktail, they were delicious!

All the girls were dressed in sombrero, short pants, ankle socks and bra. Their skins were tanned and none of them looked puny. Three of them had mandolins. They came back serenading us, singing Carmen Miranda-type songs and dancing around the tree. This was going on all over the park. Even the officers were joining in. We found three of the girls were from one family, Scots-origin immigrants of years ago. They could all speak English and went to English classes in their colleges. We made arrangements to visit their parents the next day.

Every boy and girl old enough to drive had a car, it seemed. I was running round in a sports car. It was only a two-seater, but it had a lift-up boot lid like our vintage cars.

We met the girls' family and dined with them. They gave us everything and the wines were potent and rich. We had to return to ship each night, but the families were by the dock entrance to pick us up if we were not on any type of duty. I had never seen such hospitality. Everyone you spoke to had enjoyed a wonderful time. I thought they were a wonderful nation.

The ship was being repaired. It had a massive hole in its side, the ducting, wiring, steam pipes, communication wires, everything had to be re-established. Our equipment was unloaded and some of it was put on show. The landowners were offering us, as operators of the machinery, a lump sum and a guaranteed wage to desert and teach their people to drive the machinery. We only had 97 men in our section and nine deserted. No one knew where they went. We were all interrogated when we set sail again. The inhabitants had the money, but had no one to tell them how to work the machines they could buy. It was getting time to sail again, this time across the Southern Atlantic to South Africa. We left on the Tuesday morning and were on the move when some of the families came to pick up their friends. Nobody knew a damn thing until we sailed. All we could do was to wave them goodbye from the ship. I walked to the other side to see the last of the beauty of the Bay of Bahia.

We sailed right out, with no waiting for tides. We were all discussing what had happened to the missing lads. McKellar was one from our table. He was a born comedian. We all missed his Yorkshire humour. He ran the market stalls in Leeds before being called up, and on the ship he would pick up a pair of boots or some cigarettes and start flogging them. He kept us all going. Anyway he was gone, and I wouldn't see him again – or so I thought.

The South Atlantic was as calm as a sheet of glass. We were travelling as though we were still in the same convoy. It had reduced by half as we sailed to Durban, South Africa. We were still spending time out on deck, sleeping and doing a little bit of letter-writing to post home when we got to Africa. I entered a competition to describe what we saw of Bahia. You were allowed 200 words, and I put mine in poetry form. I entered it and came third, but sadly I never kept a copy. I've scrapped the paper where I'd written it so I am only able to remember a line or so. I called it 'Bahia':

We expected native buildings such as corrals on those hills
Not a city of high skyscrapers like America builds...

I can't remember any more. A day or so afterwards I wrote another piece describing my home which I remembered as we left Liverpool. I kept scribbling a few words and kept it in my writing case. Quite a few of my mates tried to grab it to take the piss out of me, but I always kept it safe and they wouldn't go in your kit for anything.

I suppose we had another 10 days' sail to the Cape. I had plenty of time to sit and write. I wrote to my mum, and one letter each for my sisters. I couldn't write to George because again we didn't know where we were and where we were going. I thought of Alice and her poetry to me, so I dropped her a line too.

The following day I wrote another poem which I called 'The Western Hills'. I included it in my mum's letter and forgot about it. I did keep a copy this time. We were nearing the Cape of Good Hope. We had not seen any more of Jerry, but we had heard quite a lot of Lord Haw-Haw. We thought someone ought to find him and shoot the swine! He was a morale breaker, if you took any notice of him.

The seas started to get rough. You know what that means! We were nearing the Cape and it showed.

Early morning brought a sad sight and we were asked to refrain from hindering the task of rescuers on the ship lifting men out of the water. I saw two of them and didn't want to see any more – they were blue and not a pretty sight either. We found out later that they were Germans. Twenty-nine of them, we heard, and probably from a German submarine. Twenty-eight survived. One died the same day as we landed in Durban.

This was another surprise. It was a vast city. Cosmopolitan in a way, yet there was a definite class distinction even then in 1941.

Durban was huge and after the weeks we had spent at sea we were getting a bit edgy with one another. It was nice to find one's 'land' legs again and walk down the gangplank to earth. As the ship entered port it was a fine harbour. There were other vessels coming and going.

Everyone who has been to Durban during the war will know and have heard the lady singer on the quayside, singing 'Land of Hope and Glory.' I started singing 'Land of Hope and Caegwrle'! She sang and her partner played a fiddle – maybe he was her husband. I never tried to find out who they were until many years later. It was a nice welcome.

I clambered down the gangplank to go ashore for the first time in Durban. We were advised to try to get a rickshaw into the town, but to keep together. Lofty New and I went together in a rickshaw. The driver took us to the centre of the town, or what we thought was the centre. This again was high skyscrapers – not what we expected. Woolworth's took our eye, and many more shops and chemists. It was like shopping at home in Chester, only better. I can remember going to Stella Parade. I saw my first snake of any size, all kinds of animals in cages, went to see a film, and of course had a drink or two.

It was very warm and I think I was standing outside an air-conditioned store when an officer in A.T.S. uniform tapped me on the back. It was a Miss Stennet from Penyffordd, the Guide Mistress! We shook hands and she introduced me to her escort, a captain in the Guards. We talked for a while and she arranged to collect me at the Dock Gates the following night and take me to her club – Madagascar Officers' Club – for a meal and a cabaret show. I had to find some civvie clothes from somewhere, so the Guards' captain loaned me some white cricket togs of his to enable me to get in. They picked me up at the dock gates and off we sped through the black area of the city and out towards the uplands. I have no idea where we ended up, but it was a club for the girls all right. The whole night's entertainment was well beyond my pocket and my way of life. Nevertheless, I had a wonderful night – or night and a bit – because I didn't get in until 4.30am!

We only had four days' shore leave at Durban before we sailed on the Thursday with the morning tide. When we did get out of the harbour, we thought something was wrong. We seemed to fly and we realised we had lost the rest of the convoy. We went up the Indian Ocean, just the two Castle liners and a battleship. The two Castle ships could leg it. We must have been doing 28 to 30 knots. We still did not know where we were going. Eventually we arrived into Bombay Harbour (I think it was Christmas Eve 1941). There were ships everywhere, and the harbour was full. Unbeknown to me at the time, my brother George was on one of the other ships.

I think we were three days waiting to go in to tranship onto the *Volendam*. What a bloody crate, after being on an ocean liner! This was a welded cargo ship. Every effort it made, it creaked. It's a good job it wasn't turning corners, because it would have folded up. It was a bloody awful thing. We were transhipped and pulled out of the quay by the tugs.

Anyone wanting to go ashore had to have a pass and was transferred to a water boat. We all went ashore, Lofty, Merryfield, Hank, Gibson and myself. We went to see the cages where they cage and chain all the evil women, then went for a meal in a

European restaurant, so they say. We were all three-parts cut and we went to have a tattoo on our arms. You had to make your mind up what name you wanted on your arm. Everyone had 'Mary'. Don't ask me why, but for me 'Mary' it was and it still is today. I can't remember going out again. Bombay was horrible. Pungent cheap perfume and donkey shit was all I could find there.

We didn't know it then, but our next seven days were to be the worst part of our voyage – on the *Volendam*. We had a Greek captain. The O.C. troops was a Turk or Greek. He couldn't understand English or didn't want to. He treated us like animals. The ship was dirty, there were cockroaches as big as locusts and they were everywhere. You couldn't put your foot on the floor without squashing one. They were in our beds, shoes and kit. The ship was heavily laden and it creaked all night. I was sleeping right on top of the hold. There was a 24-hour guard on the holds and I had no sleep because they were up and down all night. We still didn't know where we were going. No-one told us a thing.

It was over three months now and we were getting ill tempered. Lads were fighting and squabbling. I was ill with a kidney infection and one of the Sergeants on duty roster awoke everyone up by digging the hammocks with his stick. I was excused duty because of my ailment and he came round on Reveille and dug my kidneys with his stick. I was semi-asleep and put my foot out of my hammock onto his chest and pushed him down the hold about forty steps. I didn't know and of course I was automatically charged with striking a senior rank. What could I do? What could I have done? Nothing, only report sick which I already was.

I went to see the ship's doctor and told him, and he said: "Leave this to me, and if you are charged, refer them to me," which I did and be damned I got away with it.

We were half way up the Persian Gulf, because we were in the Straits of Hormuz on the Gulf of Oman. It was time we were getting off the damn ship. Because of the transhipment we had no Christmas dinner and it was arranged for it to be held that evening. We were like pigs in a pen. Anyway, the Christmas dinner came round and the officers waited us on. Everyone was served, and a Turk came round with the duty officer.

"Any complaints?" he asked.

He had his own personal knife, fork and spoon in a leather case. It was a lovely thing. The Turk put his pack down to take a taste of something, I think it was a drink, and his eating irons had disappeared in a flash. I can't remember the name of the lad who took them but he was a crafty swine.

None of us saw what happened, but it spoiled a lot of Christmas fun. The Turk was very upset naturally, but he searched and searched. He left the deck and within half an hour we were ordered to have a kit inspection right away. The lad who was responsible told us he had thrown the stuff through the porthole. He buggered our Christmas up for us. Every man had his kit spread out all over the decks. Each one was searched thoroughly to no avail. The sharks were hiding it by now. It was real silver, according to the Duty Sergeant.

We were plodding up the Gulf at about 10 knots, fed up with Christmas and New Year celebrations. The weather was scorching hot, and everyone was wearing shorts. At least there was something to see, as we were close in to the left side of the seaway of the Gulf. Women were collecting fruit all the way up the banks, some were cleaning down, some stoning, some packing, some wrapping and the donkeys were all overloaded by the look of things.

I said to Lofty: "I'm looking forward to getting off this bloody thing, aren't you?"

He said: "I am, and I don't want to see another ship as long as I live."

I asked him, how about going home? He said he didn't think we would see home again. We did, but it was four years and three months later.

Chapter 9

THE SINKING BRIDGE

We came to the mouth of the Shatal-el-Arab, Marguill. This is where the Tigris and Euphrates rivers meet. We saw some kind of a jetty and this is where we disembarked in January 1942. The jetty was so fragile that if a wind had blown I'm sure it would have taken the jetty with it.

There were about 30 lorries waiting for us. Each man carried his own kit and was ushered to the lorry. We sped off into the sunshine and the scorching desert somewhere. We learned later it was Iraq and that we were going to a transit camp at Shaiba.

After we left the dock area, we saw nothing but sand, sand and more sand. Sheikh drivers – Indian – were driving the lorries.

As we proceeded towards Shaiba, the road, although tarmac, was not wide enough for two vehicles to pass in comfort, and there was a donkey coming towards us. It was fully loaded with all kinds of fruit. I suppose it was going to market. I had never seen anything so cruel in my life. The driver of the lorry kept his hand on the horn and kept going. The donkey cart just had to stop. The driver of the lorry got out of his seat, tipped the donkey cart up and just drove off. We were flabbergasted.

On we sped towards our destination, and we pulled up outside a very large barbed wire fence. It was a transit camp. It had a large perimeter, coiled safety wire all round it, a broken down kitchen unit, and a thatched building called a coffee shop. There was no accommodation at all, not even an office, just a derelict camp that looked like an old P.O.W. camp. We were told that this was our home for the next few weeks.

We were glad to get our feet back on the ground, but this was terrible. After an hour or so the tents arrived and we knew the quicker we could get them up, the better. It was six to a tent. We were told to get settled as soon as we could and we would be served a meal as quickly as possible.

Artist's impression of 'The Barracks' in the 1920s by M P Roberts

Left: A very creased picture of me taken from a school photo at Abermorddu in 1928: aged six.

Above and above right: 'The Barracks' nowadays. Only the ground floor of the houses remains and the play yard has gone

a

Stella and Mum pictured in 1940: a very dark sepia portrait

Me, aged 11, posed at the wheel of a vehicle – already showing my love of anything mechanical

Betty (aged 11) and me (aged 15), pictured in the garden. (The original snapshot is rather scratched).

A recently-discovered studio portrait of my father.

b

Ivor, my teenage pal, died in 1937

The Rev R Theo Jones

Me as a young man

Hope parish church, 1936

My good friend Les Lloyd

C

Right: Cole Island, where I lived while building the bridge

Left: the abutments to Shatal-el-Arab "sinking" bridge built by 660 GEN/Const. CO. R.E. in 1942. The bridge was actually down in the river when these snapshots were taken.

Right: the bridge held two railroads and two roads, open and closed, when up. It sank to the bottom of the river and ships passed over it.

d

Left: The plant park at Salachia

Below:
870 M.E. COY

Below right: my mate Lofty New

Below left: At Baghdad

e

Captain Fountain (left) and
Lance Corporal Walker (right)

Dick Elliott

Bert Garlick

Lofty New

Above: On the train to Egypt across the Sinai Desert, three Welshmen met up: Bert Davies of Keri, Abermorddu, Tiny Roberts of Summerhill and myself from Hope Village.

Left: Me at Ismailiya

On the beach at Alexandria, 1943

9

Left and below:
My beloved Mac where I lived for almost four years

Above: Harry, my trailer mate

Above: Me

Above: Bedouin girl

Above: Dromedary carrying corn

h

Above: Snow on the way to Damascus – taken through the windscreen of the Mac

Above: Mitchican mobile crane hoist

Above: Barber Green trencher

i

Above: Jebel Mazar snow post

Above: Home from home, inside the rear of my Mac

j

870 M.E. COY Royal Engineers helped build the Chekka By-Pass

Above: The Chekka Landslide Tunnel

k

Above and below: Deepening the river bed in the Bekka Valley, near King Solomon's Mines, so logs could be floated downstream

1

Above: D8 Caterpillar being loaded on to trailer

Above: Part of our massive 55-ton load

m

Above and below: Chilly work - snow clearing on what we called The Pitac, north of Tehran, Persia. I think it's the Elburz Mountains.

Above: Awaiting convoy to go to Tehran to transport Polish refugees from Russia via El Dory
Below: Salvaged plant scavenged from the desert

Above: Ready to set off for a month's leave at Christmas 1945. I took the train to Baghdad, Nairn transport to Haifa, a train to Port Said; a ship (below) across the Mediterranean to Toulon, a train through France to Dieppe, sailed across to Newhaven, took the train to London, and thence to Crewe and Chester - then home...

Above: Climbing aboard a Spitfire in the plane 'Graveyard' at Shaiba. I thought about the men who had been killed in all the wrecked aircraft

Above: Time expired after five years and three months! Me and Taffy Landler

Jerusalem

Above: Thorp Mills Triangle near Halifax, where I did my Military Transport training in 1940 – as it is now.
Below: Our HQ Mech Equipment Co R.E. at Castle Brewery, Newark Town Centre, as it is today. I scrubbed those steps doing 'jankers'.

Trucks like the ones I drove have become collector's items

Below: I drove this type of Scammell across the Sinai Desert. It had a 12-speed gear box, and high and low boosters

t

We still kept to our gang as much as we could – Eric, Lofty, Bowen, Merryfield, Paddy McDade and me. We had to sleep on the sand, on the only groundsheet we had. There were none with any of the tents. That was it and down you got. The O.C. called a parade to warn us of our do's and don'ts. We all had a guard duty and were told, in no uncertain terms, to be vigilant and, by God, he was proved to be right.

We were issued with rifles, given ammunition, and told to use it if we needed. Guard for the next 24 hours was two on and four off. I was on the second stint, from ten till midnight. There was a perimeter all round the camp with searchlights. At dusk we managed to start the generator up and get the lights on. It was obvious from what the C.O. had told us that we were thought of as greenhorns and would be an easy target for pilfering on the first night in Iraq. They would certainly have a bash at us and so they did.

I was just getting off to sleep, but of course, not undressed, lying on my groundsheet in the sand in the I.P. tent, when I heard shots being fired. I grabbed my rifle, tin hat and bullet pouches, and raced to the Guard Room at the entrance to the camp. We saw three men crawling along the inside of the dannet wire. We called for them to halt, but there was no reply and they made a dash for it. We all fired one shot in the air and they still didn't stop. We took aim and fired.

There was a lot of 'material' found on the ones that had been shot. One was clutching a bar of white soap costing about 1/6d, so his life had gone for 1/6d. One of the senior officers, on his own in an I.P. tent, the same size as ours, was fast asleep. The whole tent was taken from over him and his portable table, with his watch, cigarette case and lighter, all gold, were still on the table. The whole tent was taken, but nothing was missing from the inside. With men on guard, how could they do it? They were the craftiest baskets living!

I remembered this the whole time I was in the Middle East and wouldn't trust any of them. It was a useful experience and made me cautious for the rest of my tour of duty. The C.O. commended us the following day. Three Iraqis were shot, and we were lectured on the difference between killing or wounding an Arab. If you killed one you were charged 10/- to bury him, but if you only wounded him you could pay for that as long as you lived.

If a thief is stealing from you, you have the right to shoot to kill. It's a subject I don't like thinking about, let alone writing about.

The next day we noticed the heat and from 12 noon till 2pm we did nothing. The temperature must have been in the 80s then, all the tent flaps were up and we were still sweltering. There was little to do, we were miles from anywhere and none of us knew what was going on. There were still 76 R.E.s left in the section. We were now on our own and, I suppose, awaiting posting. There were bricklayers, plasterers, painters, joiners, all sorts. Some had no trade at all, but you couldn't do without them.

The postings came at last and I was hoping I would stay with my section. I didn't. I was posted to a construction company as a bricklayer! I pointed this out to the officer and he said to go where I was sent and to sort it out there. I was really upset, what with losing my mates, and being posted as a brickie.

Merryfield said: "You don't have 'diesel bricks'! You'll sort it out and join us later, I'm sure."

I said goodbye and joined 660 Gen. Construction Company R.E.s. They were stationed on Cole Island on the Shatal-el-Arab where the Tigris and the Euphrates meet.

The company was erecting a bridge across the two rivers from the mainland to the island, and from the island to the mainland on the Iranian side of the river. This was to be 'aid to Russia' and would take two railroads of two lanes of traffic, one closed to the other alternately. Shipping was strong on the rivers at the estuaries and the bridge was designed to sink into the water when the ships wished to pass. It was the only sinking bridge in the world, or so it was said.

As soon as I arrived, before I did anything, I applied for an interview with the C.O. to try to find out why I had been posted there. They said it was a mistake, and I would be joining my company when they had finished with me. There was plant on site and I was to show their people how to operate it before I could go back to my unit. I was frustrated about this, yet I should have been glad because the rest of 39 Section had gone to reinforce 871

M.E.Co. with Monty.

The C.O. of 660 said I should be pleased. I couldn't see it at the time, but I settled down to do some work if there was any. I went on site to see the project and the officer told me to spend the day looking round, as I might get to like it and want to stay.

There were a few pieces of plant, one I had not seen before. It was a Crane Piledriver run by a D4 600 engine and I eventually used it to piledrive thousands of piles in that river bed. There were six Chicago pneumatic compressors, for the air drills, and a D2 Caterpillar which I had only ever seen once before. It was brand new and had only worked six hours (that's how plant is controlled and serviced, by the hours it works).

I had to organise the plant and move it to where it was needed in the morning, then go on the piledriver. It was a very interesting job, and I liked it, but was still annoyed being away from my unit. However, I was too busy to be concerned. I used the D2 to pull the long timbers in position for the sheikh to drill them, so they could bolt the baulks together to make them 80 feet long or thereabouts, so you had two 40 feet lengths braced together with four 6 inch wide baulks bolted to brace them up. The Sheikh Pioneer Company Indian Army did all this. They were excellent workers and did a wonderful job with the timber and bolts.

When I arrived on Cole Island work on the bridge had already been in progress for some months, so was half built. Now, whether someone was using someone else or not, I'm not sure. It looked to me that the people who had started the job had gone, or else they couldn't finish it. It seemed fishy that I had gone there as a 'brickie', yet I was so useful to them as an operator of all the plant they had...

As a so-called brickie, I was piledriving, checking the Chicago pneumatics for oil and water, draining the air from the tanks, checking the airlines for leaks, looking after the D2 and driving and maintaining the piledriver. Altogether I drove 6,500 piles into the riverbed. As you finished one, it was cut off level. It was braced with a 12 x 6 to the preceding one, and I crawled a little further across the river. Each pile was braced one to the other and a platform was put in position and the surface made.

The Arab labourers, some of them women, dug out the

abutments, and the foundations were filled with stone which was brought down the river by barge. Each barge had a team of women, and they all had baskets about the size of a large washing-up bowl to empty the barge. The stone was in pebble form about 3 inches in diameter. There were some woman filling the baskets, some hoisting them out of the barge, some carrying and some resting. The whole time they were unloading they were chanting.

There was a 'Boss Rice' in charge. He had a whip and used it. I noticed one young girl on the 'slave' gang who was heavily pregnant. She was flagging a little and the Boss Rice cracked the whip behind her a few times that morning. I watched as she went to the resting gang. The other women were concerned, so one of them took her place when she was due to restart. The Boss Rice noticed this and he whipped her across her buttocks. This riled me so I objected to him about it and he swore at me in Arabic, which I couldn't understand at that time. My Sergeant saw this and told me that I must not intervene.

About half an hour after this incident, I saw the girl going into the reeds, so I called to another carrier to go to her. Within half an hour she had had her baby, put it to rest in an old basket on the riverbank and started to work again. I still curse that Boss Rice.

I put the bulldozer on the little D2 to fill round the abutments of the bridge and then the work for the piledriver was finished. I then cleaned it down and pulled it back along the completed bridge to have the jib dismantled and taken down, ready for transportation back to a plant park somewhere.

Marguill was a pretty little place. If you saw it at night you would believe me. There was a canteen we went to down the river towards the dock where we had landed some three or four months before. It was my birthday. I walked in the W.V.S. canteen and the lady asked me what was wrong. I explained to her it was my birthday and she walked off. She didn't ask me if I wanted anything, just scarpered. I heard some muttering and she came back with a cake with a candle on it and a glass of whisky. She gave me a peck on the cheek and all the W.V.S. came out to sing 'Happy Birthday'!

I went into the Service Club for a pint and got back to the

island in the early hours of the morning. I must have had a drink from the canteen with the lads, and got to bed without putting my mosquito net right. Within three days I was lying on my back in the hospital with malaria.

I was in for three weeks and when I came out my posting had come through to join 865 M.E. Company at Salachia near Baghdad. I travelled up on my first Iraqi train – a steam train, of course. It was old, slow and dirty, with utility wooden seats and Indian type toilets – most uncomfortable. I think the journey was 12 hours or more, and there was very little on the stations. You might get eggs and chapatties. I must have smoked 2,000 cigarettes! I was on my own and it was boring. The line was rickety and the train puffed a lot.

Eventually I arrived in Baghdad and after getting in touch with the R.T.O. I had to wait for transport to pick me up at the station. I had no idea where the camp was; all I knew was that I was going to join 865 M.E.Co, to travel, eventually, to join 39 Mech. Equip. Sec. and the sooner the better for me. I was lost without my mates. Transport arrived for me as they were going to the D.I.D. for rations at El Fareit. I arrived at the camp at Salachia. It was about two miles outside Baghdad to the northwest. The camp was very clean and I had an idea it was full of bullshit – guards and strict control, saluting, etc. Anyway, I was trained for it and could stick it out with the next man. Everything was whitewashed, the latrines were clean, and the mess was a godsend after the muddle on Cole Island.

I reported to the C.O.'s office and was told to come back the next day. In the meantime I was to go to see the C.Q.M.S. and get what bedding I required, and hand my rifle in – which I didn't have because I had a Tommy gun.

"You shouldn't have that, Hughes, because you are not an Operator are you?"

I said I was an Operator and was entitled to it and that if I left it there I wanted to take it with me when I went.

The N.C.O. took me to a billet where I put my head through the door and very nearly got molested by everyone I knew. Some of the lads from the boat were there, and one came over to me and asked if I'd driven for Alun Edwards. I said I had, and we shook hands. He turned out to be from Llay! Then another lad came over, Tiny Roberts, and said he was from Summerhill.

"I remember you living in the Ffrwd and being in the Scouts at Hope," he said.

I went round them and they all asked where I had been. It was a joy to see some of them again. I was told we were moving shortly for Egypt, but not for a month or so. In the meantime I would be joining them in whatever they did, working out towards Babylon, and that if I had the chance I should go and see it. I was more interested in seeing Baghdad. I was told I could see Baghdad that night, as the duty truck was going in and if I wanted to be picked up I could put my name on the board and get a pass. It was for them to know where we were, but to watch the guard list, as there might be guard duty. If we didn't read the orders we would be for it.

I went to Baghdad with Tiny the next night. It was a very interesting place compared to the rest of Iraq. I first saw King Faizal's Palace and it was nowhere near finished off. It was by the bridge this side of the river. The bridge looked very good lit up at night. We were dropped the other side of the bridge in the town and our first call was an eating place. Whether this was a café or hotel I don't remember. We had a few bottles of Stella, a good meal and there was a billiard table there with no cloth. There were cushions and everything else except the cloth. The cues were good, so anyway we had a game. It was funny to hear the balls rolling on the naked slate. We were laughing our heads off and I'm sure the inhabitants thought we were laughing at them. I enjoyed the complete change of environment. It was great to be with my pals again.

Then, rightly so, I was clobbered for guard.

Now there were only six men on the guard, but to encourage you to turn out smartly they put seven men on. The seventh was what they called the 'Stick Man' who could fall out and that was his guard finished, unless something went wrong with one of the other guards. A Stick Man was the smartest dressed on the inspection. That meant everything. My Tommy gun was replaced for the guard only by a rifle. The rifle I was given from the stores must have been well kept, and it was in beautiful condition. I cleaned it and really went to town on it. I was after the Stick Man if I could get it. All my uniform was kept very smart for going out or special parades. I pulled the rifle through time and time again. It was polished inside as nicely as it was outside. I did my belt, lanyard and webbing with toothpaste (don't tell anyone – it was against the rules).

It was Sgt. Major Pinkey on parade and I was called as Marker, which was a good start. He gave the order 'Inspect arms.' I brought my rifle forward and he could see his face down the barrel. I knew he was impressed. He flicked my lanyard and all my webbing to see if it was powdered. It wasn't – but you could see it rise off one of the guards, just a little white powder on his fingers was enough to lose your 'stick'.

"Fall out Marker!" I had got it.

Hurrah! That was my guard for about a month, so it was worth doing your stuff for that. I was a bullshitter anyway. I nursed my best boots, they shone like a glass bottle and my Tommy gun case, too. Boots were for running with and the machine gun was for shooting – two of the most vital parts of your life in the Army.

Mail caught up with me at last. Dr. Hughes, A 2153373 Draft RG.000. I had 39 letters all in one go. I didn't know where to start opening them. My mum's first, but which one – any one – it didn't matter. I tried to date them, but this was impossible. They were very faded so I opened them at random. The first one made me cry. It told me my gran had died and she was very important to me. Why should the first letter I had received in almost twelve months tell me that? Why? Sixteen of the letters were from Mum. There were about six from my sisters, and one from D. S Davies, curate of Hope Church, telling me if I ever reached Jerusalem to visit his brother who was Bishop of Jerusalem. There were four from Alice, two stamped Denbighshire and two Lancashire, so I knew she had been to Caergwrle. She had had some more poetry published and she included a copy for me in the third letter I opened from her.

I got tired of them in the end and left the remainder until the following day.

Tiny called to me to say: "It's like a bloody library in here."

I said: "That leaves you out, because you can't bloody read."

The next day I opened one from Mum to say George had been on embarkation leave and she had received mail from the Far East – Burma.

Poetry came into my life quite a lot at this point. I read Alice's letters and her poem.

I noticed that in one letter Alice had taken over another shop. She owned two in London Road and was taking one over in Todmorden Road. I sat down and wrote her a long letter and sent her a copy of 'The Western Hills', which I had written in the Atlantic Ocean.

I had no idea how long we were going to be in Baghdad. We were working on a stretch of new road between Baghdad and Babylon. I went down with the working party, mostly for something to do. They were putting the finishing touches to the surface of the tarmac. There was an elevating grader, an autopatrol, a Barber Green Trencher, two D4's, and a Matador A.E.C with a Crane Freuhauf trailer. Each day we took something back with us to H.Q. to transfer it to the D.I.D. when the work was finished. I loaded the Trencher on the low loader and stretchered it down. Some of the tyres were slack so we used my converter to blow them up from the Ingersol Rand Compressor used for working the jackhammer.

"Who made that for you?" they asked. "It's ideal for the job."

I said I'd had it in Balham and I had looked after it, so Pinkey wanted to see it to make one like it for his workshop.

We were only about seven miles from Babylon and I wanted to see it before I moved to Egypt – if that was where we were going. I asked for leave to go and permission to travel on the work party then go onto Babylon with the 15 cwt. Morris Commercial and be back to pick the party up after work. Three people wanted to go, so we all went together, but some of us travelled down on the A.E.C. lowloader to the site and went on from there. Tiny Roberts, C.Q.M.S. Richardson and I had a fine day out. Anyone can get lost in the Vines. There were mazes all over the place. I got completely lost and I was only four yards from the other two! The stone images and tableaux, the columns of stone – how did they build them? The gardens were a mystery. I wouldn't have missed the trip for the world. We arrived back on time and returned for our

110

evening meal, which was appreciated as we were hungry. There had been little for us to eat in Babylon.

The duty truck was going out again that evening to Baghdad. Some of the lads were learning to ride horses and they asked me to join them. As we weren't going to be there very long it really wasn't worth our while learning, so Jack Hartley, Tiny and I went for a look round Baghdad. I thought I might never see it again.

There were a lot of Red Caps in Baghdad and many of the places were out of bounds to us. My mates showed me a lot of Baghdad you wouldn't know was there unless someone had shown you. The Red Caps kept the place free from trouble. We got a taxi home and, here again, I didn't know what was going on. I was talking to the driver in what Arabic I knew, together with Tiny, while the other two were watering his petrol tank. The taxi drivers used to fleece us anyway, so what did they expect?

The movement order came for us to move to Quassassin in Egypt. We were to be ready to move on the Tuesday. I was with a lad called Timmy who was on the A.E.C. and trailer. There were two Austin 3 tonners, four 30 cwt. Canadian Dodges, a Humber Snipe, the C.O.'s car, a 15 cwt Morris Commercial and a despatch rider on a Triumph 350cc motorbike.

Our trip was a long one and little did I know that I was to make that trip many times – Baghdad to Jordan, over the Seven Sisters, over to Haifa, down the coast to Tel Aviv, across the Palestine Gaza Strip, across the Sinai Desert to Kilo 196 and on to the bridge at El Qantara. Over the bridge onto the Treaty Road towards Ismailiya, up the Canal Road past Abusweire Camp 11 turning onto Quassassin. This was our journey...

Chapter 10

TO THE RIVER JORDAN

Our orders were to go down to the D.I.D. and fill up. Fill two 45 gallon drums with diesel, get 45 gallons of petrol, and as much oil as we thought we might need.

We got back to the depot, hooked to the trailer, put the fuel and oil on the trailer, tidied the back out and put our beds in for the journey the following morning. We got down and had an early night in the back of the wagon. It was great, until we heard the boozers coming in. I suppose some of them didn't want to leave.

We awoke to a nice breakfast, got washed and were ready for the off. We were told to keep in convoy until we crossed over Jordan. Once we cleared the mountains nick-named the 'Seven Sisters' we would be OK. It was always the heaviest in the front. The 'old man' had gone with the 15 cwt and his Snipe so we were leading the convoy, if you can call it that. Only six of us. We sped on and did well across the Iraqi desert into Jordan.

We stopped for the call of nature and to kick our wheels. We couldn't make out how far the Major had gone – to make the tea, I hoped. There was a small oasis in the distance and I could see smoke. I was parched and needed a Sgt. Major's brew and a bully beef butty. Maybe we were on hard biscuits again. They were generally used on trips like this. When we arrived at the oasis we found it was the Major and we pulled off the sand track. There was no road as such and every 500 yards a barrel stood as a way-marker on the left-hand side as you drove on the right. The only reason to think you were on the road was that you could see the tracks of other vehicles: there were no other indications whatsoever. It was easy to stray off the road, especially in the dark. The only way to tell was that it 'grew on you'.

While we were drinking, we checked the mileage and found we had done 140 kilos, which was good going. I topped the water up in the radiator, and was ready for the worst journey I had ever driven. It was unbearably hot and we had the mountains to climb. We didn't drive up; we twisted our way up. It was like a corkscrew, and the bends were not cambered to meet us, they went away from us. In other words, we were going around a bend tipping away from us and with a steep ravine in front of us. We were climbing 1 in 7s, 1 in 8s for about 12 miles up, and then we had the other side to negotiate too! It was vital to have two drivers to each vehicle.

Breakdowns always happen when they shouldn't and I was wondering when something would go wrong, because the run had gone so well.

My mates didn't appreciate my pessimism.

"You're proper bloody Welsh you are. Why don't you shut up? Here, have a fag and shut up," were the usual comments.

Once we started to climb there were no places where we could pull off the road, so we were tied down to getting over the top before we did stop. We paused for a quick check on our W.O.F. L. T.B. (water, oil, fuel, lights, tyres and battery) before starting the climb.

"OK lads, on your way. I'll go ahead and find a resting place for the night," I said.

I drove for the first stint. The Matador had a good selection of gears, actual 5; high and low booster and a 4 wheel drive too. When you are in low you are in low. You crawl at a snail's pace. I had very little weight on the trailer. You would expect to climb the mountain in an hour. It took five hours with the trouble we had.

The Austin 3 tonner boiled and gave up the ghost as the radiator blew up and out of the bonnet. I saw the steam in my mirror. I thought someone had pee'd on the exhaust or something. It was just like white smoke. I was on a wide left-hand bend when it went up and he was about 15 yards behind me. We both had no option but to stop. Someone suggested towing him. There is a strict rule of the road – you are not allowed to tow behind a towed vehicle and that includes a trailer. We couldn't even break the rule just to get the Austin to the top. So I had to load him on the trailer.

I dropped back 10 yards or so and got Timmy to let the winch rope out to hook onto the Austin, uncoupled the air lines to put the brakes on solid, helped Timmy with the skids and winched the lorry onto the trailer. The other lads were behind us so we had plenty of help to put the skids onto the trailer, bottle stretch the wagon down and block it. We were on our way again and as I moved off in crawler, the front wheels dug up the tarmac – it was so hot.

We got away all right and soon made good time to Jebel Mazar, which is not far from the top of the first peak. Although the mountain road is called the Seven Sisters*, there are only four really bad ones to climb. The C.O., Pinkey and the batman driver were waiting for us with something like a meal. We had iron rations for a snack, but the cook made a bit of a fire and we all had bully beef fritters and a bottle of beer before we got down to sleep. I was awake early, threw some water over my face and started up two of the Primus stoves to make some tea. I took the cook, Timmy, the 'old man' and Pinkey a drink, went for a walk to find a bush big enough to cover me to use as a toilet and then woke the rest up. A breakfast of tinned beans with sausages was soon over and we had an early start.

I thought we should make Haifa that night, if all went well. After we came off the last mountain (it's not a mountain as we know them in Wales – it's all dust, not a bit of green), we looked back over the tops and could see how arid they were. The goats were scavenging like piards for food and they came to us for any kind of scraps. We often saw piards and hyenas.

We weren't far off Amman, although we didn't go into Amman, we crossed the River Jordan and then we were in, or near, civilisation, not far from Bursa.

We made good time and could say that we would have a good feed that night. Haifa was a town with some good cafés, but a lot of it was out of bounds to troops. We could still find a good feed. I was there many times after this first trip.

We made it to Atlit, to an old transit camp about 16 miles from Haifa. We persuaded Pinkey to ask the 'old man' to let us go for something to eat in Haifa. He refused and said there was a meal laid on for us in the transit camp, but added that we could do what we liked after. I'm glad he didn't let us go, because I remember we had a belting meal.

* I have spent months trying to find out their proper name, but no-one seems to know.

We started with watermelon, fried liver and a salad, which I have never tasted the like of since. Don't forget, we were now in a country of irrigated crops, where the soil will grow anything. We had roasted sweet potato, just like parsnips, plenty of chips and a nice big banana for sweet. It was the best meal I've ever had.

We managed to get the Austin repaired at the Transit R.E. depot. It was going to be better when we did get moving for we had an almost empty trailer again. The run down the coast was terrific after seeing nothing but sand for months on end. The air from the Mediterranean Sea was invigorating and it was nice to get into the water after having not seen any since Cole Island on the Shatal-el-Arab.

We followed the coast down to Tel Aviv onto the Gaza Strip and were in El Arish for our first stop after lunch. The weather was scorching. We drove in our shorts, with no shirt, unless we were on some parade or other. It was out of the wagon straight into the sea, and we could dry off while we are eating an orange or a banana that we'd picked off a tree in passing.

Now, we had another desert to cross, the Sinai. It was a killer. The sandstorms were heavy on that desert. The C.O. asked us to rest and drive mostly overnight. It was very hot, and he said we would appreciate driving in the cool. We did and realised what he told us had been right – we think he had been there before! We passed a few camel trains on the run up to Kilo 196, which is a stop for everything and everyone about half way between Gaza and Ismailiya. There was a good eating place there and you could blow your tyres up or water your camel – please yourself.

Now the run from Kilo 196 to the El Qantara Bridge is creepy. I have done this run several times since and found it very alarming. I was told that this was where Moses received the Ten Commandments and the place of the burning bush. Perhaps as a result of my religious upbringing, I always had a queer sensation when I crossed the Sinai. It is reputed that the road runs quite near the spot of the burning bush. I have stopped there a few times, either on my own or with someone else. I can't make up my mind as to how to read it all. As soon as you pass to get to the bridge at El Qantara and the greenland of the canal bank, you feel relieved.

We stopped at the bridge, gave the weight of our vehicle and then crossed over the Suez Canal. It is green on both sides through to Ismailiya, which is a very nice town. It was well used by our troops, although there were places out of bounds to the Forces. When we entered Ismailiya, we turned right and we thought the C.O. was leading us to the Moasker Garrison, but he went past and took us to a restaurant called 'The Blue Lagoon'. He made two men stay behind to guard the trucks while we ate our hearts out. It was a nice place, one of the best I have been in.

We moved onto No.11 Camp in Quassassin, arrived and were told we could either stay in the lorry or move into a tent as we had done when we arrived at Shaiba. The tents were about 12ft x 12ft square and there were usually six men to a tent. Timmy and I decided to stay put for the time being, in the back of the Matador. It was clean and we had a radio, a Primus stove to make a drink and pictures on the wall. You were not allowed a Primus stove in the tent in case of fire.

It was a luxury to have good ablutions again. The showers were great and it was nice to get changed and go for a pint in a proper N.A.A.F.I. again. The N.A.A.F.I. was a big one, but it was almost full. There must have been a lot of troops in the camp. I met a few of the lads I had seen before – Edmunds, a Scouser, a lad from Rock Ferry, Cyril Merryfield, Paddy McDade and Ginger McQuigan. He was from Motherwell and was singing by the piano the night we arrived. He had a lovely tenor voice.

I was still waiting to join my unit. The Eighth Army was pushed back again in the desert. Monty visited the troops and he did a lot more to upset them, too. He closed the whole of the towns of Port Said, Suez and Ismailiya, making them out of bounds to troops, but allowed them into some parts of Alexandria. It seemed as if he'd shut all the bars throughout the Middle East.

Then I learned that I was to join my unit at last. I had to pick up a new vehicle – a petrol Mac – and travel up to Cairo for the first stop, then onto Alexandria into the transit camp at the docks.

I picked up the Mac from the D.I.D. yard at Tel-el-Kabia, and took it back to Quassassin to the workshop for a check over. It was a great vehicle, so I was looking forward to getting it shipshape and starting out for Alexandria. I had acquired a folding metal bed, the type the A.T.S. used. It had two 'biscuits', one shaped with a pillow. The framework folded up and it was handy when I was on the move and using the wagon to live in. It gave that much extra room in the back. I put everything I could think of into the back, filled up with fuel and was ready to go. I collected my Privileged Movement Order 'green card' from H.Q. together with my documents for the docks and Alex.

I was on my way and said "so long" to the lads, called in to see Sergeant Critchley, who turned out to be a great friend of mine. We both knew what we were about, as we knew our jobs.

I eventually headed for Abassia Barracks in Cairo along the Treaty Road by the side of the Sweet Water Canal. This went almost up to Zagazig, and ended just after the junction where you turned left for Cairo. Because it was irrigated along the canal, it was more interesting to travel on than most of the desert roads.

I made good time into Cairo and pulled into the barrack gates at about eight o'clock. I was told I could still get a meal if I hurried so off I went to the transit mess. There were other people dining there, and one lad who I had seen the day before at 11 Camp. He was 140 Workshop and Park Co., R.E. – Monty Edmonds, a Scouser. He had a wild Egyptian piard dog called Prince, which I was to meet a few times on my travels.

I was asked to accompany Edmonds and his second man, as he was driving a wagon and trailer, and he went out to Cairo for the first, but not the last, time. There were some good eating places in Cairo but, of course, Monty had buggered it all up by shutting most of the Forces' Clubs. We went up by tram and, God, could they move! The drivers didn't give way for anyone. I would have been lost without Edmonds. His mate Jock Campbell was from Scotland and he did work at the Treacle Factory too.

I was away early the next day, followed the tramlines up to Amaria by the Pyramids and turned right for Alex. From there it was about 135 miles to Alex and I was on my own, so I didn't wish to be out in the desert in the dark.

It was a peculiar road to Alex from Mina, long and straight. You thought you were never going to get to the end of it.

I didn't know where I was going, so I belted on a bit to find my way in the light. I made Alex by 3.30pm, pulled into the docks,

had a shower and walked to the canteen to see if I could find anyone I knew. My unit were to meet me there because I had no idea
where they were or how close Jerry was. An offensive had begun
and the Germans were reported to be on the run after El-Alamein.
They were pushed back beyond Hellfire Pass towards Benghazi.
This gave the Allies breathing space to manoeuvre their tanks and
equipment round for a final push. The Spitfires and Hurricanes
were more plentiful, and the boys in blue were more than thank-
ful to have the two planes side by side in combat.

The runways were too short and not sound enough and this is
where our Platoon came in. Our H.Q. was 871 M/E Co, but they
were not with us. The section was run independently by the C.O.,
Captain Fountain, R.E.

I met two men at the docks' operating company, arranged by
the R.T.O. who were to take me to the unit. They were Busty
Gardener from Rock Ferry, Wirral and a long-lost pal, Bert
Garlick, from Chapel-en-le-Frith in Derbyshire. They took me to
my new headquarters at Sidi Barrani. They said they were working on an airfield near Salum. We learned Jerry had been pushed
back beyond the Gulf of Sirte, and the Desert War was coming to
a conclusion. Rommel was on the run. The runway we were
repairing was almost finished. There were no aircraft using it yet,
but there was a mad rush to get it operational in case there was an
offensive by the Germans, so we were working two shifts to get it
completed.

The Germans had occupied this area, and when they left they
mined it, the same as everywhere else. Our lads had cleared the
actual runways that were left, but the outside was still mined until
we had got it airworthy for the planes. There was a code of practice – all clear areas were marked with white tape and there were
'no go' areas which were still mined. If one went off the lot went
off, so it was up to every man to know where they were, although
they were clearly marked and barbed off. It was always too dangerous to defuse them. It had been proved that it was best to wait
until everyone cleared the area before starting to defuse.

To build up a runway in the sand we had to dig deeper than
you might think. We went down about six or even eight feet, if it
was soft, but if the surface was hard, we could start to build on

that. Alongside the runway there was a tar pot every 15 yards or so. Each pot held about a barrel and a half of bitumen which was heated up with an individual Primus so all the pots were going, ready to use the tar as it was needed.

You started off with something of a solid base and got it reasonably level, put on a layer of hessian spread with a layer of hot asphalt, then six inches of sand, a layer of hessian, hot asphalt, six inches of sand, a layer of hessian and asphalt and you built up until you were level with the existing ground. The top layer of sand and asphalt was mixed in a mixer and had to be laid hot. It was tipped, spread out and levelled with an auto patrol grader. This machine could do lots of jobs, work in various blade angles and could work to plus or minus half an inch. It had rubber-tyred wheels, two large rear and two small front. The fronts could angle at whim. The rears were on a solid shaft. This did the final levelling of the top layer, which had to be perfect for the watering sprayer to spray it and the Huber Roller to roll it out flat. Once you started a patch, you had to try and finish it.

It was just going dusk and one of the tar pots kept missing a beat and going up like a blowlamp. This showed right over the airfield. We were still near the front and might be raided by Stukas. I was operating the auto patrol and I called to Dick Elliott to pull No.7 out and switch it off. He was in charge of tar pots and, at the time, was loading one.

"OK, I'll pull it out now."

He had a small Fordson tractor for this, so he went to collect it from the side of the compound. He was returning with it when a Stuka came out from behind me and started to shell the job – and the minefield. The only thing I can remember is being picked up in the early hours of the morning by a field ambulance, or so I thought at the time. I ended up in the field hospital and was transferred to the 29 General Hospital. When I came to a nurse was lifting pieces of shrapnel out of my face, arms and legs. I asked to get up, but was told to stay where I was, as I was not allowed to go anywhere. I stuck it out for a day and then asked why I was not allowed to move. I wanted a wash and shave. I was told I was confined to bed until the doctor said otherwise. I didn't know it, but my hair had gone white and the nurse would not let me have a mirror to either shave or comb my hair. I did not know until the M.O. told me two days later.

I got over it quickly and was glad to get back to my unit to find out about what had happened to the machine I was operating. I shouldn't have been on it by rights, although I was allowed to drive it. Jock the lancejack had gone sick that morning and Sergeant Abercromby had asked me to take over until he came back, but he was kept in for a malaria check.

When I did get to know what had happened it was quite serious. Pinkey was hit hardest. He had been blown away and his hip had gone. Dick, the tar pot man, was almost as bad. It appeared the men working on the top, instead of diving into the cutting and getting under the machine, just scattered into the minefield. The mines were the type that lifted out of the ground then exploded in mid-air, about two feet off the ground. The mine was loaded with shrapnel and could fly anywhere as it went off. It had a terrific explosion.

Dick had been blown in the air not by the Stuka's fire, but by the mines. He was badly shell-shocked and was one of the first to be flown home on compassionate grounds. Pinkey went home almost as soon as he was able to travel.

I had improved enough to get back to normal duty, but I had to attend hospital twice a week. Although we were living in the sun, I was asked to take sunray treatment to see if it would make my hair grow again as, after turning white, it fell out. They showed me how to massage water into my scalp and that worked for a bit, producing a bit of fluff, but I didn't keep it up and went bald again. I suppose I could have claimed some sort of pension for it, but even that wouldn't have made the hair grow back and the Medical Officers seemed to think I would have lost it anyway. Worse things than that have happened to me. I was lucky to be alive. Little Eric, one of the company office boys, caught a direct hit from the Stuka and I never saw him again.

Jerry had been pushed further back into Tunis. We moved to Mersa Matruh, and had the job of collecting the broken-down plant and equipment. Hank Bowen had been driving the Mac until I got fit again. I couldn't go out with it as I was still having treatment. Hank had a Matador A.E.C which had the crane trailer.

My Mac was not to replace it, but to help out with the remainder of the work of plant movement in the desert. We had started to collect from all over the desert. They had to give me a mate for the Mac and I had a new Rogers Trailer. It had a set of eight wheels on the front and two sets of eight on the rear. It was classed as a '32 ton Transporter (tank for the use of)'. The two rear skids for loading were on hinges and all you had to do was to lift them over onto the ground and travel the machines up the skid ramps. If the machine was mobile, you could load in about five minutes or less. We carried everything from a small dumper truck to a 36 R.B. Ruston. not to mention draglines and skimmers, plus a croud shovel, face shovel, back actor, tyne rooter, sheepsfoot, cable dozer, from the smallest D2, to the D8 (which was the biggest in those days). All International B.T.D.6, T.D.9, T.D.14, T.D.18; Allis Chalmers, Cleetrack, Bay City, Osgood – I had to be able to handle all this plant and to be able to load it and transport it. Once loaded, it had to be tied down with cable stretchers. If it was a dozer and scraper, you left the scraper coupled to the tractor and loaded it in the ordinary way. The scraper would have to follow behind. Altogether you would be towing about 55 tons: for instance, a D8 (24 tons), trailer (12 tons), scraper (12 tons) and the Mac (10 tons). Obviously, it could vary.

I was now on full duty and I took the Mac over again, got my old bed back and placed everything the way I wanted it in the back. I managed to get a stove from D.I.D. and paraffin was easy to obtain. My Primus was intact and my entire brew cans and frying pan were as I had left them, thanks to Busty Gardener.

Harry was pleased to come with me to get out of the workshop. He was a sort of garage hand and could drive; he wasn't fussy about that. We got on pretty well together, although he liked a pint and many a time we had to make it to a town to get Harry a drink. He was often three sheets to the wind.

Anyway, we had to go into the danger zone to collect a Huber Roller. It had been working on a runway at Mizda, south of Tripoli. I had no idea where we were going, and at that time I hadn't really known how to find out. I was scorching along at about 45 mph and a despatch rider on a motor cycle stopped me, saying:

"Where the hell are you going? Jerry is only a few miles ahead, turn round and follow me."

I followed him and after half a mile I had an idea I was going the wrong way. A Morris Commercial caught up with me and turned me round again.

The driver said: "You're heading into enemy territory."

I spoke to the Captain (Red Caps) in the vehicle and he said they had been trying to find that damned despatch rider. He was luring transport drivers into his line, as Jerry had no transport to retreat with. Now the rider who spoke to me was as British as I was, or so it seemed!

I bought a bloody compass as soon as I could. The only chance of navigation you had in the desert was the sun, and then it was luck that brought you home safely. I have travelled a long distance in the desert and you do get used to it eventually.

The Captain allowed us to follow him and he directed us to Mizda. We arrived just before dusk, managed to load up with the winch and get on our way as I did not want to stop in that area. Jerry might do a U-turn again. I scarpered as soon as I could. Harry and I agreed to drive as far as was sensible. We reached Misurata on the coast. It was more comfortable driving on the coast at night. We found a C.R.E. depot and pulled in there for the night. If you found a C.R.E. place you could rest assured you had good food and rations to go away with. There were very few heavy vehicles about, and you were too busy to mess about, it was all go. You carried a certificate in a wallet and all you had to do was show that and you got help wherever you were.

We made it back to the depot the next afternoon and I had to go in to see Captain Fountain to try and explain to the men about being lured into enemy lines by the despatch riders. I unloaded that afternoon and we were to go to Alex to pick up a D8 for Quassassin 140 W/S and Park Co.R.E. Attached to them was No.1 P.E.D (Plant Erection Depot R.E.). All plant entering the area from the docks had to go to No. 1 P.E.D.. It had to be reported and it had to have the blade altered. Without going into technicalities, it had a strip put down the sides of the blade to collect more sand when bulldozing. The alteration was done by a team of men at No. 1 P.E.D. at Quassassin in Egypt. All bulldozers had to go for alteration before entering a company's plant park.

After loading we stayed the night at the transit camp at Alex. This suited Harry as he could have another beano. I wasn't bothered; although we worked well together, we had nothing in common, so I just had the odd pint when I was thirsty, unless I was going for a night out. Alex was a place to have a night out, although Monty had closed some of the houses of ill repute. Alex was a good eating-place. Whenever I had to travel long distance I always worked out the times we would reach towns such as Suez, Port Said, Ismailiya, Cairo, Heliopolis, Tel Aviv, Haifa, Jaffa, Beirut, Tripoli, Lebanon, Homs, Damascus, Amman, Baghdad and Tehran in North Persia. All these places have been on my map and I have visited them several times.

We were away early next day, which meant there was no rush as we could hit Cairo comfortably. We always went to Abassia Barracks, where the food was good and plentiful and it was handy for the tram to go into Cairo.

We were doing about 35 mph along the Treaty Road to Cairo, approximately 40 miles out of Alex, when we saw a distinct line in the road about a foot wide. It also stretched into the desert on the left, and also on the right. There were a few vehicles on the road and I noticed they had gone over the distinct black line. As I got closer to it, I noticed the wheel marks of the previous vehicle and the line was moving like a column of soldiers. It was ants. They were whoppers. No thought for the ones run over by the previous vehicles. Remember, I had 34 wheels altogether, so if I continued, I was going to kill a lot of ants.

I sat in the cab scratching my head wondering what do. A one pipper came up behind and asked if I was all right. He spotted the ants and said you could wait for ages for them all to cross. Harry woke up from his long sleep as I got in the back to make a brew. I asked the officer if he had time for a cuppa and he agreed to stop for one. He was driving a Standard Eight van W.D. type, off to Amaria, to the newly formed R.E.M.E. by the pyramids.

The ants were still coming, then we saw what was like a break in the line. Our response was: "Sod the tea, sod the brew, let's get across before it all starts again." We did get across, waited to fin- ish our tea and be damned they came from nowhere again. I would have loved to have had a camera. The line eventually thinned out and ended, but what I couldn't get over was that the ants never gave way for any of the ones squashed by the previous cars. You would have thought they would go round them, but they didn't.

We got on our way to Cairo and made Abassia Barracks well before teatime. This gave us time to shower before our meal. Well, I did, but Harry was a smelly old thing and never bothered about good hygiene! There were quite a few cinemas, both in Cairo and Heliopolis where there was a large Yankee camp and you could get almost anything. The tram took you straight to it.

I couldn't see the low loader from P.E.D. on the park. It was an A.E.C. Matador and a Janns trailer. I knew them all and what depots they were from. We saw Monty Edmonds' dog Prince in the transit camp and thought it funny. No A.E.C. from Quassassin and the dog running round the transit camp in Cairo. I called the dog and although he was wild he came to me and made a fuss. I didn't know what to do, so I decided to take him with us back to No.1 P.E.D. He always slept on the spare wheel rack and I had my spare wheel at the back of my Mac. Monty's spare was on the side so the dog took a while before he got down at the rear. I managed to get some hessian for him and he settled. Anyway, we went to move off the following morning and he was there again and came in the back for his eats. But as we moved off, he went off too, and we never saw him go.

The run down to Quassassin was always easy, if I remember rightly. It was about 80 miles and we did it in about four hours without stops. However, there was always time for a brew and there were some handy pull-ins on this road. There were two checkpoints, and we usually stopped by the first one out of Cairo, which was near Zagazig. We hadn't been on the side road very long when Edmonds turned up, going through to Cairo. I spoke to him about Prince and he said he often ran off. He had a lady friend and when she was about you never saw Prince, but he always came back. He would even call to see us in the Barracks, but would be gone when it was time to leave. He knew that wagon and the rest of us.

We went to Quassassin to unload our machine and find out where we were going from there. The first thing we had to do was to get the workshop fitters to measure the machine for the conversion of the blade, then report to the company office for instruction. A lad came out of the workshop to do the measurements and I had no idea who he was. We got talking about mail.

"Where are you from?" I asked him.

"Just outside Wrexham, Rhosamedre in fact."

We shook hands and I told him I was from Hope. His name was Ron Thomas. I saw him at various intervals during my trips in and out of the camp. If I stayed over we got together a few times because we dined at their mess and drank in their canteen. After the war I went caravanning with Ron for 17 years.

I reported to the office and was told: "You'll have to stay over as you're going to take the D8 back with you to your unit. We don't know where they are as there has been an advance since you left, so you will proceed to Misurata C.R.E.. They will get in touch with R.T.O. and you'll get your instructions from there, but we want you to go through if you can. If you leave your trailer at the workshop it will be loaded ready for you to get an early start. Go through if you can, it's important."

It suited Harry to have a night on the pop at Camp 11. I went to Shafto's Cinema to see 'Mrs Miniver.' I came out covered in bugs, but I had a shower before going to bed, a couple of pints in the N.A.A.F.I. and slept as soundly as a log.

We were on the road early. All we had to do was to put the stretchers on the D8 and go back up to 11 Camp for breakfast. Harry didn't usually do much driving, so I asked him to take the first stint up beyond Cairo towards Amaria. I took over after our stop at the R.E.M.E. depot at Amaria. We needed air in two of the tyres and they did them all while we were having our break. This saved time, which was precious on this trip. We made Alex for five o'clock.

We had a good three hours' drive to get to the C.R.E, arriving at 9.15 pm.We pulled into the compound and had something to eat, from the guard's ration, a cup of cocoa, and retired to bed.

C.R.E. gave us the good news that Rommel had been pushed back and we were now in Tripoli. With the airfield complete, we had moved to the 9th Italian Division H.Q. at Tripoli – so I did end up on the shores of Tripoli after all!

Chapter 11

THE SHORES OF TRIPOLI

Everywhere you went it was sand, even in the mess there was sand. Whenever I had been out on a trip, I used to walk into Captain Fountain's office to see what the next mission was. He asked me to go with Hank, the Matador driver, and help him to get the fuel from a new D.I.D. There was a lot to get so we used the two vehicles to pick everything up. That consisted of diesel, petrol, all the different lubricants for the machinery; it all had to be put in the back of the wagon, and if it spilt, it smelled for days. I got all the grease and vitafilm, 600 H.D. oil for the tractors, as much oil and fuel filters as we could possibly get. Hank got the diesel and the petrol, which was used for the donkey engines on the Cats, or the Internationals. They both started up on petrol. Petrol was not very expensive and we got a lot of it in 4 gallon square tins. The spare tins were used in the workshops and you could find one almost anywhere.

When we got back to the camp, Captain Fountain told me to unload as soon as possible and get off to El Awel to pick up a D4 Cat and bring it back to the yard. I hoped I could do it and get back for dinner, so I went to the cookhouse and ordered a late dinner for Harry and myself. Hank was busy unloading the fuel and one of the first jobs afterwards was to wash your overalls in petrol. You had a 4 gallon tin and put some petrol in it, dumped your overalls in, washed them and put them to dry on the coiled wire. This was normal practice and off I went. When I returned there was no Hank. He was dead. His Matador, with Hank, had gone up. Everyone saw what had happened. He had washed his overalls, thought they were dry and put them on inside his wagon as he lived in the back. With the fumes in the back after carrying the fuel, he must have lit a cigarette, and Oomph, the lot went up. Everyone, apparently, got extinguishers from the workshop, but they couldn't get his overalls off him in time, and he must have died of shock. He was a very smart young fellow from Ipswich.

Everyone was very upset. There was an inquest from C.R.E. What there was of his vehicle was impounded – only a chassis. I couldn't even attend his funeral because it was too far away. He was buried with the rest of the Desert Force in the British War graves in Tripoli. I still have some photographs of him.

I was away the next day to Quassassin to take the D4, meet the operator at 1 P.E.D. and travel with a 3 ton Bedford towing a caravan to go onto the Sinai Desert and work there pushing the sand off the road. So it was down to Cairo and to Quassassin again. I laughed when I saw the caravan as it was like a Council one that the roller drivers used to use. Anyway, we sorted ourselves out and left first thing in the morning for the road towards Gaza.

The job was to work on the stretch from Kilo 196 towards Gaza. Ismailiya, El Qantara Bridge and across the Sinai again (I must have done that run at least once a month for about twelve months). It was a horrible run because you were in Bedouin country all the time. We got to a sensible parking area to make some kind of a headquarters for the operator, as he had to stay there.

The Bedford unhitched the caravan while I unloaded the D4, dropped two barrels of fuel off, his oil, a battery for his radio and the rations from the D.I.D.. The other driver and I stopped as long as we could to make him feel comfortable – to start him off as you might say.

You couldn't see the road in places, so all the sand had to be pushed off the road, at the same time making sure you didn't dig the tarmac up with the tracks. I watched him for a while for we had been told to stop with him until we were satisfied he was all right and doing the job. I noticed how much more sand you could move with the side guards on the side of the blade. This one had been converted and pushed a good bladeful at the end of the run, leaving a good Windrow to take on the next cut. It did work better.

We stayed overnight, mostly for company for the operator. We went back to Kilo 196 for something to eat, because he had no transport after we left. His only protection was his Tommy gun in his caravan – no telephone, nothing for miles. The Bedford driver was leaving me to go to Bate Naballa just outside Tel Aviv. I was to go back over the Sinai again to El Qantara Bridge and off to Suez. Picking up a new D6 for 1 P.E.D, to be converted, and God knows where from there. If I shaped I could make Suez by night time. Although the camp was decrepit, it had a good set of lads who looked after us and we always had good food. We went out to Suez that night and what a dead place it was after Monty had closed the cafés. It wasn't worth going down all that way, other than for a pint for Harry and, as always, we uncoupled the trailer and used the Mac for a taxi.

I picked up the D6 next day and went off to Quassassin back to No. 11 Camp again. We saw Edmonds' wagon and Prince. He must have had enough of Cairo and was going back to Tripoli the next day taking a new D7 which had been converted. There was a lot of transport at the yard the next morning and I pulled onto the fuel pumps and got talking to all the drivers.

"We're all going to Alex to pick up plant to bring it here for alteration. We haven't been before."

They were white. I know I shouldn't laugh, but they were straight out from Blighty and looked like whitewashed walls. Ginger McGuigan, Paddy McFean, Jock, Mo, Campbell, Big Eddie, Kelly from D-pool. He was a born comedian, and could make a grain of sand laugh. I can't remember all their names, but we all went back to Alex together. None of them had been before. I felt like a mother showing them around. I pulled up at the stop near Zagazig.

There was plenty of ground, hard, for us to get on, because you usually carried heavy weights. We all got our brew cans out and made tea. We had the Arabs round us wanting to buy blankets, bully, boots, rope, tyres, batteries, a wagon, petrol, tea and anything going. They wouldn't eat pig and I don't think anyone sold anything. If you did you kept it to yourself and your mate of course. Kelly couldn't light his Primus stove. We all had a go. He got hold of it and flung it into the air.

"Leave the bloody thing there," he said. It had never gone since he had it. Anyway, I picked it up and kept it for him. I did nothing to it, just left it under the bed. We carried onto the Barracks in Cairo, stopped the night and took the lads into Cairo. They were chuffed to death over being able to see a cinema.

'Night Must Fall' was being shown in one of them. God knows how many times I had seen 'Mrs Miniver' and how many different places I had seen it in.

We set off for Alex at about nine o'clock. We got to the dock area about 2.30pm, after stopping for a break in the desert about half way up the ant path, and I told the lads about it. The marks were still on the road.

Alex was two or three hours away and they had that to see yet. It had a beautiful beach. We all went for a dip and I have the photographs to prove it. After a meal in the Morocco Club I headed the transport to the docks, where they were going to load for 1 P.E.D.. I was going onto Tripoli to my unit with the D7. I said "So long", to them and to Prince the dog. He used to come to Harry and me because he knew us from meeting in Cairo.

I got back to Tripoli two days after leaving the docks. I got myself into a load of trouble – tyre trouble. If you got a flat tyre on the trailer, especially on the inside wheels, you had a job to detect it. Then one flat would lead to another, so you got a few instead of one.

We stopped for break at the halfway N.A.A.F.I.. You could get haddock and egg there, just like a transport café in England! We always had it if it was on the menu. We had a good meal, washed and freshened up and went to carry on a bit further. There was nothing to stop us now the war was almost over in the Desert, so we intended to go on until we were tired. This didn't happen. I kicked the wheels on the back row of the trailer and I found five flats. I had an idea there was a hold-up. The wagon got sluggish on the pull. I then got the bar and tried the wheels inside the well and there were five there, so I was in the mire. I pulled onto a R.E. camp and settled for the night. I was up like a lark, as I needed to get in touch with the R.E.M.E.. Harry was still sleeping after his ale, both at the halfway and in the R.E. canteen. I undid the air-lines from the wagon, which puts on all the brakes, uncoupled the Mac, then unloaded the D7 off the trailer, coupled the winch rope of the D7 to the side of the trailer and turned it upside down.

Harry had woken up by this time and said: "I've never seen that before. What have you done that for?"

"To get the wheels off!" was my reply to him.

I was annoyed at not getting any help from him now and then, although he didn't want to drive much, he could have shown an interest and helped when it was needed. I would be glad when he'd had enough. I started to undo the nuts holding the securing bars to the rim of the wheels and I got two banks off two pretty easily. I had another bank to undo for one wheel and I got them out on top. I started on the back row when Harry came back from 'phoning the R.E.M.E. to tell them we needed 10 wheels repairing. By then I had sawn the retaining bolts off one of them.

A captain came out first with a batman driver and I had the other wheel off by this time ready for repair. He was in a small Standard 10 brake with spotless seating in the back.

I saluted and said: "Sir, you can't use that, it will ruin it to start with, but the wheels won't all go in."

"I had no idea, driver, so bear with me," he replied. "I'll be as soon as I can. Have you got your Movement Order with you?"

"No, sir, I don't have to carry one. All I have is this green card," which I showed to him.

He changed his attitude when he saw that. He was off like a shot and returned with a breakdown truck fitted out to cope with any crisis. It had a compressor, all the side lifting tackle, and four men who, I must say, knew how to handle themselves. I was there three and a half hours altogether. They put tubes in most of them as these were the latest tyres to come from the U.S.A.. At the time they must have been the first tubeless tyres on anything we had. Anyway, they blew the rest up and I asked for a lift to turn the trailer over again. If you get two pieces of timber weak enough to break when the weight gets on them it will come to the floor easily without a bump. This we did, and the men were flabbergasted to see it fall to the deck.

The captain said it was the first one he had seen turned over for getting to the tyres.

I had the Cat D7 to load, stretch down, and get on my way. The officer came to me and asked for my unit reference and Captain Fountain's address. He intended to see him, I don't know what for, but that's what he asked. He had never seen a dozer on a tank transporter before, and he was very impressed with it being so simple, yet dangerous. I got hold of the skids and folded them over and was ready for off. I must have had flats for some time, because when I got going the wagon worked better.

We stopped at Heal-a-Shaiba for breakfast – although we were in Arab country, you could get a nice brecky if you knew where to go.

We were running low on fuel. There was no way we could reach the D.I.D, so I took the coast road to Benghazi and headed for Bizerte to catch the D.I.D. there before he closed down at the fall of light. He would serve you, but only if he wanted to, he had the right to make you wait till morning. I was on petrol and could do about 7.5 miles to the gallon on a flat run. If it was climbing it could come down to less than 4 mpg. It was an excellent vehicle to handle after some of ours.

The Scammel was the best British tractor. I had the long box Albion, although the Matador took some beating if you had a booster box on it. It doubled the gear selection of high and low ratio. The only trouble with the Scammel was you had to go through every gear, you could not go from second to fifth. You had to go through the box. Diamond T was a good motor. I've had them all – Federal, Diamond T petrol, Diamond T diesel, Hug. Albion Tank Transporter, White special diesel with the then new Cummings engine and centrifugal pump, International 12 speed box. They lent me one of these when mine went in for replacement oil seals. It wasn't in the same street as the Matador, which was ideal for hot climates. It had a canvas hood, metal doors and was cool, except when you were on the pull.

I arrived at H.Q. to find they were packing up everything and going to Palestine to a place called Bate Naballa.

"Where the hell is Bate Naballa?"

"About 10 miles from Tel Aviv."

That was another four days to get there.

"Hughes, load the Muirhill dumper and D4 Cat, whatever you can out of the workshop on the turntable with safety and fall in with the convoy to Palestine."

871 M.E. Coy had already moved there and had started work on a landslide at Chekka, Lebanon. We were actually building a tunnel, because the land had slid into the sea. The whole of the main road had gone and it was our job to do the excavation for the

131

tunnel. I thought I was going to Bate Naballa and stop there, but we were going to Beirut, to set up our H.Q. in a Gendarme Barracks on the West Bank. That would take maybe five days and not four. Once I got my head down I was away. Fountain knew I had difficulty driving in convoy, so he asked me to stay with the convoy till Cairo, then I could scarper.

We had difficulty going through Cairo. It was a stupid place to traverse if you took the wrong fork as you left Amaria. Everyone was gawping at the Sphinx and looking for the Pyramids. They took the wrong fork and ended up passing King Farouk's Palace. It was hell trying to get out from there and we were pestered with Arabs pinching off the back of our wagon. I led the convoy until we came to the spare ground at Zagazig, where we all stopped and had a brew of tea. We had about four hours to go to Quassassin where we would stop the night, get a shower and some good food.

"We'll follow you, Hughes, you know where everything is, so go ahead."

I pulled in to 1 P.E.D. and everyone followed me onto the fuel pumps. We all filled up and it saved time in the morning. I pulled up in my usual place in 11 Camp.

"Where do I park?" "Where can I park?" they asked.

Talk about being a mother. It's a good job some of them didn't have nappies on, I would never have finished! One of the lads with a 3 ton Dodge parked outside a tent. I was waiting for it. I told him not to park there, as it was the Sergeant Major's tent.

"Get that bloody thing to hell out of here."

It was a lad named Happy and they called him "Happy" because his surname was Gladman. He was a bloody comedian.

"Roll on death."

"Let's have a night with Jean Harlow."

We often heard that from him.

The shower, food and sleep were good. Everyone was tired and the 'old man' was chuffed next morning. We pulled out at 7am prompt down through Abusweire, and onto Ismailiya, up to the bridge at El Qantara and past the burning bush. Think about the Ten Commandments and onto Kilo 196 for a good break. We stayed about an hour and a half and I went to the counter to get something to eat for the operator on the D4, Taffy Tucker from Swansea. He was a big thickset man, like a brick toilet.

I told Fountain what I was doing and he said he wanted to stop to see what Taffy was doing. I knew where to pull up, so I asked the rest not to stop there as it could cause congestion. They all went on and Fountain and his driver stayed behind me. We frightened Taffy to death. I got on the back of the machine and touched him and he threw the clutch out and very nearly jumped off the dozer before it stopped. With the noise of the engine you have no idea when anyone is about unless you can see them. I stopped him working and told him to have a break. I gave him four bottles of beer and some sandwiches, and I got on the machine leaving him to talk to Fountain.

The poor chap was flogging a dead horse. He was pushing the sand uphill and over the brow. I sized up the job. On the opposite side of the road was a big ravine, and there he was pushing half a bladeful up an incline. This could be made easier, I was sure. I turned the machine round, spread about 6 inches on the road and started to push it into the ravine. Taffy saw what I was doing and wondered why he had been struggling all day trying to shift it. Now, it's all right if you leave enough on the road to save the tracks marking the road. Taffy was delighted with his drink and Fountain was delighted with the half-hour I had put in on the dozer.

"A great idea, but you must remember to clean up the road at night."

It made a hell of a difference to the job. It was more or less permanent, while the wind was blowing. It was like a sandstorm at times and traffic could not get through. I think an operator was expected to do about three months there, then someone else took over. It was a terribly lonely job.

I asked if we were ready to go and we got off or we would have been in the dark before we made El Arish for the night stop. Good camp there with a swimming pool, excellent food because it was C.R.E.. There were even tablecloths on the tables. Fountain passed me and had gone. He might catch the others up before they got to the beach camp at El Arish. It was about 65 miles to the H.Q. at Bate Naballa the next day. I had never stayed at that camp nor in the area. The climate was different – it had a cool air. The sea was near and one could smell the Mediterranean. It had a distinct tang about it. The men were under canvas but this was only temporary. It was an old Palestinian Police camp, dilapidated, but under reconstruction by the Engineers. They had already completed the cookhouse and the ablutions and they were putting the finishing touches to the billets. It was a nice camp.

Fountain came and told me not to unload as I was going to Beirut the next day and to stay there and move anything Abercromby wanted. I asked if it was 'Sergeant Abercromby' and it was. I knew him from Balham and was looking forward to meeting him again. I refuelled and was ready for the off, when Corporal Erskine called to me. I hadn't seen him since Balham either. He shook hands and made a fuss.

"Nice to see you, Diesel." I could not get rid of that nickname.

He told me I had lost Harry, not before time either. I was pleased that they put another lad with me. His name was Bob Townsend and I was instructed to look after him. He had had a bad time in the desert and Fountain put him with me to give him some kind of pride back. He asked me not to let him drive in town areas because he was suffering from a form of sleeping sickness and was liable to drop off to sleep at the wheel. This medical problem meant that I had to keep an eye on him all the time.

"Encourage him all you can – he may get A1 fit again."

I had to wait for Bob to get his wares into his 'home' for the next few years, and as soon as he was ready, we were away to Beirut. We went through Tel Aviv, Nathania, Hadera across the Lebanon border, and up the coast into the West Bank area. It was about 96 miles bypassing Jaffa and Haifa. This was lovely country. You were along the sea front so you could stop, clear a fence, go for a walk into the orchards, pick a nice banana, orange, watermelon, mango, anything you wanted. Have a dip in the warm sea, make a Sgt Major's brew, eat what fruit you wished. Now and again you might see a Palestinian and he would ask for buckshees, and maybe you gave him a small tin of bully. You could take the orchard for that!

Bob lit a cigarette and gave it to me. That was something Harry never did the whole time he was with me. It was nice to have a clean and tidy lad and I noticed the difference when we finished our tea break. He swilled the teapot out and put things away. We had to live in the Mac, so we needed to keep it tidy.

We had not been to Beirut and I wondered what it was like. We found the entrance to the Gendarme Barracks. It looked OK and there were palm trees around the cookhouse and the billets. There were whitewashed stones around the ablutions. I noticed this because I wanted to go and as I came out I tripped over them. I think everybody came out as we pulled into the yard. They all wanted to see the Mac and the Rogers trailer. Abercromby came out and shook hands.

"How the hell are you, Diesel?"

A few more came out. Bert Garlick, Happy, Erskine, Busty Gardener and Jock McFarlane were there. I hadn't seen him since the *Athlone Castle*. It was great to see everyone again.

"Leave that bloody thing and come and have a drop of the hard stuff with me in the mess."

"Lt. Martin! Hell, I haven't seen you, sir, since bomb disposal. How are you, sir?"

We shook hands.

"Fine."

"Captain Fountain's at Bate Naballa, sir, and is following on in the morning. I believe he's going to see the Tunnel."

"Yes, I believe he is, and that's where you're going. Take the D4 and the Muirhill; off-load it by the 19 R.B. Dragline. Someone will tell you how to get through as the road has gone and you have to do a bit of dodging to get round – and watch the landslip too."

I got as far as the entrance to the Tunnel and asked Bob to go and find how we could get through. We had to reverse and take a steep climb up the bank. We knew we wouldn't make it, so we off-loaded where we were and let the gang come and get the machines from there.

"Go and tell them, Bob."

I turned the trailer round ready for Beirut, as we could be back before tea if we shaped, and then we could go and have a look at the town. It is on an incline, has straight streets and a small promenade. It is on the sea front and the town stretches around the coast. Paths go near the sea and there are many mosques and a nice C of E church. There were a lot of streets that were strictly out-of-bounds to troops, and if you were caught you were on a 252 straight away, no messing either. It was also fatal to go to an out-of-bounds area. You could get a knife in your back and your body would never be seen again.

Nevertheless, the town was a pleasant one in which to be stationed. It sort of never went dark. It had some wonderful restaurants – Syrian, French, Christian Arab, and Greek – it was really cosmopolitan. There were plenty of licensed bars and not a big lot of trouble in them. Stella beer, Lazizar, and some kind of Arab beers were on sale. Then of course there was 'hubbly bubbly'. You could try this if you were daft enough. It was a form of *hashish*, a drug smoked out of a piped bottle. I never even thought of trying it. I had heard all about it from Happy Gladman when we were in Tobruk. You may think I am a 'goody, goody', but I was never once in trouble in the Middle East and never arrested for anything – don't forget we didn't just go into one town, we went into many of them.

The food in the barracks was good and the billets were nice, but we were on the move so much it wasn't worth taking our bedding out of the Mac to sleep in the billets because we were off again in the morning. Therefore we made our 'house' in the Mac. The weather was always nice, except for the Winter, and we managed to keep it warm.

I had some leave due to me and wanted to visit Jerusalem. I had kept in touch with the Rev Saunders Davies, Curate of Hope. As I have already mentioned, I was to visit his brother in Jerusalem. The services had a system where you booked into a hostel and if you were going to be absent you had to tell someone. I started my journey alone, but met quite a few people whom I knew on the train going from Haifa onwards. Tiny Roberts from Summerhill, Wrexham was going to Nathania Leave Camp and we got on the train together. Little did we know we were going from the same unit! The Arab train stopped at the station and everybody got out to either water their horse or find eggs and bread. Tiny and I were watering the horse when I spotted a lad in R.A.F. uniform. I knew I had seen him before, but couldn't put a name to him. He came over to me and said, "Abermorddu,

Abermorddu School, Austin ******* Hughes. The last time I saw you we were in the Choir together at Hope Church."

It was Bert Davies from Kerrie by the Co-op in Abermorddu. He was returning to Cairo where he was stationed with the 30 M.U. R.A.F., living in a hotel in the centre of Cairo. The three of us had a photograph taken (which I still have) which was sent to the Wrexham Leader.

We were not on the train long, and as I was going to Jerusalem and Glyn to Nathania, we said goodbye, swapped addresses and arranged if we could to have leave in Cairo together. I got off the train at Tel Aviv and the R.T.O. told me there was a service to the leave camp in Jerusalem.

"Is that the hostel one? I'm booked in there."

"Yes. You'll be OK on the bus, anyway."

I picked up my kit and followed someone else going there. I went to the hostel on the first night and it was beautiful. The food was good and there was no fuss – I could just relax for a whole week.

I set out the next morning to find the Rectory. I climbed 12 steps to the front entrance and a man in a black suit answered when I knocked. I told him of my mission and he was a bit dubious at first when I said: "I have called to see the Rev. Davies. I am the person who knows his brother and I was invited."

He took me in to what I thought was his study and a clergyman appeared in a cassock. I could tell who he was as soon as I saw him. Almost a twin I would think. He took me through to meet his wife and family, and took me onto his roof to see Jerusalem.

He said: "I suppose you have come to stay for a few days and you are most welcome. We will feed you and bed you and I will give you as much time as I can to take you around The Holy City. You know there is an old Jerusalem and a new one. Other than for shopping, you won't be interested in the new part."

There were beds on the roof and he advised me to sleep with a mosquito net to cover the bed. He said that with me coming from England it would be much cooler. I explained I had been out for some time – a couple of years or thereabouts – and he was very interested in where I had been.

We set off early – 8 o'clock – to go to see the interesting places. We started off at the Wailing Wall. It was weird, yet comfortable. Then we went to St Peter's Square and we passed the golden gates towards the Garden of Gethsemene. We saw the start of the steps to the Hill of Calvary and the street called Strate, which was still unsafe to walk by oneself. He showed me the tombs and the stones which were reputed to have been moved after the Resurrection of Christ. This was most moving and I can never relate to you what it felt like. As we left the old city we went out towards the Hill of Calvary and the places where the crosses were embedded for the crucifixion of the three men. I will always remember going round with him.

I stayed for four nights altogether and returned to the hostel for my last two days. I did a bit of shopping; bought some trinkets and some photographs of Jerusalem. I enjoyed the two days, but I soon had to get transport to return to the station for the run to Beirut. I met Tiny at Nathania. We settled for our trip up to Haifa and transferred to bus transport from there.

I returned to duty on the Sunday and my Mac and Bob were waiting, loaded for a trip to Quassassin to pick up a Tyne Rooter for the landslide at Chekka. There was a 19 R.B. to go to Suez Twefek, which is actually across the Suez Canal. From Suez to get over the canal you crossed a pontoon bridge and what a job we had with that lot. It was our fault of course. We had to act on our own initiative and make our own decisions.

We collected the 19 R.B. from Bate Naballa. It was a dragline weighing about 23 tons. The jib is split for transit and the bucket is pulled in behind the skid section. We loaded the next afternoon at Bate Naballa and ready to set off across the Sinai Desert again.

"Anything for the Tucker on the D4, sir, before we leave?" I asked Captain Fountain.

"Yes, fuel, grease, a battery, hydraulic oil, a track adjusting spanner and get two crates of beer from the canteen and anything he may need. He has only got a week to do, tell him, and he will be relieved, then someone else has to go there."

We didn't move off till morning and had a night in Tel Aviv. We left at first light as we had a long trip to Suez. We stopped for half an hour at Taffy Tucker's D4. He shut it down when we got

there and travelled with us to Kilo 196 for something to eat. He
had no rations and was waiting for them to be delivered from the
D.I.D.. The bloke arrived just as we were pulling away, and we
asked him if he would stop there until Taffy had had a chance to
get a meal, as the machine should not be left. He agreed, and off
we went. Afterwards we dropped Taffy off, as he would soon get
a lift back to his machine. We told him we would see him on the
way back.

"Anything you want, besides a blonde?"

"Yes", he said, "it's my wife's birthday – try to get me something in the way of a card from a town or the Lido N.A.A.F.I.
Gineifa."

We were trying to make Gineifa, as sometimes there was a
good night out there. There was always someone on the piano in
the Lido Club. We had a shower in the transit camp, got three
days' rations out of them, went for our dinner – second to none –
then got changed and went to the Lido Club. The Three K's were
on (they finished up on the B.B.C.) and they were great.

On our way down to Port Taufiq, Bob was soon to tell me that
a wheel had just gone past on my side and that if we could pick it
up we would be in for a few bob. I said it was more than possible
that it was ours.

I pulled up on the hard shoulder as soon as I could and we
were just past the place where the wheel had rested. They roll on
for ages sometimes when they come off. I had a look at the trailer
and it was from our second row or rear row. Thank goodness it
wasn't off the inside row.

We had lost three studs, but I always carried a few spares. I had
made them out of bulldog clips when I was in the workshop in
Quassassin, by cutting the 'U' bolt in half, then putting a tight-
ened nut on it. It makes a good spare, although it is mild steel and
they should be H.T. I got the rest of the studs out and had to
straighten the wheel spacers that held on the wheel. I had a vice
on the trailer, so we were OK there. We were not long and were on
our way again.

This was one of those days. I had forgotten to fill up at Gineifa
D.I.D, so after we got on the road again I had to turn back.
Although it was only 25 miles, we wouldn't make Suez that day.

I filled up 45 gallons each side – 90 gallons altogether, topped the water up in everything, and put air in three tyres which had gone down. What a good start to the day!

We stopped at El Kabrit for a tea break because there was nothing in Port Taufiq, and we might have to unload to get over the pontoon bridge. The man on bridge duty asked our weight and I said 30 tons. The bridge was classification 30 and there was a safety margin. I suspected I was 7 tons in excess of this but thought I would chance it – the biggest mistake I have ever made.

After the abutment onto the first barge, I knew we were wrong to go, but we couldn't turn back.

"Can you swim Bob? If not, now is your chance to learn," I said.

We got in a right flap and as I crawled over the first barge it dipped to meet the second one. When I went forward to the second one, the split joint between the two pontoons was like a 'V' and then the weight of the machine was on the rear of the previous pontoon. We had another seven to go.

Bob turned white, as I had to keep going very slowly. I was pleased I was in a very low crawler six wheel drive and that got me out of trouble. Talk about a snake's back! The front tyres tipped into the surface and would not give in. I kept it going until I came to the abutment on the other side. By this time the bridge guard was out. I told him to stop flapping and calm down and he went across in his boat to have words with me on the other side. The fool tried to stop me half way up the abutment. I almost ran over him, he was so stupid. I got over, but only just, and fair play, the guard could have made a fuss about it, but I shut him up with a quarter pound of Brooke Bond tea. That did the trick. I could have gone back with it for that!

I pulled into Shell Mex and B.P., unloaded and was ready for off. Bob wanted the toilet, so I waited and an officer came and tried to give me the bull – that I should report to the office etc.

"You are going back to 1 P.E.D, so you can take a dragline bucket with you."

"I am not allowed to do that, sir."

"And why not?"

"Because if I do, sir, when this machine leaves here it will have no equipment with it, and will be no use to anyone without its bucket – and who is going to go to Quassassin for it if and when it is needed?"

"Oh, maybe you're right."

I told him I knew the machine was being used as a crane and only needed the block and tackle, but the bucket must stop with it.

"So you are going back empty?"

"Yes, sir."

"I will get a load from Suez tomorrow."

"That's no good, sir, I have to be in Tobruk in three days as my officer is meeting us there to direct us to Bizerte to pick up a German digger. They abandoned it after the push and it is to go back to 1 P.E.D. I must not be held up, sir, and I have a chit to show anyone who tries to alter my schedule."

I showed him this and he said no more.

Bob put the skids up. We checked everything and were off to try and make 11 Camp for the night. We made it OK and went to the Bug House 'Shafto's Cinema' to see 'Mrs Miniver.' I came out bitten to death. I don't know why we went there, because we were in a position to go to better places than Shafto's.

We ordered breakfast for 6 o'clock the next morning and then left early, going through Cairo at 9.30am. We were outside Alex after dinner heading for Tobruk. We made the halfway by nightfall and stayed the night there. The food was good and a good canteen with some sort of entertainment. We pulled into Tobruk at 9pm the following day, but there was no sign of Captain Fountain.

Next morning we had another breakfast with C.R.E. – there was always a tablecloth on the table. I filled up with another 90 gallons of petrol, sent Bob with our mission order for a few days' rations from D.I.D and he got five days' worth. We were never short of food. I would have loved to have sent some home for our people.

I got down in the Mac, turned the radio on and had a siesta, and woke up at 3.30pm when Captain Fountain came.

"Will you try and make Tripoli tonight or early morning? How far do you think you'll get?"

"I'll make Tripoli and be ready for the last leg tomorrow, sir. We will try to load if we can that night for an early start," I replied.

Now the hostilities had ceased it was a nice run along the coast to Alexandria from Tunis.

Instead of Bob and me saying: "It's one of those days", we now said "It's Pontoon Day" and we kept this joke up the whole time we were together. Bob was a great mate and we got on so well together. Don't forget, you know more about an Army mate than his wife will ever know, because you are with him 24 hours a day – his wife or mother only ever see him at home.

Captain Fountain met us outside Bizerte. It was late afternoon so we had a chance of loading the German digger before nightfall – if we could find the darn thing. I was following Fountain and we hadn't seen it so we pulled into the ex-Italian Armoured Division H.Q.. A detachment of our unit was still there and should know where it was. We were going round in circles and it was staring us in the face.

Bob and I dropped the skids and went to try to start it up. I knew it started on compressed air, but they all had their own temperaments. You started the donkey, filled the air tank, turned the flywheel to the point, turned the air on and it should have fired. It didn't.

"It's Pontoon Day, Bob."

Captain Fountain was talking to an Arab. He had worked on it for the Germans and came and started it for us. He got involved so I asked him to load it for us. I put the winch rope on in case it went wrong and it went on like a snake with about only 9 inches of the 2 feet track on the trailer. It had about 15 inches overhang each side. We shackled it down and stretchered it both sides and I passed it as moveable with very great care. It seemed huge on the trailer. We braced it with a wire hawser and tied it to the turntable. It looked good.

By this time it had gone dark and the engine was still running so I lifted the dragline bucket and managed to drop it right under the cab between the skids which helped to hold it in place. I turned the engine off compression after filling the bottles for restart to unload.

"Best of 35 tons there, sir," I told Captain Fountain.

"More, I should think."

He suggested we stayed the night and there were some of my old friends there, including Bert Garlick. Bob and I had a couple of drinks and then went off to bed. All the lads were going to Beirut the following week so we could have a night out when we were there.

We retired to the Mac, were up early the next day and had started off before Fountain had got from his mess. He stopped us and gave instructions, but said we could do as we wished and he would see us in Beirut in perhaps a week's time.

It was a long drawn out task with the load we had. It weighed 35 tons all right. The Mac towed it well and we made good time to the halfway towards Alex. It was dark plus two hours and we shouldn't have been on the road at that time, but the tracks were straight, like in Canada and America. But there was a difference. There was no tarmac on most of them.

Next day we made Abassia Barracks. When we arrived we couldn't get into the Barracks through the arches. We went round onto the officers' part which brought us nearer to the facilities. Everyone was having a good look at the dragline. It was German and came from Tobruk.

The next day was a 'Pontoon Day' all right.

We did well heading for No. 11 Camp at Quassassin. We had to pull in to 140 W/S and Park Co. for fuel. Bob had his hand out to turn left into the Camp and I had checked my mirrors (which were very good), when Bob shouted: "Hold it!"

I tried to stop, but had pulled a car with me for about 10 yards or so. We both got out. The car was an Opel driven by a gentleman in a black shirt, who was also wearing a lot of jewellery. He smelled of expensive perfume and garlic. He was bleeding from the chin, his hands were scratched and he looked shaken up. The Opel was buried under the draw bar of the trailer. There was a beautiful lady in the passenger seat, wearing a green outfit, fit for a queen. It appeared she was not injured, but she was very upset and didn't speak English to us. I knew it was Arabic, but although I understood quite a lot of the language, I couldn't speak the 'gentry type' Arabic which, no doubt, these people were.

Bob dashed into the yard to telephone for the Red Caps. I

stayed with the vehicle and was asked to move it a number of times. I refused and it was a good job too. I had collided with King Farouk and his Queen. When they came to they were very pleasant towards me and bore no malice. The Military Police came and called an ambulance. When they knew who it was for they jumped! They took particulars of the road, etc., and I drove my lorry into the 140 W/Shop and Park Co..

I left Bob with the Mac as I was detained immediately and put under close arrest for my own protection. This was because of the difficult position I was in. Someone might have wanted to take revenge. Mr Davies came to see me and told me to ask for anything I wanted. I was treated well by everyone, the Red Caps included The chief of the Red Caps gave me instructions to be out early. I would have an escort out of the Canal Zone. My wagon had been off-loaded overnight and re-loaded with a Muirhill dumper and a D4 to go to Beirut and then to Chekka on the landslide.

We were on the road early and I kept out of sight as requested by R.T.O.. Bob drove through Ismailiya over El Qantara Bridge, where the Red Caps left us. I am quite sure I could have been attacked if I had been on my own. Bob didn't usually drive much, so I was enjoying the break.

We reached Kilo 196 and stopped for a meal. I picked some food up for Taffy – 'food' as in 10 pints of Laziza beer as this was always best for him. He always paid for it, and he always had plenty of money. He couldn't spend it on anything in the sand.

We intended to have a drink with Taffy and stop the night but when we got there we received a surprise. They had been down from Bate Naballa and changed operators. It was another Taffy, Taffy Landler – 'Squib' we called him. He was very tiny, but you've never seen a smarter young man in your life. He was a 'Stick Man.' Whether he was on guard duty or not, he always looked smart even in his denims. Not the denims you see today. He made a fuss of us and was pleased with the beer. We had enough of our own as Bob didn't drink much and if I had two pints it was enough. The price was 47 piastres. If Taffy had paid us he would have been skint so I told him to owe it to me and he said he might not see us again. I told him he must be joking as we 'lived' along the route and would probably see him in less than a week.

We arrived in Beirut late evening the next day and had our usual shower, meal and a pint, and then we walked down to the town. Next day we took a run to the tunnel, off-loaded and came back to Beirut to await instructions from the office. It was Sunday the next day.

"You can have a couple of days off Saturday and Sunday, but come into the office, both of you," said Captain Fountain.

I thought it was something to do with King Farouk, but it wasn't. The Allies had started to repatriate Polish people from Russia. The Captain wanted three men to go who were capable of using their own initiative with both people and machinery. They were to go to 1 P.E.D, and pick up a converted snowplough, a D8 caterpillar, with two winged blades in the shape of a plough, about 4 feet high. It was to go through The Sinai, Gaza Strip, over Transjordan and into Iraq, through Iraq to Iran, up towards the Caucasus, over The Pitac and into Russian border territory.

"You will travel in convoy at all times and the snowplough will be in the front at all times. In the event of a landslide or an avalanche of snow, the convoy will stay put until the way is clear and the plough has been reloaded onto the trailer again. There will be 30 lorries en route, canopy covered, one ration and clothing, fuel and oil, stores etc. Everyone will meet in the transit camp at Tehran in northern Persia for the first journey," he told us.

So, Taffy Tucker, Bob Townsend and I had the chance to go. I would be I/C transit, on and off loading, Bob would be second mate on the Mac and Taffy would be the machine operator. Although we could all do each other's jobs, this was how it would read in the event of the responsibilities needing proof.

The three of us met in the canteen. We had a pow-wow and decided we were going to do it. We saw Captain Fountain that evening at 7pm and made arrangements for the Mac to be fitted with a wider front seat before we left for Quassassin to pick up the snowplough.

We left at lunchtime the next day and we were to pick up our passes and documents for the trip to a camp outside Tehran called El Dory. It was an old military camp set up to accommodate all the refugees.

Our first task was another trip across the Sinai Desert again to pick up the D8 snowplough. En route we called to see Squib who was on the D4 shifting sand off the road at Kilo 196. (By the way, he did pay me the 47 piastres he owed me for the beer).

We were soon over the border into Egypt through Ismailiya, up the side of the Sweet Water Canal, Abusweire and once again in Camp 11 in Quassassin. We saw Phil Phil – an Arab lad who worked for the workshop at 1 P.E.D. He was a real good lad, about 23 years old, and always said he would invite me to his wedding.

We picked the snowplough up with as many spares as possible in case of a breakdown, including a spare seat, in the event of one getting wet. You always carried a spare seat. That's where the operator sat for 10 hours a day, so it was important that it was comfortable and dry. And two large hawsers for towing. All our personal equipment was to be picked up in Homs in the Bekka Valley, I suppose in two days' time or thereabouts.

We filled with fuel, an extra 45 gallon drum on the winch rope, as much oil as we could manage to put in our side storage space, checked all our tyres and we were ready for the long long trek. Although we were loaded, we could do 200 miles a day on easy ground. It was the climbing that took the time. The D8 with the plough was about 27½ tons, the trailer was 12 tons and the Mac was 10 tons, so the whole lot weighed a total of 49½ tons.

We made Bate Naballa the first night from Quassassin, which was very good going. We had a night in Tel Aviv, saw a film called 'The Star Spangled Banner', had a couple of pints and then went to bed early for a quick start to Beirut the next morning. We were in Beirut just after lunch on the Sunday. After a meal, shower and change, we found the liberty truck for the races in Beirut. Talbot was the lad to go with. He knew all the answers – how to bet, what to bet on. It was a wonderful day out after being on the road for weeks. Several of us formed a syndicate and bet on the 10 races from that. You could have a side bet if you wished and see how well off you were if you listened to Talbot. We each put in 10 Syrian £s and came away with 70 each. Talbot, McDade, Busty, Walker, Bob, the cook and myself. We all made money on our side bets too. I had 150 Syrian £s on me so I didn't have to draw any more cash before I went off on Monday morning.

We decided not to start off the big trek on the Monday because as you left Beirut you started to climb straight away on the way to Chatura over the Jebel Mazar Pass. It was a long ascent and took 12 hours' solid climbing. There was no stopping either or you would never have got started again. When we were tired we swapped on the move. There was no way I would be able to sleep going up there, because I had to keep an eye on Bob and take command if I saw him nodding off with the sleeping sickness.

Chapter 12

TREK TO NO MAN'S LAND

We took off at dawn on the Tuesday morning. We left Beirut heading through the Christian Arabs' area – the worst part I have ever travelled through out of all the places I visited. Although Beirut was the best place I was stationed in, it was the worst for pilfering. Someone would be on your trailer pinching stuff out of the back of the wagon before you realised it. Nothing was too heavy for them.

You got about a mile of level road before starting to climb over the terrain of mountains towards Damascus. The Mac was the ideal vehicle to tackle the job in hand.

Bob started the climb as it was more tedious towards the summit. I was going to let him drive while I was capable of keeping my eye on him, not when he and I were tired. We were on terrific climbs and drops so we couldn't take any chances, with carrying the weight we were.

So, "Jebel Mazar here we come."

The Mac got very hot as it climbed. It had a petrol engine so it would show up greater than a diesel, and sure enough it did. The floorboards felt white hot at times and it was boiling in the cab. We had no side windows, and the windshield was opened as far as it was safe to do so. Climb, climb, climb, the camber of the road was no better than going over the Seven Sisters. At times you thought you were going to tip over, looking at the front of the Mac.

We reached Jebel Mazar in 11 hours and so had to stop the night. It was very weird, an Army patrol passed and came back to us to ask if we knew what we were doing staying the night. They were R.T.O. officers and persuaded us to carry on driving down to Chatura.

"It will take about seven hours, but it will be safer from the Arabs there than staying over the top all night to sleep," they said.

We had our break, a meal, a bit of a walk, a smoke and were ready for the off. I had never descended so slowly at any time like this, it was frightening. Our headlamps shone over the sides of the mountains as we negotiated the bends, illuminating through nooks and crannies and down to the bowels of the earth, it was so steep. Again we thought we would go over because of the camber of the road. It seemed a such long way down.

I stopped to kick the wheels and water the horse. It was so still, every sound carried, even Bob's snoring as he had gone off a while back. I took a good puff on my cigarette, put it out and climbed in again. It was scary and I heard a clicking noise. I investigated it and it seemed so far away, yet so near. Click, click, click, click. What the hell was it? Then I heard a puff, puff. It was a railway line running alongside the road and the clicking was the safety ratchet on the line for climbing. It scared me to death.

I saw a light near the bottom of the descent which had gone on for six hours – we were near Chatura. A light appeared on my left and I found it to be the Royal Corps of Signals. At last, I was in a civilised area again. Thank goodness we got over that mountain for the first but not the last time. Although it never went really dark, it was a bright moonlit night. Even the road was shining. I pulled into the N.A.A.F.I. park and, to my surprise, it was a 24 hour service. Was I pleased with the officers who told us not to stop on the top!

I went in and ordered two breakfasts. Bob was fast asleep with his head on the metal door for a cushion. I went out and kicked my wheels and woke him.

"Come on, breakfast!"

Bacon, eggs, fried bread, sausage, a pint mug of tea, real Players cigarettes and a proper box of matches. We got a few bottles of beer for the next night's halt, wherever that might be.

I let Bob take the wheel on what turned out to be a proper Pontoon Day. We were on the start of the Bekka Valley, eventually to head for Homs and Aleppo, so I was sure it was flat land and if Bob did go off the beaten track, it was best for me to have a rest. He was full of beans and willing to drive, so I let him go on as long as he wanted.

I don't know how long we had been there, but I woke to find

crawly things all over me.

Bob had gone off the sand track, off the so-called road, and had buried the head of the Mac into a sand heap. The Mac must have stalled and I didn't hear a thing until I woke. I couldn't move for bloody locusts. They had got everywhere as we didn't wear anything other than shorts, socks and plimsolls. I couldn't see Bob, he was covered.

He was fast asleep, his head on the steering wheel, and you could hardly see that. The canopy was covered and if you walked away it was a perfect camouflage. They were in the beds, under the beds, in the brew can, on the snowplough, everywhere. It dawned on me to try to shift them by getting the airline, running the engine and trying to blow them off. This we did after I'd spent ages trying to awaken Bob. It did move them, but only for them to land again in another place.

We also had the task of getting out of there. We had to unload the plough, unhitch the trailer and put it out. The Mac came out on its own. We had to hitch up again, load the snowplough and tie down. It was a bit heavy on the front set of wheels, so I loaded it reverse onto put the weight further back. We just managed to get the skids up, but it rode a lot better after our tea break.

I drove to the D.I.D. at Homs to stay the night and wait the next day for Taffy Tucker. He was coming from a forestry job from round King Solomon's mines near Syr in North Beirut. He wasn't there when we arrived, and we had a good sleep the next day waiting for him. I was very pleased as I caught up on my letter writing.

We refuelled with petrol and I calculated we had done 4.5 mpg. We had to swap the barrel on the winch rope and fill the two tanks. We had 135 gallons altogether. We got rations for three people for two weeks. God knows where we would get the next from or where we would be. Russia is a long way off. That's where we were heading.

Our next call would be about Rutbah in Iraq, if we could make the transit camp on the Syrian Desert, off the parallel pipeline. We saw a brake coming into the camp. It was a Dodge 15 cwt. I noticed the hard face of Taffy Tucker peering through the side window.

"They've got here, Bob, at last. We can get ready for morning."

"Hi, Taff."

We shook hands and spoke to the driver who had brought him. He was a great lad named Andy Gill whom I met later in Shaiba.

Taff got his clobber into the Mac and cluttered the place up. We had to move round a bit to give him room amongst all the stuff we had acquired, won, or snaffled. We made a bed for him which fitted in just right as long as he didn't mind sleeping nearest the door. I don't think it made any difference, as it was a canvas cover anyway. There was only one canteen there, so we went for a pint. A lad was playing a banjo and doing a George Formby impression.

It was an excellent night out considering we were in the middle of the Syrian Desert. The Syrian Desert was the worst one of all to cross. It was so barren, there were no oases on it and it was so open. Dry, arid, lifeless and quiet. Eerie, I suppose.

Next day we were off. Our aim was to get beyond the desert that day, then onto the mountains beyond Ramadi. Habbaniyah or Salachia would be a good stop if we could make it. The old camp was sure to be there. Maybe we would touch for a meal too.

There wasn't much room with Taffy sitting in the middle. It was an awkward cab to seat three people. The steering wheel was huge compared to, say, one of our Albions. We managed and had a good run through to Baghdad.

Salachia is two miles outside Baghdad. I took Bob and Taffy down the town to show them some of the places of interest, if there were any.

We had a good reception. I reported to the office and told them who we were. They were part expecting us and we were running a day late according to them. The company was 865 ME.Coy. They had a contingent of men working on The Pitac, and one of their D8s had gone over the top as it was clearing an avalanche. They wanted to replace it. They had a load of rookies. Not that there was anything wrong with rookies, other than their white legs. They had no idea how far you had to travel out here, so they wanted to tag along. It was a hell of a pull from here on, so it was nice to have company in the event.

After another day and a half we arrived at their detachment camp outside Tehran, Persia. There were only nine men there, all operators, and it was only crawler plant. They were keeping this side of the overpass of The Pitac open for timber hauling from the mountains. They were attached to Ninth Army C.R.E, so it looked like tablecloths and a dhoby to do some washing, before we went onto the Russian frontier.

The meal we had was wonderful. It was venison, probably gazelle, a little bit nicer than roast rabbit. We were waited on and had a drink with our meal.

We left the 865 lads and headed north to the transit camp to pick up the rest of the convoy for Astara on the Russian frontier. It was the Caspian Sea coast all the way up to Astara. We met two miles out of Tehran.

The main convoy was under the command of an Indian officer. We were controlled by our own orders which we were carrying. He was responsible for his men and the drivers of his Indian crew. I made it plain to him that the vehicles had to stay at the rear of the snowplough all the time. They were not to pass us, as if there were a landslide we would not be able to pass them. It was important to keep to it.

The officer wanted to dictate the speed of the convoy too, but it was up to me to determine that. I could possibly average about 24 on flat country and well below that climbing – bearing in mind that we were to negotiate the Elburz Mountains, and would have snow avalanches and landslides to contend with. If we had to deal with six landslides we could do 150 miles a day. None of us knew what was in store, so it was up to me to decide to how far we went in the day.

I said: "You look after your men, sir. I will get on as fast as we can. I should think the round trip will take about 12 days. It will become boring for your drivers if we have a lot of trouble. If we have a stop I will sound the siren and nobody passes me. Please make that clear to everyone."

The following morning we left early. The sun was scorching hot even then. We hadn't started to climb yet. From where I was sitting, I could see the snow on the peaks. These were not main roads, so you expected anything. Off we went and did well for the first 50 miles.

I spotted a couple of trees tipped at 45 degrees. This was a sign we did not want, and as we got closer we could see the reason. Every inch of the track had gone. Slurry and sludge were running down the ravine. It was a case of: siren on, stop, offload and get on with it.

"Get the tea on, Bob."

Taffy started the donkey as I lifted the skids down; up with the blade and down she came. We were there for four hours' hard graft. We could all operate the dozer, so one had a tea break as the others worked. I also got an hour on the bed and fell fast asleep.

"Can we go now?" asked the Indian officer.

"No, sir, not until we load the dozer," I told him.

"Well, you can catch us up."

"What if there is another one round the next bend, sir? How will we get past you to get to the landslide?"

"Oh yes, of course, I see what you mean," he replied. "When do the men stop for a break?"

"At the next landslide."

"Oh that's no good. They want a break."

"If we have no more trouble, sir, we'll stop in four hours."

"You go on and we will have our break and follow you."

"Now you know that's no good, sir, a slide can happen anywhere, anytime. If I have gone and you get one before you reach me, how do you get through?" I pointed out. "When I travel, you travel, when I stop, your men get their breaks."

Yes, yes, he's learning...

We stopped for a break in four hours and Bob went round a bend for a look. We were a few hundred yards from our night stop. The slide was only a small one. We unloaded and cleared as much as to allow the lorries to pass for the night stop. We continued work until we had finished, then went up in front of them on a huge piece of spare ground.

The Indian officer came over to see me after we got our meal on the way and he apologised for being a bit awkward, but he hadn't understood why he couldn't go on without us. He knew the score now, and was pleased with what we were doing.

We made good time the next day and found the way gradually to the Camp at Astara. I was driving and Bob and Taffy were on the lookout. They saw some movement ahead. We were on strange ground, and very cautious. We hoisted our Union Jack and I put the siren on warning and hoping for the best. I was on the left and Bob was on the right with Taffy sort of leaning over Bob's knee.

Our first encounter with the Russians was a burst of gunfire. Three bullets through the cowl of the radiator, over the top of the engine, through the bulkhead, and they buried in the winch rope, dead centre of the wagon.

Thanks very much, Joe Stalin!

There was all hell let loose. The Indians behind us ran for cover and we ran under the blade of the plough.

Someone came towards us. A Russian explained that they had changed the guard and no one had told them we were expected. He spoke perfect English and, as we found out later, he spoke perfect Hindustani too. He had been selected for the job of looking after us and I told him, in no uncertain terms, that we had been shot at by Germans and didn't want any more. He apologised, but Taffy reported it on our return to El Dory.

When we approached the dannet wire of the camp, we saw thousands of people, most of them Polish refugees from the invasion of Poland in 1939. The Russians had regained the territory and the people and could not accommodate them. They had been under slave labour both by the Germans and the Russians. They were devastated. The whole camp was a marshalling yard with high dannet wire all round, guarded by soldiers.

There was an area sealed off for the convoy and we moved out of their way to let the Indians get on with their lives. The thirty lorries made a circle and kept together, which suited us. There was no accommodation for the drivers, they just slept where they could. There were thousands of people the other side of the wire, children, older women and a few men who were really dejected.

We started to get our breakfast ready, which included toast, and our usual bacon, eggs, etc. Without thinking, Bob threw two pieces of bread out over the end of the trailer. The wind blew them over the fencing and there was such a commotion. The refugees fought for the bread, and a voice came from the fence, a voice speaking excellent English, and it was a girl of about 24 or 25. She spoke to me and asked us not to do that again, as the people were starving and would kill for a piece of bread. She was very pleasant, clad only in an old Army overcoat and a pair of boots which were much too big for her. She wore an old Glengarry hat. As far as I could see, she wore no underclothing either.

These people were destitute, of that there was no doubt, and they needed help. You could see the girl was upset at speaking to us, and as this was the first consignment to come out of Russia, they trusted no one. I didn't blame them. She was a pretty girl, her blonde hair cut square, with a fringe, and clinging alongside her was a little girl. Perhaps a sister or even a daughter. She knew what was going on, that they were to be shipped to another country.

The actual movement of the refugees had nothing to do with us. We three were only responsible for the condition of the roadways. We got on well together and we knew our job. We mucked in with work and cooking.

The girl who had spoken to me happened to be the interpreter for the whole Polish contingent. Her name was Yanina. She was a schoolteacher in Poland and had taught English in Warsaw before War broke out.

On the return trip she had to deal with every query and told me that she did not like the Indian officer in charge of the convoy. She complained that he tried to get fresh with her and asked what she could do if he continued to behave like that. They argued about toilet facilities, which were non-existent. Food too was a problem. The Polish people had had hardly any for months and, because it was now so plentiful and they didn't eat it all, the officer wanted to cut their rations down, either to sell what remained or to have some gain out of it. She asked us to have a word with him, which we did.

Yanina was riding in the first truck. There must have been a thousand people on this convoy and this would mean about 34 standing up on a lorry. They were well organised. Some moved over for the few to sleep for a while. They were exhausted and had a difficult task to keep alive. When they had done this trip they might be able to live again.

The refugees were infested with lice and fleas. They were scabby and unclean, but not through their own fault. Yanina had nothing to wear, only her stinking overcoat and heavy army boots. Her feet were blistered and the other child, who never left her side, was the same. She had not a stitch on under her matted overcoat. The three of us went through our kit to find anything that might do to make them underclothing. We'd had winter kit given to us before we left, so we all had our summer kit and most of mine was fairly new. Bob gave two pairs of Aertex underpants. I had two pairs to spare. Taffy had two shirts and we gave them vests, too. I passed Yanina my 'housewife' and she sewed the shorts up so they fitted. The girls were more than grateful. We sorted some socks out and gave Yanina some soap and a towel for each of them. Bob had a new toothbrush and we gave her some tooth-paste. But with all these new things, she had to be ever so careful how she conducted herself with her own people.

We had three heavy slides on the way back and did the whole run in 40 hours, driving as long as we could. We arrived at El Dory at approximately 4pm, said goodbye and were glad to have a shower and clean clothing. We went to the mess for our first meal and it was a good C.R.E. meal – tablecloths, a pint of beer, served at your table, with all the trimmings.

We were interested to know what the people were doing the next day as we prepared for another trip. The first task was to de-louse everyone. It was so sad to see the children naked and thin for the want of care of nourishment. They were lined up to go through a door to be 'dipped'. All their clothes were incinerated. They walked through a deep trough over their heads in a fluid-like sheep dip. They came out of there into a hot bath and a com-plete change of new clothing. They were so grateful and the ones who could understand us couldn't thank us enough. I felt remorse that the world was so cruel and these people had had to suffer so much. It was the end of their suffering now, they had got out of Russia.

Yanina and I met before we started the next trip. I didn't know how many we were going to have to do, but she asked me to find her uncle. He was in the transit camp at Astara. He wasn't on the list for the first trip. I was to find him if I could and try to look after him. He was the only relative left of the whole family, and was a Major in the Polish Army. The Russians didn't recognise their refugees' military rank at all. There was no favoritism. The

156

officers walked and were pushed to get on the transport, just like the others.

We had a heavy fall of snow and the pass was blocked twice. It was easy to move it and we did the trip two days quicker than the last one. As we arrived back at El Dory I sounded the siren and saw Yanina running towards us. She was disappointed; her uncle was not with us. There were quite a few more people to come, so I was sure he would be there on the next trip. She brought every-thing for us – cigarettes, toothpaste, matches, razor blades, soap and chocolate.

The next trip took two days longer. We had trouble with the D8, a broken injector pipe, and had to wait for the R.E.M.E. to come to us. Storbat was the nearest depot and we were lucky in that we caught a lorry en route there. We were soon on our way, then we turned a bend, only to find another snow slide. Anyway, we did the trip a day quicker than we expected after the break-down.

I had a good description of Yanina's uncle, and I called to an old man who fitted the bill to see if he was the one, and sure enough it was him. He shook hands and made a fuss when he found out she had gone on before. He didn't speak English and I had no idea of his language, so we had to do our best to tell each other what we wanted to say. He was worried in case she would be moved on somewhere else without him. I assured him she wouldn't be, as she had been selected as interpreter for the whole group. We started another trek through the desolate land of nowhere.

We stopped at a wide clearing for a tea break and had to spread ourselves out a bit so we were a good way from the rest. Because of our weight we had to select our ground, the others were all right. If they sank a bit, there were plenty of us to pull them out. If we sank down, we had to unload to get out.

The day was much brighter and the ground had dried up. We had our break and were tidying up when we heard a funny noise. There were some creatures in the long grass, and they were not human either. We looked and saw what looked like a family of apes walking upright but covered lightly with fur or hair.

We watched their capers and I'm sure they saw us and tried to surround us. I was in the cab like a bullet, sounded the siren, started up and was ready to move as Bob and Taffy jumped into the back. As the siren sounded, they formed a circle, had a kind of conflab, then moved off in the opposite direction.

We passed it off as 'one of those things' and made good time on the way back because we knew the road and there were fewer landslides. We were getting to know every corner of the track, taking more risks. In fact, we were too far ahead of the convoy at times.

It was nice to know we had done something to help these poor people in their plight. The convoy eventually cleared more than 8,000 refugees altogether.

After leaving El Dory, they were transported to Quassassin in Egypt first of all, then those who wished were joining units of their choice. Some joined the Red Cross or the Polish Air Force and I met quite a few of them again all over the world. Some of them had lost everything – identity, money and all their belongings. Some were poor peasants, some aristocrats. How some of them managed to get their money out of Poland I will never know, but a few were rich people.

As we arrived back this time we had Yanina's uncle with us and we were getting to know how the Polish people relied on each other. Each trip we returned from, our clothing was collected from the Mac and dhobied for us, and Yanina was always there with our goodies. They were most dedicated people. We did feel we were doing a worthwhile job.

Eventually, after eight trips over three and a half months, our long treks were over and we headed home to our unit in Beirut. It got more civilised as we got nearer to the coast, although we had a long way to go yet. Baghdad came and went quicker than we thought, but we had the worst to do yet. Baghdad to Damascus was a long trek, then we had the long run to Bekka Valley before we climbed the track to Jebel Mazar. We were trying to do a bit extra so Taff and Bob did more driving than usual. D.I.D. Homs was our aim, so we could get some nice food down us. C.R.E. would look after us, and although there was nothing to do in Homs, we had a safe haven and a day of rest. The next day it was Chatura, the climb to Jebel Mazar. A night in the snow and then down to Beirut the following day.

We stopped at Chatura for a long break, kicked our wheels, watered our horses and got ready for the pull up to Jebel. Sausages, baked beans, eggs, black puddings were all still on the menu at the Halfway House. We were still digesting these as we climbed the Pass. It was an eight hour climb non-stop. There were very few pull-ins if anything went wrong.

We were nearing the top when we met a civilian on his hands and knees praying to Allah to get him out of his mess. His lorry had gone over the cliff. What made matters worse was that the train was on its way up the Pass. The train was on ratchets but dare not risk stopping as it was so steep. Luckily we were opposite a pull-in just big enough to accommodate our length, so we stopped. We haggled for half a minute as to how much it was worth and we went to pull away. He soon relented and what we charged him was peanuts to what it would have cost him if he'd had to call someone out to him. Even then, I doubt if they could have got him from there. Then there was the train too. His lorry was loaded with sheep and goats. They had tipped over each other and they were blarting. The wagon was almost at right angles and luckily enough hadn't tipped over. How he got there I will never know.

He said: "English Asskarrie, he cut me up Johnny, then my brakes would not hold me."

We uncoupled the trailer, that meant it was solid on the brakes, we coupled the Mac to the trailer and let out the winch rope to winch the lorry from there. The civilian wouldn't get in the cab, he was too scared, so Taffy took the reins, and as I took the strain it started to move very slowly forward and we got it out. We wanted 300 Syrian lire from him (about £30) and he only had 100 on him. He was from Beirut and told us where to call to pick it up. We told him to leave it for us the next day as we were going to Beirut anyway. If he didn't pay, we threatened that he would be off the road if we saw him anywhere again.

The man's lorry was very well maintained. The brakes were good, but nothing would have held it the way it had gone down that cliff. We heard the clatter of the train's ratchet as we pulled the vehicle clear and we were only just in time. He was really grateful and kissed our hands. We followed him to the top to see if he could continue down that night into Beirut. We were going to stop the night at Jebel Mazar anyway, so he stayed till morning. He said he would never stay there on his own as the Arabs would have had him and his sheep. They were even scared of their own kin! They cursed us, generally, but they always asked for our help.

It would be very difficult to try to describe Jebel Mazar. It was a peak on the top of the Lebanon Range. It was a snow post, desolate, arid, barren, still and motionless, weird in the still of the night. No man with any sense would stop there, never mind stay overnight, yet during the day it was always a place to cool down after the great climb from either way – Chatura or Beirut. It was a haven to hot engines – they all cooled down there. The snow was as crisp as crystals in the hot sunshine. The air was clear and fresh. There was a beautiful view either down the Bekka Valley or looking across to the sea over Beirut. To think you could drive 49 tons down that mountain into the sea, with wrong cambered roads and twisty bends made you shudder with fear in the event of a mishap. Do you know, the four years I went over that Pass I never even had a puncture! I slid sideways a few times, and had one wheel off the road, but never had a mishap.

On returning from Damascus, entering the Christian area of Beirut, we had to slow down almost to a crawl. This meant whoever wasn't driving took to the rear of the wagon and watched the trailer. Bob was dozing as usual and a cluster of starving kids were on the prowl for lorries carrying anything worth taking. They would jump on the trailer, onto the back of the wagon and throw out your kit, food, the stove, anything they could lay their hands on. I called to Bob who jumped to it and went into the back. Kids had got on and were throwing stuff out. Bob called and shot a warning bullet in to the air. One young lad fell under the front wheels and was killed outright. We could see he was dead. It was a case of out of the cab, pull his body to the side before the two sets of eight wheels went over him, back in the cab, and drive as fast as we could out of the area into the military zone before anyone could identify us or our vehicle.

It was a terrible accident, and an ordeal for us, but what could anyone do? The boys were thieving and if you stopped you would be set upon and probably killed for no fault of your own. Our strict instructions were to scarper in an event like that. I always hoped it would never happen to me, but it did, and that's what we had to do. It was shocking and I've never forgotten it.

We arrived at the Gendarme Barracks to find our unit had moved to another camp. They had gone to a coastal camp right by the sea at Needle Rock on the West Bank left of Beirut city. We were re-directed by the R.T.O. and only had another mile to do before we were back in our camp. We had a shower and a meal, good food served at proper tables. I would have to wait until the next day before I could go to the office. I had the fatal accident to sort out with the C.O. and thank goodness Captain Fountain was still there. He already knew about it and it was cut and dried other than my formal report to go to the R.T.O. at G.H.Q. Ninth Army. Ten shillings would be deducted from my credit in due course, to bury the boy. Psychologically it can affect you if you worry about it, but the lads were thieving and trespassing, and there was no way we were to blame. If we had stayed there we might not have been around to tell anyone about it.

The camp was beside the sea and we could dive out of the mess room window into the sea. It was beautifully situated, half a mile from the centre of town, next door to a top class restaurant, which was much too expensive for us to visit and you had to speak French to get served. The town was a fair place in which to be stationed. It had three cinemas, and about six bars, run mainly by the Greeks. It was on the seafront but there was not much of a promenade. There were some good shows in some of the bars, and always some kind of belly dancing, if you liked that sort of entertainment. The bars which served food were good. I had my favourite, run by the Christian Arabs. You got a square deal.

It seldom went completely dark. I had a photo taken at midnight and it came out all right. I still have it. Beirut to me was OK. I remember the happy times there. The long trek was over, but we were still on the move. Where to this time?

Chapter 13

IRRIGATION SCHEME

We had a premonition that the war was getting towards the end and we might see Blighty again, sooner than we expected. We had had reinforcements, two more transporters in the camp. A Hug timber hauler, another Mac and a Crane Freuhauf Trailer. I reported for instructions.

"Take the D8 snowplough back to Quassassin, and pick up a new D7 and 12 yard onion scraper. The other Mac will go with you to pick up a Tyne Rooter, and the rest of the tools," said Captain Fountain. "How is Bob? Have you had any problems at all? Do you want to keep him?"

"Yes, sir, he's a good lad and we get on very well."

"OK, keep him. You know these lads are rookies. Show them the ropes. Where to stop and so on; fuel, how to get more rations than you should. You know how to look after yourself – so keep your eyes on them."

'Charlie the Mac' was a nice fellow. He was a good driver and would listen to what you told him about the safety aspect of being out on your own. You had to keep to the rules, if you could find any. I'd learned the hard way, and found you couldn't stop on the side of the road, leave your vehicle and expect no one to invade your 'house on wheels'. You couldn't leave it unattended except under military supervision.

The first stop was just below Tyre, by the banana forest. It was the place to take a dip in the sea, pinch an orange and a banana, grapes and watermelon, dry out and head off towards Tel Aviv.

The weather in Palestine was warm after the long trek over The Pitac. I enjoyed the sea and the clear waters of the Mediterranean. The coast was with us for the next two days except for the trek over the Sinai Desert once more. Our two guests were quite amazed at the length of the journey, and enjoyed meeting the Bedouins near Kilo 196. Our machine was still there, operated by a new recruit, Dave Shut. We stopped at 196, as this was the last stop before you got to Ismailiya, after the El Qantara Bridge. There was nothing at 140 W/S & Park Co. or P.E.D. unless you went up to the Camp. At 11 Camp there was a good N.A.A.F.I., but it was a good way from the workshop so we had to offload the snow-plough and load the D7 and the onion scraper towing behind the 54 tons.

Charlie's Tyne Rooter had to be lifted on by crane and I noticed the German machine I had brought from the Tunisian Desert had been overhauled and was now in use for the heaviest lifting in the yard.

We decided we could make Kilo 196 if we didn't go up to the camp, so when we were loaded and fuelled up, we were off. Charlie hadn't had much experience at roping down or the use of the stretchers. He was learning, like we all had to, but he had never seen a stretcher put on a rope before, so I roped him down and we were off to the Sinai again.

We had a meal at 196 and I uncoupled the wagon and went off to see the D4 operator along the Treaty Road. I took him a couple of bottles and Charlie asked who they were for. I asked if one of them would stop and guard the rest of the machines while three of us went to see Dave Shut. We took him a feed of something cooked and his beer. It was almost dark and he was adjusting a track on the D4. He was pleased to see us – well, pleased to see anyone. It was so boring there. You were not allowed to leave the place unattended. Many W.D. drivers had got bogged down in the sand, left their vehicles and gone for help only to come back to find their vehicles ransacked, and everything gone. This was the reason for the machine being there. C.H.Q., C.R.E. told us how much better it was since the machine had been stationed there. We got him mobile for the morning, had a bottle of beer with him, and listened to the Forces network, which was his only contact with the outside world after we'd left.

I'd thought Shut was a rookie from Blighty, but he had been in Baghdad about the same time as me. He must have been on detachment when I was at Salachia. He was with 865 M.E.Coy, and had worked on The Pitac, when I was crossing over to Russia from Tehran. Major Jackson was I/C and a machine went over the top and was reputed to be a write off. It had gone so far down the ravine it would have taken months to remove it. I will tell you what happened to it later in the story and this is where I had dealings with Jacko. The fact was that the machine was new, worth £8,000. It had only toppled over so it was probably repairable.

We headed back for Beirut across the Gaza Strip to Tel Aviv, up the coast to Haifa, over the border to Lebanon and onto Beirut. We arrived at about 8.30pm, tired and ready for a shower and a feed. The cook was very good when we got in from a long run, if he was there. We had bubble and squeak, a pint and his best rice pudding. I think he made his own sausages – they were excellent.

I was too tired to go down to the town so I answered some of the mail I had received. I soon hit the hay. The Hug timber hauler was in the yard and another lad named Charlie was ready for the forestry in the morning. This lad's name was Charlie Cull. The first time I met him he was white. He asked me every question in the book as he had no idea of the routes we had to take, because we were not allowed to go off the beaten track. He was leaving for King Solomon's Mines. We still had about eight machines there and were still deepening the river bed to float logs down stream. Anyway, Charlie Cull didn't know his way out of the camp let alone to Damascus.

I had the two Charlies with me on the run to Damascus. Cull was going to the forestry while 'Charlie the Mac', who was carrying the Tyne rooter and compressor, was coming with me. I was to drop them off and to stay there with Bob and Taffy Tucker, the operator for the D7 and onion scraper. We had instructions in an envelope, not to be opened until we got to the N.A.A.F.I. Park in Damascus.

We arrived there after tea the following day. We had problems with Cull and the Hug transporter. He hadn't closed his trailer stays up to shorten his length, which I had suggested to him before we left. He couldn't get round the bends with it like that. He didn't know how to shorten it. I had my own problems with them and the scraper. Anyway, we were on the climb and he failed a gear first and, although he was empty, he couldn't get off again and gave his clutch a bashing. He was too erratic and should have changed as he saw me drop a gear. There were two nasty bends about two-thirds of the way up and you had to wait until the road was clear and get right over to be able to negotiate them with a long load. His back end went over the side. I'm sure he felt stupid after I'd asked him to close it up. He told me he hadn't known what I'd meant!

I went to the top to Jebel Mazar, dropped the trailer and left Bob with it. He sat on the D7, in the sunshine, while I went back to tow Charlie out. I explained to him that always on this pass he must use a short haul. It didn't matter if the timber overhung the bend, as long as his follower was a sensible distance and he could alter this even if he was loaded before he stretchered his load. The follower will always move backwards or forwards. This is the idea of it.

I got him out and to the top. We adjusted his follower and he began to grasp what it was all about. The other Charlie (I can't remember his surname) was a good and better lad. In some ways I would have liked him for a mate instead of Bob, to do a bit more driving. But Bob never varied. He was a stone-waller and an excellent mate.

Bob woke up and said: "I couldn't brew up, I had no gadgets." We made a brew and started the descent. I told Cull to stay behind for a quarter of an hour and not to get too close. I had 55 tons on mine and he was empty. I told him not to go down on his brakes, but to drive it down on his gears.

We continued our journey for Charlie Cull to go through to the forestry job and 'Charlie the Mac' and myself to go onto Damascus to the N.A.A.F.I. later that afternoon. Our job was to report to a sheikh in Damascus. His name was Effendi Hibbish, a landowner who seemed to own half of Damascus. He was a Christian Arab, with one wife only, three daughters and one son. Mr Hibbish was educated in the U.S.A. and he based his living on the American way of life. His home was superb.

Our orders were to meet him on his land, which was a huge expanse. His crops were being ruined, either by flooding or poor irrigation. The whole area of the Bekka Valley is green and careful irrigation can bear fruit, properly controlled, and Mr Hibbish was trying to do that. How we managed to get the job I don't know, but we were instructed to excavate a dyke through his land. This was a 10 feet deep dyke, the width of a scraper, and we were to complete it as quickly as possible. The land was chiefly chalk stone and ran in layers – some very hard and some very soft.

We started by taking as much of the topping as possible, then tried the Tyne Rooter to get down to the shape of it. Anything too hard, we had to blow. All the excavated earth was put on the lowest part of the land. Taffy knew how to "muck shift" and we did well.

Hibbish was more than pleased with the way we had tackled it. He came to see us. He spoke excellent English and always brought some cans of Yankee beer when he visited us.

Thursday was a day off. Thursday was 'shooting day'. He sent two shooting brakes, three rifles, and plenty of .22 rounds of ammunition. We went shooting for gazelle. It was his land and it was rich in everything. Even the water from the wells was drinkable and it was beautiful and clear. Some of the wells were being modernised from the oxen bucket, escalator type, to the modern diesel pump type. When the dyke was completed it was to be kept full of water at all times and all the various waterways were interlinked to the dyke.

As we worked, we saw some of the crops ruined by flood and drought. We spent many days doing the job we had to do. Who sanctioned it I will never know, and how Mr Hibbish paid I will never know either. Every Thursday we went shooting and had plenty of wine and venison, Yankee canned beer, excellent food and, after Mr Hibbish knew how we were cooking, he sent a servant out to us. He lived like a Bedouin and did everything for us, including washing, cooking, made our beds, kept everywhere tidy and brought us our breaks during the day.

We all got dressed up to go to the house for dinner, and it was like a banquet. There was plush carpeting and we could go where we wanted to in the house. Hibbish's three daughters were beautiful. They had all had a college education and spoke perfect English and, as far as I know, perfect French as well. They were amiable people and they treated us like lords. To get to their homestead you had to go through an Arab village not far from the Y.M.C.A. in Damascus and to negotiate the turning in the village we had to move all the cars. The scraper just came through with inches to spare and I knew it was going to be difficult on the return trip. The job was almost finished, so Bob and I went for a walk to the village to have a look. There was a mud house right on the corner, so to be able to get round, all the cars would have to be moved, then it dawned on me to take the Mac and let the D7 and scraper travel to the village and load it there.

"Good idea, Diesel", said Bob. "You must have been born with a brain after all."

Eventually the dyke was complete and the water was turned back to its natural channel. We must have hit the level just right. It flowed from its source to the end of the dyke. In no time Mr Hibbish was there to see the big turn-on. He was pleased with what he saw. The waterways filled up and his men were amazed with the flow of the water. They had been using tankers and donkey carts to irrigate the land up to now and one of the Arabs came in front of me, knelt down, and thanked me.

"Very, very good for water, Sahib. Before we all work too hard to get water. This is very good."

They were all chuffed; the job was finished.

The next day we were ready to move and asked Mr Hibbish if it was all right to travel to the village with the D7.

"How about the road surface?" we asked.

"Don't worry, it has to be done and it's not tarmac anyway, so it will settle in a day or so," he replied. "You might even drop the blade as you come down with it. It may take a bit of the crown off the road. It's a bit high in places."

Taffy never failed and we travelled to the village with the Mac waiting for the scraper to follow us through. We were loaded by 10.30am, and I think everyone in the village was out.

Taffy never loaded. It was a frightening experience, and he avoided it while I was there. The skids were down and we were ready to load. Taffy beckoned for me to get on and load. I crawled up slowly and got up first time. It was dead centre, which it had to be because the scraper would run out of line if it wasn't. I moved forward, the skids were put up. I came back on the skids, put the stretchers on and parked up awaiting the arrival of 'Charlie the Mac' to pick up the rooter and the compressor.

Mr Hibbish came to us and handed us an envelope each. We

were to open them when we left. He shook hands, thanked us for what we had done and, in fact, he offered me a permanent job after I left the Forces.

I'm afraid it wasn't my kind of life, so I didn't take him up on his offer, but I did keep in touch with Mr Hibbish himself for about two years after the work was finished.

Charlie came so we helped him load and left to go into Damascus. We all had a meal in the N.A.A.F.I. before the short trek to Chatura, then the climb up to Jebel Mazar. We were back in Beirut the following day.

While we were at Chatura, Taffy asked if I had had a look in the envelope.

"No," I said.

"Well have a look, you'll have a shock."

It contained 5,000 lire. 100 lire was about £10 so we did well and we hadn't expected anything, anyway. We all had the same, except the other lorry of course. He also got the cook, Akmoud, to load as much beer as he could under the beds. We did very well.

Taffy went back to his billet. Bob and I moved round again and were glad of the extra space. The D7 and Scraper were to go to Bate Naballa the next day, so we had the usual shower, gave the dhoby man our togs for washing and went to spend some of our money.

We had a night in Beirut. Tomorrow Bate Naballa. Our orders were to go from from there to Kilo 196, to take another D4 for Shut and take that to Quassassin for a complete overhaul. Then bring a new D6 back from Quassassin and drop it off for Shut at 196 and bring the D4 back again to Bate Naballa.

We were up and down this coast all the time. There were manoeuvres in Nathania. We delivered a machine there. We went to the leave camp at Hadera, did a quick job, back to Bate Naballa, then to Beirut, up to the tunnel at Chekka then onto the Forestry job at King Solomon's Mines. I was like a spider crawling all over the place.

On one particular run to Damascus we stopped for a break about 20 miles away. Bob was cleaning the brew can on the trailer. It was dusk, so we were making our way to the N.A.A.F.I.. We could park there and go up to the town for a meal. Bob was engrossed in his task and didn't notice a pack of hyenas creeping up on him. I spotted them and called to Bob to tell him to come inside and he started to laugh with the hyenas.

I said: "They'll get you."

This made him laugh all the more, but I was serious.

"They will bloody well get you!"

The hyenas were laughing and so was Bob. In the end I got up and grabbed him and pulled him inside. The hyenas were nearing the wagon and were now laughing their heads off. They were yapping outside, so I started the engine to build the air up and sounded the siren.

"Yap, Yap, Yap."

They flew into the rocks and everything went quiet. A pack of hyenas will hypnotise you if you are daft enough to let them. The bedouins told me this and I'm sure they were right. They creep up on you and pounce, especially if they are hungry. Bob didn't believe me for a long time.

We were soon in Damascus. We parked the lorry for the night, had a wash and changed and went to Damascus to our usual restaurant. We knew there was a film on at the open air cinema, so we decided we were going to go. As we were eating our meal on the ground level, there were some girls upstairs in uniform. There was a nice balcony and they were looking over the top and throwing things down.

Bob said to me: "I'm sure that's Yanina in the Red Cross uniform."

Sure enough it was. I was ever so pleased to see her. There was no chance of us going to the cinema. We had too much to talk about. She told me the whole story. She had left Tehran about three months before after all the documentation had been completed. Her uncle had joined the Polish Army and had a flat in Damascus. Her young sister was attending the Christian school in Damascus and she was based for the time being at the Military Camp at El-Faide. She insisted that I went to her uncle's flat to see him. He had something for me.

I went and Bob returned to the N.A.A.F.I.. This was about 8.30 pm. There was a show in the N.A.A.F.I. so Bob was OK.

Yanina called a taxi and into the hills we went. It was a high rise flat, we were up about four storeys. I met her uncle again, who had a vodka in his hand as we walked in. We shook hands and I had an embrace from him. He was most grateful for what we had done to help him. We sat and tried to talk with what English he could muster. He had a chess board and I told him to set it up and I would have a game with him.

He had an excellent manner. The flat was expensive and he wore a solid gold watch, ring and a gold chain. His uniform was hung on the adjoining wall and a Major's shoulder badge showed me his rank. I literally hammered him at chess the first time. I played him many times after that, but he never let me win again! We met up in many parts of the Middle East.

He made it clear to Yanina that I was to have a Golden Eagle from his birthplace in Warsaw. He brought it out to show me. It was glistening in the artificial light. I examined it, not that I knew anything about it, but it was marked on the bottom inside. It was about the size of an electric light bulb. I was pleased to accept it, and I really looked after it. Later on I will tell you how I lost it.

Whenever we went to Damascus we always tried to buy Damascus silk. We could buy it for a lira a yard and sell it in Haifa for three lire. We got friendly with a Huhudi in Palestine, and he asked us to tranship some Jews from Damascus back over the Lebanon border and said he would pay us 10 lire a head for them. The gendarme didn't stop us as we passed the border. I am not going to say how many we brought through. Quite a few in fact. They had free movement in any country, but couldn't get from Lebanon to Palestine without showing their identity, and some of them didn't have that document. We did it for a while, but I think we overdid it. It was getting a bit 'hot'.

The following day we spent at King Solomon's Mines. There was a D7 which had broken down in the river bed, so we had to cancel our previous orders and when this was pulled out of the river bed, we loaded it and took it to Beirut for repairs. Eventually we winched it on and were in Beirut the next day.

It was the same boring run over Jebel Mazar and down the Pass the other side. You went down on your head for at least a mile into the Christian side of Beirut, then made your way south of the city to the West Bank down to the seafront. I unloaded the

D7 and took it straight over the pit ramp for immediate inspection. On doing this we found that the sprocket had just come loose and it could have been repaired on site. This was maddening because we were busy. This machine had to go back as they were struggling as it was, so it was back over the top again to Chatura, into Bekka Valley onto the R.A.F. Camp at Homs and pick up a Roller No. 7 for Bate Naballa. And this is what we did for almost two years.

Chapter 14

HOME ON LEAVE

umours were rife that men were to be sent home for a month's leave. In the end, it was my turn and, although I didn't expect it to come so soon, I was next in line for a trip to Blighty. Captain Fountain sent for me to give me the gen.

Transport to Haifa, train to Port Said, ship from there to Toulon on the south coast of France, train from Toulon to Dieppe, troop carrier across the Channel to Newhaven, train from there to London and London to Chester.

What a ruddy journey! Documentation, finance, passes and travel vouchers. I was fed up before I reached Haifa.

Ever travelled on an Arab train? The passengers were everywhere. They were like rubber balls elasticated to the train. The train was packed, and down to Gaza there was no chance of two of us getting together to talk. I travelled with Jimmy Booth from St Helens. We eventually met up with lads we knew, but you could expect that on the length of service we had all done over four years.

We were advised to pack our kit bags and let them go ahead. They would be put on a ship to Toulon, South of France. We were to pick them up there. It left Port Said a week before us and it was due to be in Toulon when we got there. It didn't arrive. It had hit a mine alongside the Island of Moza. Much of the kit I had saved for years had vanished. The Polish Eagle, Damascus silk, all the trinkets I had from all over the world – Bahia, Durban, some I had picked up from Asher, Basra, Baghdad and Bombay. I had a present from Yanina she had given to me in Tehran, a replica of a hubbly hubbly pot. It was dressed in a kind of gold braid, and had a golden pipe and a mouthpiece. It was only in miniature, but was a perfect keepsake. Anyway, it went down with the rest of the belongings I'd wanted to take home.

We thought someone was kidding us and that the kit bags had

172

been stolen, but we were assured after we got back that the ship had sunk.

What a difference it made, travelling the desert by rail rather than by road. I was always used to stopping when I wished and doing the things I wanted to do. I have never had such a long journey. We left Haifa at 11am and stopped at Kilo 196 for a break, only 10 minutes. The queue was a mile long. It was dusty as there had been a sand storm. The sand was everywhere on the train. Dry, arid sand. There were no carriage windows as such, and they were open both ends. The seats were solid wood, like a utility seat on the buses after the war finished. They were horrible. The old steam locomotives were 'shot at' long ago. It was dark as we got to El Qantara Bridge. We stopped for the toilets and out came the Arabs. They would give you a shoe-shine if you were daft enough to let them.

At 1.30 am, with a mouthful of sand and the smell of donkey dirt thrown in, daylight came and we had somewhere to stop. Everyone stretched their legs. Who should be standing alongside me but Tiny Roberts from Summerhill! Further down the carriages was Bert Davies from Abermorddu, Taffy from C.R.E, G.H.Q. 9th Army, Lofty New from Southampton, Cyril Merryfield from Bournemouth, and Bill Bourne, whom I hadn't seen since we left Shaiba. Everyone was shaking hands and asking each other where they had been.

We eventually arrived at Port Said and weren't long boarding ship – the *Empire Battleaxe*. What a bloody crate! Every move it made it creaked. It was slow, fairly clean and a new ship. They later found it was no good for carrying passengers. It was all metal and most uncomfortable. I think we were five days crossing the Mediterranean; arriving and disembarking at 3pm we went into a hut for the night so we all had a night down in Toulon. I didn't find it very appealing. I was glad to hear Reveille and get ready for the train journey up through France to Dieppe. We left at 10am and arrived at Dieppe at 1am the following day. Then we transhipped onto the troop carrier for Newhaven, a six hour crossing, and it was a rough Channel. We arrived at 5.30pm at Newhaven, and documentation took a few hours, so it was another wasted night.

We were in England and we were not allowed out without a pass. The brains had been working again. On company notices was this sign – "No passes will be issude untill tree tirty", and that's how it was spelt on the company's noticeboard.

How stupid could the Army get? We had been away for four and a half years and to have idiots telling us we couldn't go out until they said so was unbearable. There was a pantomime when they did give out the passes. Everyone either tore them up or gave them back into the camp adjutant's office. All we were interested in was getting on the train for London and home. There was nothing at Newhaven.

We trained it to London and the next morning I transferred onto the Crewe train and sat in the compartment on my own for a long while. Alongside me there was another train with a Swaddy in the compartment. He had medals all over him. I caught sight of a porter and asked him what it was.

"Yankee soldier," was the reply.

"Where did he get all his bloody medals from? I've just come from Egypt and I haven't any yet after four years. When do I get mine and where do I get them from?"

The Yank had been on active service for two years and he was covered in the damn things.

After a while a few more of the lads arrived. Jim Booth was amongst them and I called him into the compartment. It was nice to get on an English train again and have a bit of comfort. It puffed out as fast as it could do to Crewe. I said, "So long" to Jim at Crewe and changed for Chester.

"Does this stop at Chester?" I asked a porter.

"It only goes to Chester – so you can go to sleep if you like."

I got a train to Penyffordd and walked it to Hope. It was the last train and I was glad to be on it. It was cold, dark and frosty and I was clad in everything I could wear but was still shivering. My teeth were chattering as I trudged the two miles to Hope. I got in at about 11pm.

I can't even remember how I embraced my mother after such a long absence.

While I was in Newhaven I'd strolled into the cookhouse by

Balham. My luck was in. I'd managed to get bacon, cheese, tea, margarine, about a pound of sausages and also cooking fat and some powdered egg.

My mum was over the moon She hardly recognised me, as I was almost black. We sat for ages talking, so it was 3.30am before we went up the 'wooden hills' and, of course, I couldn't sleep.

I didn't know where my brother was. I think he was spending his time at Birkenhead. I didn't see him for a couple of days after I arrived home.

The next day mum was up and I could smell the bacon cooking on the old-fashioned grate by the fire. An electric or gas stove in those days was a luxury. I got up and went down to see it snowing outside, and I said something I shouldn't have said when I saw snowflakes falling from the sky. I don't know whether Mum heard me or not; I hope she didn't.

I had a nice breakfast and I went to see some of my fellow villagers.

I thought then: "When I get out of the Forces, there is no way I am going to settle to village life as I knew it before I was called up."

I felt ten years behind my time. I had been away for four years and the country had advanced more than that during this war. Because of the war, people had come out of their shells. Girls were drinking pints and doing jobs which the men had always done, working together in factories, wearing slacks or boiler suits, and even driving buses. Young people had taken over the things I used to do. All the bellringers were girls and so was the station porter. It was funny to see a girl pulling a trolleyful of cases along the platform. If you'd stayed at home all the time you would have got used to it, but it was a shock to me. I felt as if I had been lifted out of one world and dropped back into another one.

I met one friend I had kept in touch with for most of my overseas service. Although it was very cold, and I felt it, I went to the cinema in Chester wearing two overcoats, scarves, two pairs of socks. I remember standing in the queue for the Regal and I couldn't stop my teeth chattering. As we came home on the train to Penyffordd, there was ice on the windows, and I was glad of the walk home to Hope to warm me up. There wasn't much central heating in those days, and you got warm on top of a coal fire if you could afford the coal.

My mum was very quiet all through my leave. It went like wildfire and with it being a close community, everybody knew everything about everybody else. My sisters were working at Meadowslea Hospital and had been during the whole of the war. They should have gone into a factory and earned better money for themselves and my mother, but they wouldn't have been so vain.

I went to the local shop, the one for which I had delivered papers for about six years, and asked: "Got any cigarettes, please?"

"No way."

"Where am I going to get cigarettes from?"

"You will have to go to the N.A.A.F.I. for them."

"Thanks very much, Mrs Shone."

I tried the three shops in the village and failed. I knew they all had cigarettes under the counter. Was someone trying to tell me to go away, I wondered? I'd been away so long and grown up so much that people I'd known all my life were shy with me – and everything had altered. We'd been living in different worlds. It was not much of a welcome from anyone other than my mother. Nobody really wanted to know. I went to Les Lloyd's for his address, but never got it. His elder sister was there but Dorothy wasn't in. His dad said: "We will have to get it for you." But I never went back for it.

It was as if the whole village had changed. I met Joyce from Penyffordd, whom I had been writing to for about four years, but I could see she had other interests and I spotted her in the bus queue going to Chester with a boyfriend, which she hadn't mentioned to me in my correspondence.

I called at the Rectory to see the Rector, and while I was there I found out there was a dinner at the Church Hall in Wrexham. Tickets were available at Post Offices throughout the district and one had to book. I bought two tickets – why I don't know. I had been to the Odeon in Wrexham on my own and was catching the 11.20pm train back to Hope. A girl got in the compartment wearing A.T.S. uniform. We spoke, and I thought I knew her. It was Daisy, our school friend. Funnily enough I never gave her a kiss.

We shook hands. We made quite a fuss and it was great to meet someone I knew. I said I had tickets for the dinner at the Church Hall and asked if she would like to come. She said she had tried to get a ticket but couldn't and asked me where I had got mine from. I said I had bought them from Caergwrle Post Office and that Hope hadn't any. She said she would love to go and I told her it was on Thursday. She asked if I was going in civvies or uniform and I said I was going in uniform as they wouldn't let you in in civvies. I said I would see her on the 5.40pm train at Hope Station.

I walked home with Daisy and got in at 11.15 pm. Mum was up and had some turnip and potato frying for our supper. We sat till after midnight talking. Mum had altered – she had lived on her own for so long after the evacuee family left. I felt I was intruding on her, but she was worried a bit about something. I had a feeling it was George. He wanted to get married. I found out later it was Mum who wanted to get married, and she had put off seeing her 'boyfriend' because I was home. She did marry him later on.

Leave was nothing like I had anticipated. Even the people I'd worked with were embarrassed to speak to me. I had already been round the world and they had stayed among the nettles. I enjoyed my stay with mother and that was about all. I felt I was a complete stranger to everyone whom I knew before I went away.

I looked forward to the Thursday night out at Wrexham. Like my leave, it came and went. The glamour soon wore off, the chandeliers, the huge organ in the hall was still ringing in my ears, together with the band of the Metropolitan Police and the Royal Welsh Fusiliers' band. Even the regimental goat gave a song and dance! We had a wonderful night out. I couldn't dance, but I was never off the floor with Daisy, she was a good dancer. The food was plain, but very well served. The wine must have been good. That, on top of the beer and spirits we drank, was a bit too much for me, and Daisy had a job to stop me singing. But I didn't disgrace her.

I got home in the early hours of the morning and Mum was up. She asked if I had met anyone I knew and I told her I had met Daisy and that we had been to the dinner together. She went spare. I had no idea, but Daisy was being drummed out of the A.T.S.. I honestly had no idea, but I found out afterwards that she was waiting for her case to come up and was on indefinite leave. She didn't whisper a thing to me – not that I was concerned other than her being an old school friend.

I was so pleased to be given a date for the return to my unit. Back to Beirut. We were to report on 2nd February.

I'd had a nice leave, but I was so mixed up I was glad to be on the move again. So many thousands of miles again to Beirut. It just didn't make sense as the war in Europe was over. Anyway, we had to go, but this time I knew where we were going, or did I? Ha. Ha. Wait for it.

I consoled Mum and told her I was in no danger now, that it was only a formality and we would all be home soon. I said my goodbyes to the village and caught the train from Hope to Chester, changing at Hawarden Bridge Halt, then into Chester and changed there for Crewe. There were two hours to wait, so I went down to Love Street N.A.A.F.I. and got myself as many cigarettes as I could and a char and a wad. Then I went back to the station to catch the train for Crewe. There I was to due meet Boothy and I did. We both felt upset, but I also knew there was something wrong with him. He clammed up when I asked him. As the train was late leaving Crewe, we knew we were going to be late into Euston. It was dark as we got to Rugby and I noticed Boothy having a weep. I asked him what was the matter and he still clammed up. We had to wait there, so I got a char and a wad for both of us. Eventually we arrived in London three-quarters of an hour late and missed our connection to Newhaven, which I think was the train for Bournemouth.

The first job was to find the R.T.O. and get our warrants stamped, which we did. There was transport at the station to take us to the transit camp at Newhaven. In the early hours of the morning, the weather was chilly, and we were glad to get into the huts provided. We had to draw bedding and make ourselves comfortable. The Duty Corporal called to tell us there was a cuppa in the cookhouse and down there we went and had a sausage butty and a cup of char, then we went up to bed. We were to report to the troop carrier to cross the Channel again to Dieppe the following day, so there was no waiting. I scribbled a note to my mum, and posted it as we went to the landing stage.

178

The English Channel was a roaring lion – gosh, it was rough. As the craft battered against the swell, it thrust me to the side of the staging and tore my clothes, ripped the pocket on my battle-dress trousers and the cuff of my blouse. It was a fine outfit, one of the smartest issued by the Army. It was Canadian. I must have been an awkward size or something. I never had a scruffy uniform. I thought all the British uniforms were full of lime or something when they were issued. I always got a Canadian battledress that looked good.

The storm subsided before we reached Dieppe, and the pilot soon got us into the harbour and tied up at the jetty. We were able to have our midday meal in the transit camp and then catch the evening train down to Toulon. What a train journey! The British hadn't a clue how to run trains compared with the French. It was a little bit clattery until it got its revs going, then it was very quiet and it got a move on all right. I think the journey takes 11 hours or it did then in 1944.

We slept most of the time and arrived at Toulon about dawn. We were met by the transport from the transit camp and so we settled to a day of rest. After the roll call in the morning, the day was ours until the boat sailed. I think we waited two days as the ship had trouble with docking equipment on its run into Toulon.

We embarked the following afternoon, and I can say that it was one of the best boardings I have ever had. You just walked on the ship. It was a utility ship made at Clydeside for troop carrying during the War. It was all metal, and when it moved it creaked, and when it creaked it echoed throughout the ship: "Gdoing, Gdoing, Gdoing." What a bloody noise to have to put up with for the next few days.

We sailed on the evening of 6th February, heading for Port Said, Egypt. We spent six days crossing and then two gruelling nights on that bloody train. There was not much to look forward to, and you had got to go. The ship was *The Yoma*. It's a good job there was no tide in the Mediterranean to worry about. There was very little creaking when we were plain sailing, but when it got a sway on, it seemed as if was forcing itself to break up.

We got there and on time. We had a nice sunbathe and a rest. I didn't have any duties on board to do at all. I usually fell for something. Our kit bags were unloaded for us straight onto the train and we picked them up from the vans as the train stopped en route to Haifa. There was nothing in mine to worry about, and I ignored the messages I got to pick it up until we got nearer to Haifa. It saved me having to carry the damn thing about with me.

We docked at 5pm and went straight onto the train at Port Said. That meant a night, a day and another night to Haifa. This gave Boothy and myself a nice run up to Beirut with our own transport when it came from Beirut, as we thought. It was from the R.T.O's office in Beirut and we got back to our camp to find no one there. They had moved to another camp! Where the hell this time?

We kept the transport we had and reported to the R.T.O's office.

"Your company has moved to Shaiba in Iraq. You will be transported to Haifa tonight and catch Nairns transport to Baghdad. Train from Baghdad to Basra on the Shatal-el-Arab and be picked up from there by your company transport."

What a horrible run again – to go over the Seven Sisters, with someone else driving, made me go cold there and then. Anyway, they were bus drivers and they were on the run regularly, so they should know the way as well as myself. I'd passed them often enough on my runs from Damascus.

We arrived in Haifa and the bus had just left, so it gave us a night there and the next day. I wanted to see the orange packing in Jaffa, so we went to Jaffa that night and stopped in Phil Phil's hostel on the water front. We had a few jars of beer and finished off with some of Jaffa's brandy. It was like cat's pee, and absolutely bounced our heads the next day. We were not fit to ride on a night bus, I can tell you.

We clambered on with our kit and thank God we got a sleeper. It was 11 hours and not luxury, I can tell you. Nothing like driving in my Mac! I wondered what had happened to that, and if I would see it again after living in it for that length of time. I felt that we belonged to one another.

The buses were articulated, with most of the seats 'sleepers'. If you got one on the turntable it rattled you all night long. The best place was in the centre of the trailer, where you had a bit of a cushion and you were best to keep away from the rear wheels too. I managed a bottom centre bunk, while Jim was a little to the rear, two bunks away, but quite comfortable. We slept through to Amman anyway and we were over the Seven Sisters, well on our way to Baghdad.

It was boring, bloody boring. Why the hell was I going all that way out there, just to come back for demob in a few months? The R.T.O. in Beirut told me this. It was still an experience travelling about. It was nice to see some of the places you knew. The transit camp in Salachia was a dump, but one could go into the town of Baghdad and see if the billiard table now had a baize surface after four and a half years. It had, and it was now a well-run club for the Forces. It was something to do with King Faizel the Boy King who was assassinated some years ago. His photograph is in my album.

We stayed on until late, as our train to Basra was a night train leaving Baghdad at 1.15am, arriving at Marguill about 9am. It hardly went dark during the night, and we managed to get comfortable seats. The train was not overloaded as it usually was. We sat on cushioned seats, not like the last run I did – overhung by Arabs hanging out of the carriages, off the roof, even between the buffers of the couplings, mad as hatters. We even had proper coffee with goat's milk near Babylon on the night stop.

When we arrived at Marguill I could see a 15 cwt Dodge and a driver sitting in it. It was Bert Garlick, the Derbyshire lad from Chapel-en-le-Frith. He had come to pick us up, or so I thought. Actually, he had come to pick up a new intake from Blighty but, as you can imagine, we took precedence with Bert. There were only nine rookies, so they all got on the Dodge.

"Where the hell are we, Bert?" I asked.

"A place called Shaiba," he said.

"I know it, I was there before in an old German P.O.W. camp."

"That's it, you've got it in one."

I sat in the front with Bert and got a bit of gen out of him.

He said: "It looks as though you have lost your Mac. Charlie Cull is on it and he is out all the time. There is plenty of driving to do and we aren't idle at all. Everyone has got a job, but by the looks of things you will be asked to teach some of these new lads the ropes, and do the duty driving, but that's not for me to tell you. You must be the senior man in the section now, so no doubt Fountain will look after you until you are time-expired. How long have you done now?"

I said: "Five years."

Bert said: "It's down to five and six now. Most of my mates have gone, and you won't be long after them."

We arrived in the camp just before lunch and I walked into the mess to a hell of a din, glasses, bottles, tin pans, everything was clanging and who should be standing in the mess doorway but Captain Fountain, laughing his head off. He came over and shook hands, and it was nice to have such a good welcome. Fountain and I had seen a bit of rubbish together.

He called me into his office where we sat over a pint of beer. He told me the good and the bad news. Our job was to collect every piece of plant we could find right through from the whole of the area. This included the Bekka Valley, Syria, Lebanon, Palestine, in line with Jordan, Iraq, then Persia and Iran right up to Tehran and The Pitac. All plant was to come in from these areas for shipping out of the area or for selling to the respective countries. There was a terrific Plant Park, which consisted of every piece of plant there was, all lined up in their respective lines, M.E/N tractors, ME/EX excavators and so on. All had a number and a place in the system. Water pumps, welders, compressors, every one was numbered and marked, and in good working order,. If not, it went into the workshop for repair or was assessed as 'B.L.R.' (beyond local repair), when R.E.M.E. picked it up and took it to be sold at an R.V.S. spares yard.

Captain Fountain explained to me that he would like me to stay put in H.Q. now that I hadn't much time to go, and it would be aggravating if my repatriation papers came when I was in Egypt, Persia or Lebanon. They would have a job contacting me and I would be late for the most important date of my life.

Charlie Cull was on my wagon and Captain Fountain proposed he stayed on it rather than move him off for what might be a few months or so. I was to do the rations each day with a new Diamond T. It had only done 12 miles when I took it over.

"See Sergeant Erskine. All your kit from the Mac is in store and

Charlie didn't want to take any of it until he saw you, so you sort it out and anything you don't want can go back on the Mac for the long hauls."

Everything was just as I had packed it. I thought I would never see it again, but it was all intact. Even my biscuit for my fold-up bed and the bed. Remember, this was an old A.T.S. bed and I had had it for years. I'd picked it up at Tel el Kabia, out of a lorry that had been B.L.R.'d. Anyway, it was still there and my name was still on it – Sapper Driver A Hughes, T.P.T. Class 1.A. 2153373. Yes, that was my rank and I stuck to it.

So, I was to finish my time off in a billet. I spotted a nice spot by the door and asked if I could use it.

"Yes, it'll be a pleasure to have you, Diesel. Old Jenks was there and he went home a month ago. You must have passed him in the Meddi."

It was the beginning of March and getting hotter. We took a reading in the billet and it was 118 degrees in the centre, with all the fans going flat out. It would be about 11 o'clock. The boys were coming in for the middle break, for there was no work between 11am and 2pm.

Captain Fountain came in the billet to see one of the men and saw I was comfortable.

He shook hands with me: "Glad you're back, and I'll call you as soon as your papers come in. Do what you like. The Diamond T is yours. Watch the company's noticeboard as your times will change from day to day. Get a diary book from Gardner and put your times down each night, or we get no rations. D.I.D. are queer down here."

So, I was days duty driver: providing transport for swimming, fishing on the Shatal-el-Arab, days out at Basra, football, cinema, any concerts at the R.A.F. camp – I did them all. No parades, only pay parades, and that I collected from the office if I needed it. I was still in credit even after my leave.

The lads didn't know where to go fishing.

"Leave it to me, I know of a good place," I said. "Get some long canes and ask the workshop to make some spears." (I showed them a diagram of one).

We managed to get some sisal which was used for putting

between the rows on the plant park. I took 16 spears, and we all had one with two spare. You used the cane with the sisal tied to it. You threw it like a spear at the fish in the water. Have you ever tasted sword fish? It is like eating lamb's fries, fried in golden butter. It was delicious, especially when it was cooked by our cook in the mess. He was very, very good. Clean and always helpful. If a driver came in off a run after eating hours, swordfish went down 'a bomb' in our mess.

Although I had lost my Mac, I was enjoying being with the lads in the billet. We had a football team and we had a band. One or two of us were interested in singing and we formed a group like the famous Inkspots. There was a saxophone, piano-accordion, drums and an old piano left in the mess by the previous company. We had a lad named 'Geordie' McRay who could make that piano talk. It was out of tune and we had no tuner spanner so I made one in the workshop. We tuned it by ear after getting the middle 'C' from a record in the officers' billet. When we'd finished it was like a new one.

One of the worst problems we had was bugs. We did everything to get rid of them. We came up with many good ideas. We kept all the tins out of the mess and put all the bed legs in disinfectant in the tins. Bugs weren't like fleas, they couldn't jump. They were red raw bugs. They came out like an army at night time. During the day they were not to be seen, unless you searched for them, and then you would find them up inside the tubes of the legs of the beds, not a few, but thousands of them, so we had an idea of burning them out of the metal framed beds. If you used disinfectant it stank all night and every night. The bugs were not in the blankets, they were storing their energy for the onslaught at night when you were in cloud cuckoo land. They crawled from their hideouts to dig into you while you were asleep.

Next day it was fishing.

"Where are you taking us to, Diesel?"

"On the Shatal-el-Arab in Marguill. It is where the rivers fork and a bridge goes over to Cole Island."

"How do you know that?" said the Captain.

I said: "I built the damn bridge before I joined the unit."

He was so interested, he came with us to see it. It was still sinking in the water for the ships to pass and it looked as good as new. Rail traffic was still crossing it, and it must have been a great asset to all the countries in the area. It was the only crossing so near to the estuary. Its aim was aid to Russia. Shipping docked at Marguill, to be offloaded and transported to Russia via Persia, into Tehran and over The Pitac to Russia.

"Where's the fishing? Come on Diesel, we'll have no dinner."

We parked on Cole Island. I walked with Captain Fountain and half the gang to show them the fish. The water was full of fish. You could see them in the strong current of water of the Tigris. They varied in length from a foot to three feet. You struck slightly ahead of your prey and it was not often you missed.

I left the gang fishing then went back to the truck to find the rest of them had done their own thing and got hang of the idea. On the abutments of the centre bridge they had three fish already, almost enough to feed the mess. I walked around to see where the mosquitoes used to dig their heels into me when I had malaria some four years previously, sandfly fever twice and had injections for blackwater fever.

The Island was dead compared to what it used to be. 660 General Construction Company was a large body of men, so the Island had been overcrowded really, and Marguill at that time had been well occupied with troops at night. Remember, this is where I spent my first months abroad.

I gathered my thoughts together and got back to fishing. The lads had caught too many, so I said we could give some to the Arabs who worked in the machine shop. It would be a change to give them something. We were always taking from them and giving nothing in return, and we all knew what low wages they were on.

They had 22 fish in all. We got back early enough to have them cooked for evening dinner. We never ate much at lunch time as it was always too hot. We gave the Arabs eight fish and had enough for two days if Cooky could get them in the freezer.

We got back in time to get into the billet before an electric storm. It went black and all hell was let loose. It was as bad as when Rommel retreated from Hellfire Pass. The shit-storm broke

185

loose and the sand billowed everywhere. Although we had good shutters on the billet windows to close, the sand got everywhere, even down your ears; your hair was full of a spent earth which we seemed to wash away for days after a shit-storm. You felt it on everything you touched afterwards. Pick up anything either outside or inside, and a cloud of dust would rise from it. You could smell it too.

You always saw a civilian with a chin cloth so he could raise it to his mouth if it was dusty. We were stupid as none of us wore anything, and then we were chewing sand for the next few days.

That evening it was dark and we had a sing-song in the mess. It was too dark to go out. Normally it was quite light until midnight, and then it started to get even lighter again.

Always after a shit-storm the compressors had to be used on the workshop and the Plant Park to blow all the dust off everything. This started another storm. You could see the clouds of dust a mile away from the compressor pipes used to blow the dust away. It rested like a fall of snow on everything and it took longer to get rid of than snow. Snow melts, sand doesn't.

We had to blow out the billets as well, so it kept some of the plant park staff occupied, not that they had nothing to do. I remember the whole of my term abroad was busy. I was not idle during the whole tour, and I had very little leave. Captain Fountain told me to relax and let someone else have the work for a change. He told me I had done my share, living in a truck for that length of time. Four years is a long time.

It must have been the King's birthday or something special. Everyone had to be on Sunday morning parade. We fell in, called the roll, inspected and marched to Church. The Church was underground and I had a camera with me – a new Woolworth's camera. I think it cost more than 6d, but at that time all goods from Woolworths were only 6d.

Anyway, I took a few pictures of the platoon 39th Mechanical Equipment Pltn. R.E. C.O. Captain Fountain R.E. These photos are still in my album. I took a snap of the Church altar. I gave it a time exposure of five seconds and it came out OK. I also took it to the graveyard of the British and American planes. We clambered onto the wings. This was the first time I had been in a plane. They were tattered and torn apart, and I thought about the pilots and the crew. How many had died in the planes we were messing about in? I took photos of a hat parade (see how soft we were), lamp shades, bush hats, helmets, all sorts of daft things. We were a load of crackpots by now, and we were all waiting our turn to return to civilisation.

Then the "old man" sent for me.

"You are next to leave us, you and Taffy Landler. I think I'm wasting my time, but I must tell you: if you wish to stop on, you can sign for a further five years and you would be promoted to Sergeant, as from when you sign."

I rejected his offer and he agreed with me. We had had enough, and he was on his bike as soon as his papers were in his office.

So, we were to leave on the Tuesday. Another boring trip. Truck to Shatal-el-Arab, train to Baghdad, Nairn's transport to Haifa, train to Port Said, ship to Toulon, train through France, troop carrier across the Channel to Newhaven, train to London Euston, train to Chester. At least two weeks again.

That afternoon my old Mac came into the yard. What a funny feeling. Charlie Cull was on it and I gave him a dressing down for not looking after it. He thought I was mad.

He said: "You don't wash it if you're out with it."

I said: "I was always out in it, but it was always clean, both in and out. You're a dirty bugger."

Captain Fountain was standing behind me.

"I know how you feel, Diesel, but you're going home. After a few days, you'll forget it."

There was no harm in him thinking that. The next few days Landler and I packed our kit – I don't know how many times.

Throw this out...

Keep that...

You can have that...

No, I'll keep that...

The last of the summer wine...

Goodbye Iraq.

I had seen enough of it anyway.

We were mounting the truck for Marguill. I can't remember

celebrating. I can remember Taffy Landler singing: "Roll on the boat, the boat that takes me home, far from this land of shit and jankers, mosquitoes, bugs and flies get in your bloody eyes, so roll on the boat that takes me home."

We must have sung that for the first two miles on the truck, to Marguill station to the tune of "Gone are the days."

It was a funny thing, going back from whence you came. I could remember as though it was yesterday how the man had been tipped out of his donkey cart on the very same road that we were leaving on. Landler of course, was not with me then. He was going home on compassionate grounds and was only a rookie compared to me.

The Shatal-el-Arab soon came up and we were on it. The station, if that is what you could call it, had no platform, just where the train came in, that's all. We said our goodbyes to Mo Kella as the train came to a halt. We were lucky, it was half empty and we got a seat. It was wooden, but a seat.

We threw our kit bags in the baggage truck and settled to the most boring trip of the whole run, from here to Baghdad. Bloody awful. We were in Baghdad for 6.30pm. We had plenty of time for the night run to Jordan and Haifa.

So, it was a few bottles of ale, plus a drop of the hard stuff to get you off to sleep on Nairn's buses. Over Transjordan, over the Seven Sisters into Palestine and the Mediterranean. I was lucky enough to get a bed off the turntable or the rear axle. It wasn't as bumpy as the last run. I slept some of the way, until dawn any-way. Just going over the Seven Sisters now. Thank God for that. There was only one more boring run now across the Sinai, up to Ismailiya.

We made Haifa a bit early, so we had time to go into town and have a meal and a drink before the two days' train journey to Port Said. Well, really a night and a day. It seemed more like a week. Every stop, eggs and bread, eggs and bread. The seats were so hard, you looked forward to every stop to stretch your bum.

The train was always packed. Arabs all over it clinging to the sides and hanging through the windows where there were any. Most were without glass. I can still hear that sound of a train whistle in my ears, such a hated and weird sound. I had served

188

my time travelling on this damn thing and the Sinai Desert. The train would stop for water and the Arabs were buzzing to see what they could pinch, so not only was it boring, you had to be on guard all the time. I warned Landler to keep his eyes on his kit, and if we were to have refreshment one of us should go and the other watch the kit. If we didn't do that it would be gone, and I had quite a few presents for my family and a gift from Phil Phil which I didn't want to lose.

I attended Phil Phil's wedding in the end. He was the most faithful person I have ever met out of the U.K. He gave me a pair of his own goat's bells from the goat he gave to his intended father-in-law, as part of his dowry. He told me, in Arabic, to take them to my mother with his blessing. I don't think I grasped it all, as they have a different meaning to their words than we do and they are more sincere. I only ever saw his wife on the wedding day, and that was just her shape and her forehead. She looked very pretty. One never discussed anything to do with a family, and she was never allowed to speak to me, although she knew of me and that Phil Phil was friendly with a British soldier. I would love to return to Quassassin sometime to see if he is about, he was a little younger than me.

The train had come to a stop at El Qantara Bridge. This was where we took a lot of water on, as the water holes were rationed through the desert, and because the El Qantara was by the Suez Canal, everything was watered. So then onto Ismailiya and up to Port Said. We should be there by tea time. We were, and how funny it seemed to think you were not going back after five years and three months.

I recall wondering: "What's going to happen to me, when I finish in the Forces?"

The train puffed through the dock gates at Port Said. I remembered the scramble on my leave trip, how everyone dashed to be first. I told Landler to slow it down, not to be first off. Last was best because all the bedding would have been used before. If you went last, you got the new stuff and last in the dining room you got the fresh food, so experience counted.

We both enjoyed the two days before the *Empire Battleaxe* sailed out of Port Said on the afternoon of 6th August 1946. It was strange to think we were not going back to the land of shit and jankers again. Then it was five days across the Meddi to Toulon and across France seeing the fields getting greener every day, and then the White Cliffs of Dover. May I say that it is only the folk who have left the country who know what sight that means.

I cried twice, once when I returned on leave and then when I came home "time expired." The last was the more thrilling as I knew I didn't have to go back to wherever they had sent me in the first place. At least I knew where I was going this time. But, did I? Was I to cross the Channel again?

Chapter 15

OFF TO FRANCE

We landed at Dover, trained it to London, and then went on to Andover. I had been to Barton Stacey before during my days in London, so I knew what to expect. It was a 'bullshit camp'. I had never been used to it, so you had to be careful or trouble was around the corner.

We got into a nice billet. The beds were all ready with pillowcases, covers, sheets and blankets. The toilet blocks were attached and we were not far from the mess. We were allowed out that night as we had an evening meal at 6pm, so we went down to Andover to see what a pint of beer tasted like out of a thin glass.

We got outside the camp to catch a bus and arrived in the town. The beer was on ration. I was never a big drinker, so I didn't mind having one here and one at another pub. When we came out of a pub near the Town Hall. I wondered what the noise was. It was the Town Crier calling "Nine o'clock and all's well!" He repeated this again and again.

I never went out scruffy. If there was an occasion to be smart, I could and would rise to it. As it happened, I was not in my best battledress as we were going on leave for a month, so I managed with my No. 2 suit. It was all right. There were two Red Caps standing on the corner. One stopped me and told me I was improperly dressed and would be charged for not having my battledress clipped up. I told him I was wearing a tie so I didn't have to have my top button fastened. It was no good. He was going to charge me, and make no mistake, he did. I was on orders the following morning when I should have been on the train for home. I pleaded "Guilty" and got one day's C.B., which meant me losing a day's leave out of my 28 time expired. The Red Cap was only a bit of a kid. I told him afterwards I would get him, and quite by chance I did – some time later when I was a civilian.

The officer in charge of transport was a Captain Martin who

was with me in Balham, London. I went to see him and told him I had been on orders and lost a day's leave. He asked where I lived, and because of the distance he granted me two days travelling, one up and one down, so I lost nothing, only my pride at having a stain on my crime sheet to go out of the Forces. I was still livid with that bloody Red Cap.

Anyway I went to get my Rations Book to go on leave and spotted Sergeant Erskine, the cook who used to be in Bowbridge Road, Newark. He shook hands and made a fuss, "Where have you been," etc. He gave me a bit of sugar, bacon, butter, dried egg powder, bags of tea and a tin of bully, for my mum. I offered to pay, and he kicked my backside.

It was best to go on the train to London, then to Crewe, from Crewe to Chester and then home somehow from there. I managed the train to Mold via Penyffordd and walked it to Hope. I left my kit at the station and got it home on the bus the next day.

When I arrived home, the back door was open and a soldier's hat with a respirator was hanging on the mangle. Mine joined them, and I walked in and shook hands with my brother, George, whom I hadn't seen for about five years.

I made the usual fuss of my mum and gave her the rations. You should have seen her face light up when she saw what I had to give her.

I can remember chatting until the early hours, then it was up the 'wooden hills' to bed.

I was sad because I could see how our family was broken and had drifted since Dad died. All the girls were at the hospital in service, and I knew then that we were never going to be together again like before.

I went for a night out with George to Wrexham, and we both came home singing. This didn't suit Mum, as she hated booze and would run a mile from it. We had gone away boys and come back men. Five years is a long time to be separated and then expect everything to fall into place again just like that.

We all had a lot to discuss. I would have liked to have pooled our resources, which would have amounted to about £300, put it as a deposit on a new bulldozer and George and I work together. I would do the work on the machine and George could get out looking for the work (work of this nature would come to you at that time). It would have gone like a bomb. Another person who did the same thing sold out for over £1 million and he only had two machines.

George refused point blank, as he was getting married, and wanted his gratuity to pay for his wedding to Doll. He had met Doll through the evacuee family we had to take in as the war started. Fred and Elsie had one son Billy. They lived with Mum until the danger in Liverpool had passed. They left and I didn't see much of them after that. Dolly used to come to see them and got on well with Mum. Whether George was home at one time I don't know, but he met Doll and he married her, and went to live in Bidston somewhere round Sherlock Lane.

On the second day of my leave, George went off, and I only saw him at his wedding when I was best man. Do you know, I had no idea what my duties were. I didn't prepare a speech, had no money and didn't know what was going on!

I finished my time expired leave of one month and went back to Barton Stacey. The camp was full of R.E's, some with overseas service, some quite raw recruits. Out of the whole of the camp, there were only six drivers.

"Fall out on the left all the drivers and Sapper Drivers."

I was a Sapper Driver with T.P.T. Class 1 Operator / Excavator. You had to drive everything.

"You will all report to the Military Bus Depot at Woking tomorrow, 8am, find your buses and go to Southampton Docks to pick up troops returning to England. Most of them are officers so be on your best behaviour."

I was on it for a month or so, then I went with my old mate, Cyril Merryfield, to work in the company office. Me in an office? Buzz off. I really enjoyed it.

"Drivers fall out on the left – you, you and you. We want volunteers to go to France. It is to do an R.E. battlefield tour of our advances during the offensive. It will be a pleasure trip and it will give you men with Middle East service a bit of a break. I would go if I were you, Hughes."

Merryfield was going, so I went. Across the bloody pawny again. I knew every wave on the English Channel. This time it wasn't so nice. Woking was the R.E's Depot for everything. We went there first to pick up the transport. There were six vehicles. I had a small 15 cwt Morris Commercial, but I had all the booze on board. Our job was to drive and look after the officer on board. Not quite a batman, but to help him as much as possible. May I say I couldn't have had a nicer officer. He was a Canadian and treated me like his equal. He could see I had a fair amount of experience, and was very interested in what I had done and where I had been. We were embarking on what was part of an officers' pride to find out what went wrong, or vice versa, during an offensive in battle. I was about as interested as Paddy McDade, and Paddy McDade was the comedian of the drivers. He made us all laugh, the type of lad you had to have in a group. We loaded the transport onto the troop carrier and began the crossing to France at about 6pm, arriving after 1am. The crossing was rough, and some were sick, but not me, I was a good sailor.

We embarked at Dieppe and went off somewhere to a Yankee Camp. All the transport, except the fool (me), went into the camp for a meal, but the fool had to stay with the booze until the officer returned. He did so after half an hour and I went to the mess for one of the best breakfasts I have ever had in the Forces. Tea was tea, proper Cornflakes, sugar, proper fried bacon with egg, just like Mum did it, toast that was not burned to a cinder, all laid out like I was used to at C.R.E..

That morning we went off on the tour which was to last 10 days. I had never seen so many Brass Hats in one heap before and from the various Services, too. We started, I think, at Rouen and did almost the whole of France, as far as Toulon. We had good time off, so we were able to see some of France. We were paid in francs, and I remember getting a wad of notes to the value of £5 and every time I managed to lock up the booze wagon to be able to go out, the officer always gave me 3,000-4,000 francs. "Go and enjoy yourself." I looked after him and he appreciated it. We got on very well.

We went into a hotel at Nantes. I was able to leave the Morris safe in a lock-up and go into the hotel to sleep, and at the same time be up early enough to see to my officer. I knew which room he was in and had to take him coffee and clean his shoes etc, so I bumped his door to find him in bed with a blonde filly.

"Can you find another cup, please?" he asked.

I said: "I already have one, sir. I saw you last night coming in and had an idea the lady wouldn't be gone at 7.30 in the morning."

"Good for you! Many thanks."

We were all down for a continental breakfast, and on the road again for 9.30am, heading south. While the officers went round their viewpoints we had a rest and plenty of time to ourselves. We ganged up where we could and had a bloody good time. Our last day was around Toulon and we were heading back towards Dieppe. One stop on the way back was a transit camp near Bordeaux, but I still had to sleep in the booze wagon. It was a good bed and I was warm. I was not very interested in the trip, although I found out later that it had been quite important. As far as I was concerned, it was a good time waster for me to bring my release nearer. I was to be demobbed in three weeks' time. Then what would I do? Work for a living.

We arrived at the Docks at Dieppe late at night, probably after 9pm, so we bedded down for the night ready to load up the following morning. We were all up early and got aboard our military craft and ready to set sail, only waiting for the Brass Hats now. In five hours we were to be home again at Barton Stacey. From Newhaven we went to Woking, then dropped everything off, and got on our bus up to the camp. It all reminded me of my tour of duty in the Middle East when I was away for long periods from the H.Q. I would get back to a log of mail. I was lucky this time, I had seven letters.

We were all too tired to do anything other than have a pint and get our heads down. We were excused parade the next day, read all the orders and had a day off, so we all went into Andover. I will always remember the showers at Barton Stacey. They were the best I have ever had. It was lovely to get cleaned up. I caught the decker to Andover with Merryfield and McDade, found a good café, had a meal and then a couple of pints.

We came out of the pub in the Market Square and heard the damned Town Crier again. What a stupid noise. We never found out what it was all about.

We read orders when we got into camp. The demob had started: Men A to D were to report after first Parade to Coy. Office with full kit, everything they possessed: "You are not coming back." From here to Aldershot. Documentation. From there to Woking, civilian clothes, identity card, ration book, your last travel warrant and a smile from the Sergeant Major. There was not much more I wanted to see in the Forces anyway, and my turn came the following Wednesday.

Chapter 16
DEMOB AT LAST

I had sorted my kit for the big day. Was it a big day? At times during my tour I had thought of nothing else. When I was in the desert I wanted my papers and now the time had come, I wondered what the hell I was going to do. Nothing was like what I'd left in 1940 on that dark October day. It was now 15th May 1946 and I had been into and served in 18 different countries. I was supposed to be going back to my country village to carry on where I had left off six years ago.

I hadn't got much civilian clobber, only a pair of shoes that we were allowed to wear. I had no suits, even though I wanted to wear one, but it wasn't usual for any of us to wear civilian clothing, because early on in the war you had a job to buy a suit and then you couldn't get one as everything was on coupons or dockets. I jumbled everything in my kit bag because when you handed them in they were usually burned anyway.

On parade for the last time. Full pack, and I thought back to the day we all marched to Liverpool, with full kit, whistling 'The Shores of Tripoli.' Nearly six years had gone quickly.

"Get on the bloody decker, Hughes, standing there dreaming. You go out today and become 'Mr Hughes' once again."

I was in a whirl. We all had our big valise on our back, small valise tied to our webbing, complete with water bottle and polished dixies in the small valise. My Tommy gun was handed in at the armoury in the camp, so I didn't have that to carry around with me. I went round the decker shaking hands with my buddies. Some I would never see again. I went downstairs and said goodbye to Howarth who was always turning up at these sort of occasions because both our surnames started with the letter "H."

We lined up outside the decker at Aldershot, filed in as called by name, and started to hand stuff over as it was called out. You kept a battledress, boots, overcoat, gloves, scarf, and webbed belt.

I was wearing my cheese cutter, so I put my Glengarry in as I didn't need that. Everything cleared, we went for our civilian clothes – a suit, I had a very good one. Officer's in fact, as there were none there to fit me. It was a nice brown tweed. I also got brown brogues, a razor, hat, underclothes, as well as the ones you kept, a brolly and a brown paper bag to put it all in. Now to Woking to be given the bullshit.

"Thank you very much for the six years of your life."

Get your medals and a gratuity of £86 in the P.O. Savings Account. Ration book, identity card, a demob book, telling you that you are reserved for the next seven years, and would be liable for call-up in the event of hostilities flaring up again and, the most important book of all, The Great Pay Out, the Post Office Savings Book. I had £87.17.6d all to myself. After all that time away from home, I had more than that in credit, to be paid out by the Pay Officer. I was also allowed to keep my A.B.64 Part One (I have still got it), the red and battered old thing I had carried with me all round the world. Oh, and a meal ticket to get your last meal if you had time before your train went to London. Stuff their meal up their bums, I thought – I'm going home to my mum, I don't want to miss the bloody train eating the last meal. That's how bewildered we all were.

Merryfield and I were in a tizzy. We had no idea what was hitting us. So, once again I shook hands with him as he boarded his train to Bournemouth. I was waiting for the London train. Then I was off, on the train to Euston and a train up north, changing at Crewe for Chester. I managed to get a Wrexham connection and got off at Hope Station. I was lucky for once.

I grabbed my few belongings and walked up from the station feeling dreadful. I got home and there was no one in. Mum had gone out somewhere, and I had no idea if a key was planted anywhere, so I had to wait. I went to Penyffordd to visit Joyce. I knew her mother well and our relationship ended when I came home, as she was to marry someone else that year. I had a chat to her mother, but Joyce was out, and I eventually got home on what we knew as 'The Buckley Flier' to Hope.

Mother was in when I arrived back home and she knew I was home by my baggage. I had 165 days' leave and no idea what to do with myself. Everything seemed such a big anticlimax after what I'd been doing in the Army, especially as I had been looking forward to coming home for so long. I went for walks in the village, but it felt as if no one wanted to know me. I went to see everyone I knew. Lots of people had left, some were dead, some were married, some had moved away and some had forgotten me.

It was very unsettling to be in the bedroom I'd had as a kid. There were so many things I hadn't got, that I needed, even a mirror to shave. We had no bathroom and had to manage with hot water boiled in an electric kettle. A bath had to be arranged days before. You had to put the boiler on, get sticks and coal, get the water boiling and ladle it into the bath across the back kitchen, lock the door, and make everyone go round the front.

"Sod this," I thought, "I'll go to the Town Baths in future."

I lived at home but found it difficult to settle down. I returned to the Church routine, but even there I couldn't settle. I was a bell-ringer and I knew they were short of ringers, so I tried to join them, as I had been ringing bells since I was 13 and had done quite a bit for my age. I didn't get much of a welcome, so I gave up.

I felt as if I no longer fitted into the jigsaw of village life.

I had to find some way of getting back to what was maybe called normal. What was normal? I was entitled, by law, to be able to go back to the job I'd had before I was called up and I could have demanded them to take me back.

"You can have a job on the shovel until a vehicle becomes available, that's the best we can offer you."

I said: "Your best isn't good enough. I could demand that you put me on the wagon."

"You'll have to come back in a week's time and we'll see what we can do."

I said: "If I come back in a week's time, it'll be for you to tell me I'm starting work on a lorry, otherwise you can stick it. I will see the Labour Exchange" and I went there.

"Have you just come out of the Forces, Mr Hughes?"

I said: "Yes."

"Why do you want to go back to your old place? There are better jobs than that. They want drivers at Bishops at Broughton. Why not go to see them?"

I went the next day, got there at 8am, and was interviewed at 9am. I went out on the yard for a test on an articulator and passed. I started the following Monday at 7am. I had found a job!

It was 1/9d per hour, 4d a mile bonus after 400 miles and you were expected to do 200 miles a day at least. The job was delivering prefabricated houses being built at Broughton by Vickers Armstrong. The houses were made in four sections, and fitted perfectly on the trailer of the artic. The four sections of the house came out of the factory together, and had to stay in that order and group. If for some reason, accident or otherwise, one got damaged, the other three sections had to go back to the factory. In other words, they were not interchangeable. If another driver had an accident with his house, you all had to go back no matter where you were. If you were on site, you would still have to go back and lose your mileage bonus. This happened to me once, but I was only at Northwich. A lad hit a brewery wagon on Middlewich roundabout, it only clipped the corner of the house, but we had to go back.

Bishops had 'snoops' everywhere and you were told what to expect if you did anything wrong. The 'snoops' were also there to help control the likes of an accident, to tell you all to go back and perhaps find a driver who had gone on. He had to be turned round to go back. Routes were very strict, and if you were caught off one for no reason, you had a 'snoop' behind you and you were sacked there and then. No messing, you had gone.

My best week's wage was £39.7s.6d. I can remember giving my mother £15 and she wondered what had hit her. I don't think she had ever seen £15 all in one go before.

I was enjoying myself all over the country: Newcastle, Birkenhead, Southampton, Bristol, South Wales, the East Coast, Bridlington, Liverpool, Shotton. You name it, we went there and I enjoyed every minute of it.

On site you had to be careful you didn't get bogged down, and the crane had to be in position before you went on. The four parts of the set had to be present on site before the crane driver started to unload you, you had to stay until all four were offloaded, and then it was a scramble to the base to get another one. And this is how it went on, every day, but you could earn a packet. I saved nothing. I gave most of it to Mum and she lived a better life than when she was on her own. At least she could go to the shops if she wanted to.

I started to get settled and wanted to improve our standard of living in the house. I hadn't any inclination to get married, because all my friends were missing and I knew the girl I'd corresponded with had already been spoken for – but I wanted to get some new furniture in the house. All we had was old. I started to decorate and I had quite a shock when Mum said if I wasn't satisfied with the place, I could go.

It really shook me to hear that coming from my mum, as we always got on together so well. Anyway, the job at Broughton was coming to an end. They were tightening up on hours and people were being sacked for the least thing, so 'keep your nose clean' was everyone's motto. Then I picked a passenger up, the bloody 'snoop' had me and I was sacked. Two weeks later everyone had finished. Production had stopped two months previously so we all knew we were to go. I got paid up and left.

I went to the Labour Exchange in Wrexham and got on the Crosville buses passenger service. Now I had a problem, I had to be in work for 4am. The routes were 'Colliers' (round the five pits in the area), and to Wrexham Trading Estate. It was a long drawn out schedule spread over 15 hours, with a stupid break at midday, so I told Mum I had to go into digs in Wrexham. That was a big mistake. The job was not rosy, the digs were as good as you got, but I seldom had the chance to go home and when I did, Mum was either out or didn't really want to be bothered with me.

I stayed in digs for a few weeks and met a lad there called Bob. He was OK, but he boozed too much for my liking. So I found a girlfriend, my dear Mary, who was working with my sisters at the hospital. I later married her, and we were together for 46 years – but that is another story, and one I would love to write some time, too.

ABBREVIATIONS

A.T.S.	Auxiliary Territorial Service
D.I.D.	Daily Indent Depot
R.T.O.	Transport Officer
140 Workshop & Park Co. No.1 P.E.D.	Plant Erection Depot
Char and a wad	Tea and cake
N.C.O.	Non-commissioned officer
A.M.T.	Advanced Military Transport
L.D.V.	Local Defence Volunteer
C.R.E.	Command Royal Engineers
W.V.S.	Women's Voluntary Service
S.I.B.	Secret Investigation Bureau
M.E.P.	Mechanical Equipment Plant R.E.
R.E.M.E.	Royal Electrical & Mechanical Engineers.
W.R.A.F.	Women's Royal Air Force
W.A.A.F.	Women's Auxiliary Air Force
K.D.	Khaki Drill
+(D) = D2, D4, D6, D7, D8	All Caterpillar bulldozers
R.B.	Ruston Bucyrus = 10 19 21 22 32 & 53 Electric

Index

Where people listed are contemporaries of Diesel Taff they have been indexed just by name, unless they have a military rank. Where they are his "elders and betters" they have been given the appropriate title Mr, Mrs, etc.

An imprint of
ANNE LOADER
PUBLICATIONS

Other books published by the Léonie Press, an imprint of
Anne Loader Publications, 13 Vale Road, Hartford, Northwich,
Cheshire CW8 1PL, Gt Britain, include:

Memories of a Cheshire Childhood by Lenna Bickerton
(ISBN 1 901253 00 7), price £4.99

A House with Sprit: A dedication to Marbury Hall by Jackie Hamlett
and Christine Hamlett (ISBN 1 901253 01 5), price £8.99

A Bull by the Back Door by Anne Loader
(ISBN 1 901253 06 6), price £8.99

*The Way We Were: Omnibus edition of Les Cooper's Crewe memories
'Over My Shoulder' and 'Another's War'*
by Les Cooper (ISBN 1 901253 07 4), price £7.99

A Nun's Grave: A Novel set in the Vale Royal of England
by Alan K Leicester (ISBN 1 901253 08 5) price £7.99

The Duck with a Dirty Laugh: by Anne Loader
(ISBN 1 901253 09 0), price £8.99

Nellie's Story - A Life of Service
by Elizabeth Ellen Osborne (ISBN 1 901253 15 5), price £5.99

Summer 2000: *Woollyback* by Alan Fleet (£8.99)
The Muck Birds by Geoffrey Morris (£8.99)